The Rise and Fall of the Aramaeans
from Their First Appearan

Gotthard G.G. Reinhold

The Rise and Fall of the Aramaeans in the Ancient Near East, from Their First Appearance until 732 BCE

New Studies on Aram and Israel

PL ACADEMIC RESEARCH

Bibliographic Information published by the Deutsche Nationalbibliothek
The Deutsche Nationalbibliothek lists this publication in the Deutsche Nationalbibliografie; detailed bibliographic data is available in the internet at http://dnb.d-nb.de.

Library of Congress Cataloging-in-Publication Data
Names: Reinhold, Gotthard G. G., 1945- author.
Title: The rise and fall of the Aramaeans in the ancient Near East : from their first appearance until 732 BCE / Gotthard G.G. Reinhold.
Description: Frankfurt am Main ; New York : Peter Lang, [2016] | Includes bibliographical references.
Identifiers: LCCN 2016016580 | ISBN 9783631675991
Subjects: LCSH: Arameans—History.
Classification: LCC DS59.A7 R45 2016 | DDC 939.4/302—dc23 LC record available at https://lccn.loc.gov/2016016580

Cover Image:
The House of David inscribed on a Victory stela, Têl Dan, Israelite per 9th c. BCE, Israel Museum, Jerusalem: Images Resources & Copyright Management, Jerusalem, Israel

ISBN 978-3-631-67599-1 (Print)
E-ISBN 978-3-653-06922-8 (E-Book)
DOI 10.3726/978-3-653-06922-8

© Peter Lang GmbH
Internationaler Verlag der Wissenschaften
Frankfurt am Main 2016
All rights reserved.
PL Academic Research is an Imprint of Peter Lang GmbH.

Peter Lang – Frankfurt am Main · Bern · Bruxelles · New York ·
Oxford · Warszawa · Wien

This publication has been peer reviewed.

www.peterlang.com

Contents

Preface[1]

In the early nineties, after the publication of my dissertation at the Johann Wolfgang Goethe-University Frankfurt am Main *Die Beziehungen Altisraels zu den aramäischen Staaten in der israelitisch-judäischen Königszeit* (EHS.T Bd. 368, Frankfurt am Main: Peter Lang 1989), a significant archaeological find came to light with the sensational broken pieces of the Têl Dan Stela, Israel, which greatly illuminated the portrait of Aram and ancient Israel's history. Ever since, I have closely watched the international scholarly debate and investigated the new materials myself. Further motivation for this project came from Dr. Izaak J. de Hulster (University of Göttingen/University of Helsinki), during the archaeological excavations of our ABA team (= The German Study Group for Biblical Archaeology, Schorndorf, Germany) in Jerusalem, Israel, from 2009 through 2011.

I owe my sincere thanks to Dr. Pieter Gert van der Veen for enabling me to lecture on the subject matter at the annual conferences in Schönblick, Schwäbisch Gmünd, Baden-Württemberg, as well as at our specialized ABA conferences in Germany and to collaborate on the publication Peter van der Veen/Uwe Zerbst, *VOLK OHNE AHNEN? Auf den Spuren der Erzväter und des frühen Israel,* (STUDIUM INTEGRALE, Holzgerlingen: SCM Hänssler, 2013).

---

1   This essay builds upon research conducted over the past several decades on the Aramaeans, from their presence in Mesopotamia and Syria to their relationship with ancient Israel. For the Têl Dan inscription of discovery preceding study, see Gotthard G.G. Reinhold (1989).
    For discussion of the Melqart/Bir-Hadad and Têl Dan stelae, see Excursus I and II in particular and Reinhold 1999; 2003 in publications, and 2005; 2008 [a] in lectures. Regarding the earliest attestations of Aram see Gotthard G.G. Reinhold 2006, 2008 [b], and in publication: Reinhold, Die Aramäer und Altisrael. Zur Frühbezeugung Arams in Schriftquellen des 3./2. Jahrtausends v. Chr. aus dem syrischen und mesopotamischen Raum (Exkurs), in: Peter van der Veen, Uwe Zerbst, hrsg., VOLK OHNE AHNEN? Auf den Spuren der Erzväter und des frühen Israel, STUDIUM INTEGRALE, Holzgerlingen: SCM Hänssler, 2013, 204–206.

I am also grateful to Mr. Paul Michael Kurtz (University of Göttingen / Max Weber Center for Advanced Cultural and Social Studies), who has translated an earlier version of this text on behalf of Dr. Izaak de Hulster – for the latter's once intended volume – and subsequently helped me improve the English after I had modified and expanded the text.

In addition, I would like to thank Prof. Dr. Manfred Oeming and, once again, Dr. de Hulster for the invitation to participate in the Heidelberg Colloquium *Aram and Israel: Cultural Interaction, Political Borders and Construction of Identity during the Early Iron Age (12th – 8th Centuries BCE), September 1–4, 2014.*

However, I alone bear responsibility for any errors in the volume.

Finally, I am grateful to the following persons and institutions for their helpful cooperation in my publication of colour photographs in the present volume:

Dr. Haim Gitler, Chief Curator of Archaeology and Curator of Numismatics at The Israel Museum, Jerusalem, Israel;

Bella Gershovich, Image Recources & Copyright Management Department, The Israel Museum, Jerusalem, Israel;

Prof. Dr. ord. Stefania Mazzoni, Director Italian Archaeological Mission Tell Afis. Archaeology and Art History of the Ancient Near East, Universita degli Studi Firenze, SAGAS. Dipartimento di Storia, Archeologia, Geografia Arte e Spettacolo, Firenze, Italia;

Marianne Cotty, Le Départment des Antiquités Orientales Musée du Louvre Paris. Centre du documentation du Départment, France;

Hanna Nelson and Leila Audouy, Agence photographice Réunion des musées nationaux Grand Palais des Champs-Elysées Paris, France; and

Jan Böttger, Bildrechte und Archiv (bkp), Bildagentur für Kunst, Kultur und Geschichte, Berlin, Deutschland.

On the occasion of my 70th birthday, December 19, 2015, I would like to make the present study available to the experts. This investigation of a history of Aram and ancient Israel encompasses new archaeological sources and their evaluations as well as previously known finds, which were researched with new methods. Furthermore, a number of specific analyses should be highlighted here: a renewed evaluation of the oldest written sources from Syria and Mesopotamia and their contribution to the early testimony of Aram, researches on the succession of the Aramaean kings from Aram-Damascus, and Excursus I–II, which consider Melqart or Bir/Bar-Hadad Stela from Syria and the broken pieces of the Têl Dan-Stela from Israel.

The results conveyed in this volume could always be adapted or replaced by recent discoveries, of course. In this sense, I hope the present volume will serve as a basis for the future research.

Gotthard G. G. Reinhold, ABA, Sulzbach an der Murr, December 1, 2015.

Foreword

by Izaak J. de Hulster, University of Helsinki

The relationship between the Aramaeans, especially Aram-Damascus, and the Kingdom of Israel was a dynamic one, characterized by both rivalry, military conflicts, and domination as well as alliances, military cooperation, and economic exchange. This relationship forms an integral part of the history of the Levant and left its traces in both biblical and extra-biblical sources. The Aramaeans are a topic of renewed academic interest, as can be illustrated, with the recent volumes edited by Berlejung and Streck (2013), by Niehr (2014), and the forthcoming one by Sergi, Oeming and de Hulster,[2] as well as the establishment of the Max Planck Minerva Center for the Relations between Israel and Aram in Biblical Times.[3]

Gotthard G.G. Reinhold's first monograph on Aram and Israel dates back to 1989.[4] Since then he has continued his historical, archaeological, and epigraphical research in Israel, Syria, and Jordan.

It was in 2008 that my countryman Peter van der Veen brought us together. While working on individual research projects, yet sharing common

---

2 Angelika Berlejung and Michael Steck (eds.), *Arameans, Chaldeans, and Arabs in Babylonia and Palestine in the First Millennium B.C.*, LAOS 3 (Wiesbaden: Harrassowitz, 2013); H. Niehr (ed.) The Arameans in Ancient Syria, Handbook of Oriental Series. Section 1 The Near Middle East 106 (Leiden: Brill, 2014); Omer Sergi, Manfred Oeming, and Izaak J. de Hulster (eds.), *In Search for Aram and Israel: Politics, Culture, and Identity*, Orientalische Religionen in der Antike (Tübingen: Mohr-Siebeck, forthcoming 2016). Likewise three monographs could be mentioned on the Elija-Elisha cycle and the Arameans: Hadi Ghantous, *The Elisha-Hazael paradigm and the kingdom of Israel: the politics of God in ancient Syria-Palestine*, Bible Word (Durham: Acumen, 2013); Hillel I. Millgram, *The Elijah Enigma: The Prophet, King Ahab and the Rebirth of Monotheism in the Book of Kings* (Jefferson: McFarland, 2014); and K. Lawson Younger Jr., *A Political History of the Arameans: From Their Origins to the End of Their Politics*, Archaeology and Biblical Strudies (Atlanta: SBL, forthcoming 2016).

3 A collaboration of the Bar-Ilan University (Israel) and the Universitya of Leipzig (Germany): http://aramisrael.org/ (accessed 26 November 2015).

4 Gotthard G.G. Reinhold (1989).

11

interest in Aram and Israel, the three of us regularly exchanged different approaches and opinions. We planned a volume together and had hoped that Gotthard Reinhold's contribution could have signaled the dynamics of researching this topic 25 years after the publication of his monograph. For various reasons this volume could not be released.[5] Meanwhile his chapter has grown into a new monograph and his 70th birthday is yet another honourable occasion for a book that celebrates decades of devoted study. His research is marked by his diligence, enthusiasm, and originality, as well as by the imperative to publish to bring science forward and the humbleness that our knowledge is preliminary and future research can lead to new insights.

---

5   A preliminary publication on the iconographic exegetical contribution I had planned myself appeared as Izaak J. de Hulster, 'A God of the mountains? An iconographic perspective on the Aramean argument in 1 Kings 20:23 MT', in Izaak J. de Hulster and Joel M. LeMon (eds.), *Images, Text, Exegesis: Iconographic Interpretation and the Hebrew Bible*, Library of Hebrew Bible/Old Testament Studies 588 (London: Bloomsbury, 2014), 226–250.

1 The Attestation of Aram in the Oldest Written Materials from Syria and Mesopotamia during the 3rd and 2nd Millennia

According to the textual evidence of the ancient Near East, West Semitic seminomadic tribes infiltrated Mesopotamia and Syria from the Arabian Desert as early as the third millennium BCE. Cuneiform sources first attest the root *aram* in designations of a particular geographic region as well as cities and villages—all most likely referring to proto-Aramean tribes. Regarding the precise referents of the terms Aram, Arame, Aramu, and Arami, these denominations initially serve as toponyms and thus allude to the names of villages, cities, or urban areas along with their immediate settlements and hinterlands, against a minority of scholars who advocate for a "city-state Aram" during this early period. Stemming from the region of Nippur (Nifur) during the time of Naram-Sin of Akkad (conventionally 2254–2218), tablet AO 5475 comments on the king's victory over Harshamatki Lord of Aram and Am (= Armânum)[6]. F. Thureau-Dangin has transcribed the relevant passage as [*Na-ra-am-ᵈ*] *Sin* | [*šar*] [*ki-ib-ra-t*]*im* | *ar-ba- im*| *i-nu* |*Har-ša-ma-at-ki* | *bêl A-r[a]-am* | *ù* | *Am* |......., and, hence translated: *Narâm-Sin, roi des quatre régions lorsqu'il combattit Haršamatki, seigneur d'Aram et Am....*[7] Aram, then, stands for a region or settlement west of the Tigris in this Akkadian royal inscription dating to 2200.[8]

---

6   Ignace, Vol. OIP, Vicinity and Alishar from Inscriptions, Gelb, J. XXVII (Researches in Anatolia Vol. V), Chicago: University of Chicago Press, 1935, 6, differentiated "Armânum = Am" from "Amânum = Amana Mountains". See also M. McNamara, De populi Aramaeorum primordiis, *VD* 35 (1957): 129–142, esp. 132/133.

7   F. Thureau-Dangin, "Une Inscription de Narâm-Sin," *RA* VIII (1991): 199–200, esp. 199.

8   I.A. Gelb, *Sargonidic Texts from the Diyala Region* (MAD 1; Chicago: The University of Chicago 1952), 110, 112. Text 217 ln. 8 (Kh 1934, 22= Iraq Museum) reads [A-r]a-meᵏⁱ ik-mi-ME (sic). Likewise, text 220 ln 9 (Kh 2934, 25=22021) attests Ar-ra[meᵏⁱ]. See further Conn Grayson Davis, "The Aramean Influence upon Ancient Israel to 732 B.C." (Ph.D. Thesis, The Southern Baptist

As for Syria, Tell Mardikh (ancient Ebla) has yielded an archive with thousands of cuneiform tablets, wherein the toponym A-ra-mu appears (TM.75.G.2231).[9] Other evidence for such a city has come from Tutub (ca. 2200)[10] as well as Drehem, near Nippur west of the Tigris (end of the third millennium). More detailed statements come from the Drehem material, specifically the private collection of Baurat Wengler (= Wengler 22), which cities erín A-ra-mi^{ki}—a military convoy (or retainers) of the municipality or region—as providers of sacrificial animals.[11] On the third day of the eight month of the Puzurish-Dagan calendar in the forty-sixth year of Shulgi, the second king of the Ur III Dynasty, animals, and the sacrifices of other neighbouring groups and individuals were reportedly taken to Puzurish-Dagan, i.e., Drehem, near Nippur. Constructed in year 37 of Shulgi's reign, Puzurish-Dagan served not only as the region's administrative centre but also—and indeed chiefly—as central depot for the reception and distribution of sacrificial animals for the land's individual cities and temples. Transcribed by A. Deimel and translated by N. Schneider, the obverse of the most important tablet from Wengler 22 reads as follows:[12]

6(?) gu(d), 40 udu, 20 máš-gal, erín Áš-nun^{ki}
6   gud,   52 udu, 8 máš-gal, erín A-ra-mi^{ki}
6   gud,   42 udu 18 máš-gal, erín Kaš-da-dun^{ki}
    ugula A-ḫu-ni

Theological Seminary 1979 (University Microfilms International, Ann Arbor, Michigan, 1984), 3 f..
9 Giovanni Pettinato, "L 'atlante geografico del Vicino Oriente Antico attestato ad Ebla e ad Abū-Ṣalābīkh (I)," Or 7(1978): 50–73, esp. 58 and 70, which display reference to a-ra-mu^{ki} (XI, 4) and a-ra-mu^{ki} (233α), respectively. See also R. Zadok, Elements of Aramean Pre-History, in: M. Cogan and I. Eph'fal, (eds.), Ah, Assyria...Studies in Assyrian History and Ancient Near Eastern Historiography Presented to Hayim Tadmor (Scripta Hierosolymitana 33, Jerusalem: The Magness Press, 1991): 104–117, esp. 106.
10 C.G. Davis, "The Aramean Influence,"4.
11 The tablet Wenger 22 is transcribed in P. Anton Deimel, "Miszellen", Orientalia O.Ser. II (1922), 62.
12 Ibid.; Nikolaus Schneider, "Aram und Aramäer in der Ur III-Zeit," Biblica 30 (1949), 19–111, esp. 110. Die Keilschrifturkunden der Ur III-Archive und die Bibel, St Ans 27–28 1951, 473–475, esp. 467/68.

6 Ochsen, 40 Schafe, 20 Ziegenböcke (eingebracht von) Kolonen von Áš-nun[ki]
6 Ochsen, 52 Schafe, 8 Ziegenböcke (eingebracht von) Kolonen von A-ra-mi[ki]
6 Ochsen, 42 Schafe, 18 Ziegenböcke (eingebracht von) Kolonen von Kaš-da-dun[ki]
Anführer (war) A-ḫu-ni.

The tablet's reverse lists the animal offerings from individuals whose names indicate specifically Akkadian descent. While Eshnunna once stood within the current tell of Diyala, the so-called A-ra-mi[ki] lay east of the Tigris.[13] Finally, an Old Babylonian tablet from Yale University's Morgan Library Collection, which dates to the sixth regnal year of Ammisaduga (conventionally 1582–1562/revised 1483–1462)[14] refers to a city called 'Ar-ra-mu[ki]. J. J. Finkelstein has transcribed the relevant portion of the text: SAG.GEMÉ Ta-ga-ša [M]U.[N]I (2) 'Ar-ra-mu[ki]3) ma-a-at SU.BIR$_4$[ki].[15]

Additional studies have found in the early cuneiform sources not only toponyms (GNN) but also personal names (PNN) bearing the root *aram. Accordingly, already by the end of the third millennium and during the transition into the second, the names A-ra-mu-i-ku (=Aramu)[16] from the sixth to ninth regnal year of Shu-Sin of Ur (conventionally 2037– post 2029)[17], A-ra-mu (= Aramu) in a list of rations recorded on a table from Zimri-Lim contemporary with King Hammurapi of Babylon (conventionally 1728–1686)

---

13 See A. Pohl, "Kurze Bemerkungen zu den Ortsnamen der Tafel Wengler 22", *JFK* 11 (1965): 363–64.

14 See David Lappin, Neue Untersuchungen zur Chronologie der Ersten Dynastie von Babylon auf der Grundlage der Venus-Tafeln des Ammizaduga und überlieferter 30-Tage-Mondmonats-Reihen* (Anhang C), in: Peter van der Veen/Uwe Zerbst, VOLK OHNE AHNEN? Auf den Spuren der Erzväter und des frühen Israel, STUDIUM INTEGRALE, Holzgerlingen: SCM Hänssler, 2013, 279–325, esp. 311.

15 J. J. Finkelstein, "Subartu and Subarians in Old Babylonian Sources," *JCS* 9 (1955), 1–7, esp. 1.

16 C. E. Keiser, Cuneiform Bullae of the Third Millennium B.C., New York MCMXIV (Babylonian Records in the Library of J. Piermont Morgan, ed. By Albert T. Clay, Part III Plate 45, No. 159), New Haven: Yale University Press/London-Humphrey Milford-Oxford University Press, MDCCCCXX; see further McNamara, "De populi Aramaeorum primordiis,", 135.

17 See A. Dupont-Sommer, "Sur le débuts de l'histoire araméenne," *VT.S* 1 (1953), 43; other than those names with A-ra-mu, he also finds the designation La-ba(?)-an. Three cuneiforms tablets from Mari (time of Zimrilim) also testify the PN Aḫ-la-mu. See Ibid., 44 and S. Moscati, Sulli origini degli Aramei, *RSO* XXVI 1951, 16–22.

at Tell-Harîri in Syria (ancient Mari) and A-ra-am-mu (= Arammu) at Tell Atshan (ancient Alalakh) all manifest themselves.[18] Moreover, while PNN A-ra-am-ma-ra (= Arammara)[19] and A-ra-am-su-ni (= Aramsuni)[20] appear again at Tell Harîri in cuneiform sources, the Hurrian PN Arampate[21] and Aram-uzni[22] have surfaced from the middle of the second millennium in Yorgan Tepe (ancient Nuzi). Despite the potential desirability of identifying either groups and individuals who came from these specific cities and towns or PNN that indicate certain ancestral lands significant for the history recorded in cuneiform sources, scholarly inquiry cannot legitimately secure an Aramaean ethnicity within this early period. Cuneiform texts in the very least would have to suggest such an ethnic group. Thus, Mahmud Mufaddi Abu Taleb concludes, "Consequently, there is no ground for dating the appearance and settlement of the Aramaeans to the first dynasty of Akkad and the Ur-III-period."[23]

---

18 Jean-Robert Kupper, *Les nomades en Mésopotamie au temps des rois de Mari* (Paris: Society d'Edition Les Belles Lettres, 1956), 113; D.J. Wiseman, *The Alalakh Tablets* (London: British Institute of Archaeology at Ankara, 1953), 128.
19 S. Moscati, "The Aramean 'Achlamu' ", *JSS* 4 no. 4 (1959),: 303–307, esp. 304.
20 Ibid.
21 I. J. Gelb, P. Purves, and A. MacRae, *Nuzi Personal Names* (OIP; Chicago: University of Chicago Press, 1943), 203b, 235b.
22 Ibid.
23 Mahmud Muffaddi Abu Taleb, "Investigations in the History of North Syria 1115–717 BCE," (PhD. Dissertation, University of Pennsylvania), Philadelphia, 1973 (University Microfilms International, Ann Arbor, Michigan, 1983), 35.

2 The Development of Aramaean Tribes during the Second Half of the Second until the Beginning of the First Millennium BCE in the Ancient Near East

As Iris von Bredow[24] has demonstrated, during the end of the third and beginning of the second millennia B.C.E.—i.e., the transition from the Late Bronze to Early Iron Age—nomadic tribes from northern Syria called the MAR.TU (i.e., Amurru, "people from the west")[25] likely entered Mesopotamia and menaced even the strongest dynasties of the cultivated territories, adumbrating a similar process that would occur with the "onslaught of nomadic Aramaean tribes on the cultivated lands of northern Syria"[26] during the second half of the second until the beginning of the first millennium BCE. Description with the term "onslaught,"[27] however, should not indicate a unified military act, process, or occurrence but rather one aspect of the various territorial and political takeovers by new populations from the desert's fringes. Indeed, many indicators from various regions at the end of the Late Bronze Age evince either the direct conquest of intact cities from older cultures by nomadic incursions or the transition of Aramaean tribes— settled on the outskirts and wont to migrate as "semi-nomadic pastoralists," i.e., shepherds between desert and cultivated land—to longer sedentariness, which thus precipitated the collapse of the Late Bronze Age economy.[28] Settlements otherwise intact were thus overtaken or created anew, now in the hands of tribal leaders. Significantly, these conflicts arose most frequently

---

24 Iris von Bredow, *Die Geschichte Syriens vom Neolithikum bis zum Ende der Bronzezeit* (Abteilung Alte Geschichte, Historisches Institut der Universität Stuttgart; Stuttgart WS 2004/2005), printed manuscript.
25 Robert M. Whiting, "Amorite Tribes and Nations of Second-Millennium Western Asia," in *Civilizations of the Ancient Near East* (ed., Jack M. Sasson; New York: Charle Scribners Sons, 1995), II: 1231–1242.
26 Iris von Bredow, see note 19.
27 Ibid.
28 W. Schniedewind, *The Rise of the Aramean States* (JSOT Supp 341; London: Sheffield Academic Press, 2002): 276–287, esp. 279–280.

in times of drought or famine.[29] Other regions, by contrast, saw gradual infiltration of tribes into cultivated areas as an increasing symbiosis of pastoralists and sedentary inhabitants developed. Nevertheless, early Aramaean tribal leaders availed themselves of such natural conditions early on to gain dominion over sizable tracts of land. Judges 3:7–11 reports of a certain Cushan-rishathaim, an Aramaean ruler from Aram-Naharaim—an area of the Upper Euphrates, the Ḫabur region north of Jebel Bishri—who beleaguered ancient Israel for eight years and was eventually routed by Othniel. Although A. Malamat seeks to associate him with the usurper Jarsu (Ḫ'-ru) in Egypt at the end of the thirteenth century, there are no certain extrabiblical sources that secure such an historical connection.[30] Had this Aramaean actually exploited Egypt's weakness at the time, the conquest of Ramses III (1195–98) over those Aramaean territories, including Qsnrm, would occasion no surprise. In any case, the toponym Kushan-rom in northern Syria remains well known. Evidence of the Aramaeans' increased significance in ancient Near Eastern history at the end of the second millennium comes from Babylonia as well. At this time of Assur-bel-kala (1073–1056), an Aramaean usurper named Adad-apal-iddina, son of Itti-Marduk-balatu, came to the throne in Babylon.[31]

Middle Egyptian, Ugaritic, and Akkadian sources intimate a distinct Aramaean ethnicity only at the end of the second half of the second millennium. Such a designation seems to emerge from the region of Biq'a, in the fertile oasis of Damascus (Ghouta), already toward the end of the fifteenth and beginning of the fourteenth centuries, since this region in particular suggests a migration of Aramaean segments of the population. From the list of GNN on the mortuary temple of Amenophis III at Qom el-Heitan (Thebes West), where Cartouche 7 of the statue pedestal List D attests p; 'rm, Elmar Edel[32] contends the Aramaeans receive clear acknowledgment

29 In particular, see Peter M.M. Ackermann and Glenn M. Schwartz, *The Archaeology of Syria* (Cambridge: Cambridge University Press, 2003), 367.
30 A. Malamat, "Cushan Rishataim and the Decline of the Near East around 1200 B.C.," *JNES* 13, no. 4 (1954): 231–242, spec. 231.
31 ARI II, 62.
32 Elmar Edel, *Die Ortsnamenlisten aus dem Totentemple Amenophis III* (BBB 25; Bonn: Peter Hanstein Verlag, (1966), 28, 93, 96, Table II; Manfred Görg, *Aram und Israel*, *VT* 26/4 1976, 499–500 and Namenstudien III: Zum Problem

already at this time. Criticising such a conclusion drawn from one isolated instance of "Aram" within these Egyptian sources, Ran Zadok declares, "If this proves correct, then the *terminus post quem* for the Aramaean penetration into Syria is to be fixed a century earlier than other sources would allow."[33] Support for this interpretation, however, comes from Manfred Görg[34] who suggests the list represents a "Syrian-Mesopotamian direction," and W.M. Schniedewind[35], who considers this attestation the earliest for Aramaeans. Ugaritic and Akkadian cuneiform texts from fourteenth- and thirteenth-century Ras Šamra (ancient Ugarit) provide additional evidence for incipient sedentariness of Aramaean nomads. Accordingly, a Ugaritic census table describes Aramaeans armed with bows and slingshots, further connected to the city ubr'y: *bn. | army | š t | qštm | [w] [|]q[l'] (Col. III, Rev. ln. 22)*.[36] The four graphemes clearly allow for interpretation as an ethnic designation.[37] A. Dupont-Sommer, for instance, offers the following translation: *"Fils-de-Army: deux arcs et une fr[onde]."*[38] Discovered in 1952, the royal edict of RS 16.178 refers to a number of localities that includes a certain eqlêt[meš] a-ra-mi-ma (i.e. "fields of the Aramaeans"), which lay under the control of the Ugaritic king(!), whose territory likely stretched as far

einer Frühbezeugung von Aram, *BN* 9 1979, 7–10, esp. 10 and Elmar Edel, *Die Ortsnamenlisten im nördlichen Säulenhof des Totentempels Amenophis' III.* (ÄAT 50, Wiesbaden: Harrassowitz, 2005), 122, 144; otherwise see 'rm in another context: Karl Heinz Priese, Studien zur Topographie des 'äthiopischen' Niltales im Altertum und zur meroitischen Sprache, *EAZ* 17 1976, 315–329, esp. 318/19 and 'rm and ';m, das Land Irame. Ein Beitrag zur Topographie des Sudan im Altertum, *AOF* 1 1974, 7–41, esp. 18.

33 R. Zadok, 1991, 106.
34 Manfred Görg, "Namenstudien III", 10.
35 W. Schniedewind, 2002, 276.
36 On this census tablet, see already F. Thureau-Dangin, "Une tablette bilingue de Ras Shamra", *Revue d' Assyriology et d'Archéologie orientale* 37 (1940), 97–118, esp. 107(cuneiform), 115 (transcription and translation); see also Cyrus H. Gordon, *Ugaritic Handbook* (AO 25; Rome: Pontificium Institutum Biblicum, 1947), 174 (transcription), 215:292 (word index); idem, *Ugaritic Manual* (AO 35; Rome: Pontificium Institutum Biblicum 1955), 174 (transcription), 242:254 (word index). For this city, see P. Sacchi, *Osservazioni sul problema degli Armei*, Atti Acc Toscana Sci Lett 25 1960/61, 85–142.
37 Mahmud Muffaddi Abu Taleb, 1973, 38.
38 A. Dupont-Sommer, 1953, 46.

as the Orontes.[39] For John Van Seters, this expression indicates the steppe region of northwestern Syria, though such a localisation has not received confirmation.[40] As for analysis of Assyrian cuneiform tablets concerning the Aramaeans at the end of the second millennium, one find in particular proves quite important: the appearance of "proto- or early Aramaean tribes" of the Sutu, Aḫlamû and Aramaeans. An interpretative question then emerges: whether these tribes stand as differentiated nomadic groups or a single aggregated Semitic people. While Conn Grayson Davis distinguishes them, arguing both Sutu and Aḫlamû designate early tribal elements of later Aramaean populations, Van Seters maintains that soon after the emergence of sedentary Aramaean tribal groups, Sutu and Aḫlamû became a general sociological term for nomads, losing its earliest ethnic meaning.[41] R.A. Bowman connects the rise of the Aḫlamê-Ar(a)mâia to the decline of the Sutu and with good reason, since later sources attest to the Sutu migration first into the more stabilized regions of northern Syria and subsequently on to Mesopotamia.[42] As with the Aramaeans, evidence for the Aḫ-la-mû appears quite early through PNN, but the term occurs as an ethnic name only later, in cuneiform documents of fourteenth-century Dilmun in the Bahrein-Failaka region, for example.

More detailed inquiry confirms this portrait as well. Although the Mari letters allude to the designation Aḫ-la-mû as an ethnic group.[43] This latter assembly consists of a fragmentary Amarna letter (EA 200:8–11) and two dispatches from an officer stationed in Dilmun to the governor in Nippur, both missives dated to the time of Burnaburiash III (1375–1347). Before 2200, Dilmun lay within the Qurna region north of Basra, later within the

39 See J. Nougayrol, *Les Palais Royale d'Ugarit III Textes, Accadiens et Hourrites* (MRS 6; Paris: Imprimerie Nationale/Klincksiek, 1955), 48.

40 John Van Seters, *Abraham* (New Haven, London: Yale University Press, 1975), 30.

41 Conn Grayson Davis, 1979, 8, 21; John Van Seters, *Abraham*, 30.

42 Raymond A. Bowman, "Arameans, Aramaic and the Bible," *JNES* 7, no. 2 (1948): 65–90, esp. 69.

43 A. Dupont-Sommer, 1953, 4; so also M. Noth, "Die Ursprünge des alten Israel im Lichte neuer Quellen," *AbLA* 2 (1971): 267.

Failaka region.[44] The following transcription and translation of the cunei-form comes from A. Goetze:[45]

Ni 615:14–15

14	*[K]A.LUM Aḫ-la-mu-ú it-tab-lu*
15	*ú it-tu-ú-a-a mi–im-ma*
14	Around me the Aḫlamû have carried away the dates,
15	thus with me there is nothing that I can do.

Ni 641:12–1o.e.

12	*Aḫlamû*
13	*ša na-ka-ri*
14	*ú ha-ba-ti-im-ma*
1o.e.	*it-ti-ia*
	lu i-da-ab- [b]u-bu;...
12	The Aḫlamû
13	certainly talk
14	to me
1o.e.	only of violence
	and plunder;...

While Adad-nerari I mentions the Aḫlamû when recalling the victory his father, Arik-den-ilu, over them (1319–1308), further associating this population with the area north of Babylon, the group emerges later in a letter from the Hittite king Hattushili III of Hatti, which he wrote to the Cassite king Kadashman-Enlil II of Babylon (ca. 1270–1265). In this second text, the Hittite king expresses surprise that Kadashman-Enlil could not receive any messengers "because of Aḫlamian hostility."[46] Shalmaneser I (1274–1245) reports the defeat of King Shattuara of Ḫanigalbat (Mittani), who

---

44 T. Howard-Carter, "The Tangible Evidence for the Earliest Dilmun," *JCS* 33 (1981): 210–223; R.R. Stieglitz, "Ebla and Dilmun," in *Eblaitica 1* (Essays on the Ebla Archives and Eblaite Language ed. by Cyrus H. Gordon, Gary A. Rendsburg, Nathan H. Winter, Winona Lake, Indiana.: Eisenbrauns, 1987), 43–46, esp. 43.

45 A. Goetze, "The Texts Ni 615 and Ni 641 of the Istanbul Museum," *JCS* 6 (1952), 142–145 (Appendix), esp. 145; P. Cornwall, "Two Letters from Dilmun," *JCS* 6 (1952): 137–142.

46 KBo I 10, 36–54; Roger T. O'Callaghan, *Aram Naharaim—A Contribution to the History of Upper Mesopotamia in the Second Millennium B.C.* (AO 26; Rome: Pontificium Institutum Biblicum, 1948), 101; Mahmud Muffadi Abu Taleb, 1973, 37 and C. Vandersleyen, L'Euphrate, Aram Naharaim et la Bible,

21

had allied himself with groups of Aḫlamû and Hittites; Shalmaneser's son Tukulti-Ninurta I (1244–1208), moreover, conquered the "mountains of the Aḫlamû" along with the territories of Mari, Hana, and Rapiqum in the Euphrates region (ARI I, 82/119).[47] Finally, Ashur-resha-ishi (1133–1116) details battles against the Aḫlamû, who by this time had inhabited wide swaths of the Syrian desert and Mesopotamia. Transcribed and translated by E. Weidner, the following text comes from the inscription on clay knobs:[48]

Nr. 60, 6: ṣa-ab.[..] . ša-giš ummânât^{meš-at}
 aḫ-la-mi–i   rapišati^{meš} mu-par-ri-ir el-la-te-šú-nu

šá i-na siq-ri   ^d nin-urta qar-di ilâni^{meš} e-liš u
šap-liš [....]

.....[..]., der hinmetzelte die weit ausgedehnten Völker der Aḫlamê, ihre Truppen zerschmetterte, der auf Geheiß des Ninurta, des Helden der Götter, droben und drunten [......]

Importantly, the form Aḫlamê-Ar(a)mâia seems to offer clear testimony to that commonly attested combination of the proto-Aramaean tribes the Aḫlamû and the Ar(a)mâia—first mentioned in the annals of the Assyrian king Tiglath-Pileser I (1114–1076) during his fourth regnal year—although precise interpretation of this designation has seen considerable debate. The question of reference thus comes to the fore, namely, whether the appellation alludes to a confederation of nomadic and seminomadic groups based in the district KUR bi-eš-ri (Jebel Bishri), southwest of the Euphrates, as far as Tadmor (Palmyra).[49] W.F. Saggs affirms such a hypothesis, and

---

in: Le Museon. Revue d'études, 107, Louvain-La-Neuve: Peeters, 1994, esp. 5–14.

47 KBo I 10, 37. For the document dating to the time of Tukuli-Ninurta I, see E. Weidner, *Die Inschriften Tukuli-Ninurta I und seiner Nachfolger* (AfO Bei. 12; Graz: Weidner, 1959), 27–28 and Hayim Tadmor, Historical implications of the correct rendering of Akkadian dâku, *JNES* XVII/1 Jan 1958, 129–141, esp. 139 ff.

48 Ibid., 54.

49 The Aramaean Aḫlamû stemmed from this region according to Wolfgang Leineweber, *Die Patriarchen im Licht der archäologischen Entdeckung* (EHS.T Reihe XXII Bd. 127), Frankfurt am Main: Peter Lang, 1980, 28; cf. Glenn M. Schwartz, "Pastoral Nomadism in Western Asia" in *Civilizations of the An-*

J.A. Brinkman goes so far as to suggest this reference concerns seminomads affilated with the Yaḥmadiu within the Ur-III texts.[50] For a more detailed explanation of this specific term, several witnesses prove particularly significant. Since A. Grayson translates aḫ-la-me-e with the general sense of "nomads, barbarians" and since Assyrian cuneiform texts always designate gentilics with *KUR* followed by *MEŠ*, Manfred Weippert renders the term "Aramaean Bedouin."[51] Other scholars like R.T. O'Callagan, A. Malamat, and Mahmud Muffadi Abu Taleb, by contrast, understand the locution Ar(a)mâia in reference only to a "branch" or "sub-unit" of an Aḫlamû confederation.[52] Accordingly, Klaas R. Veenhof

cient Near East I (New York: Scribner, 1995), 249–258, esp. 256; Paul E. Dion, "Aramean Tribes and Nations of First-Millennium Western Asia" in *Civilizations of the Ancient Near East II* (New York: Charles Scribners Sons, 1995), 1281–1284, esp. 1281.

50 Henry W. F. Saggs, *Babylonians* (2nd ed; London: British Museum Press, 2000), 128–139, spec. 129; J.A. Brinkman, *A Political History of Post-Kassite Babylonia 1158–722 B.C.* (Anal Or; 43; Rome: Pontifical Institute Press, 1968), 277–278, n. 1799; cited by David. I. Owen, "Some New Evidence on Yamadiu = Aḫlamû" in *The Tablet and the Scroll: Near Eastern Studies in Honor of William W. Hallo* (ed. Mark E. Cohen, Daniel C. Snell, David B. Weinsberg; Bethesda, Maryland: CDL Press, 1993), 181–184, esp. 181.

51 Albert Kirk Grayson, ARI II:13; Weippert, *Die Landnahme der israelitischen Stämme in der neueren wissenschaftlichen Diskussion* (FRLANT 92; Göttingen: Vandenhoeck & Ruprecht, 1967), 103. This goes to confirm with the comments of R. Zadok, The Aramean Infiltration and diffusion in the Upper Jazira, ca. 1150– 930 BCE., in: Gershon Galil, et al. Eds., The Ancient Near East in the 12th – 10th Centuries B.C.E.: Culture and History. Proceedings of the International Conference held at the University of Haifa, 2–5 May 2010, AOAT Bd. 392, Münster: Ugarit-Verl. 2012, 569–579, esp. 570: "The West Semitic semi-nomads, who are labeled 'Suteans' (mostly in Middle-Assyrian sources) or Aḫlamites (mostly in Middle and Standard Babylonian sources) then, were very probably the ancestors of the Arameans. This can be argued in view of the fact that the latter first appear as Aḫlamû Aramâyu in Middle-Assyrian sources. Aḫlamû Aramâyu means 'the Aramean semi-nomads.' This means that the Arameans were regarded as a group of Aḫlamites (= Middle-Assyrian Suteans)."

52 Roger T. O'Callaghan, 1948, 95; A. Malamat, "The Arameans," in *Peoples of the Old Testament Times* (ed. D.T. Wiseman; Oxford: Claredon Press, 1973), 134–155, esp. 135; Mahmud Muffaddi Abu Taleb, 1973, 173.

glosses it "Aramaean Aḫlamû."[53] The parameters of usage for *KUR* and *MEŠ* and the consistency with which the denomination ar-ma-a-ia falls among them demands analysis as a gentilic for these attestations.[54] Indeed, examples from the end of the second millennium up until the ninth century B.C.E. confirm this proposition:

Tiglath-Pileser I (1114–1076)

	aḫ-la-me-e	*KUR ar-ma-a-ia*	*MEŠ*	(ARI II:13)
(KUR) aḫ-la-me-e		*KUR ar-ma.ia*	*MEŠ*	(ARI II:23)
KUR aḫ-la-me-e		*KUR ar-ma-a-ia*	*MEŠ*	(ARI II:27)
É.MEŠ KUR		*ar-ma-ia*	*MEŠ*	(VAT 10453+10465)
		See[55]		

Aššur-bel-kala (1073–1056)

KUR [a] ḫ-la-me-i	*KUR ar-ma-ia*	*MEŠ*	(Frag. BM 134497)[56]

Adad-nerari II (911–891)

KUR aḫ-la-me-e	*KUR ar-ma-a-ia*	*MEŠ*	(ARI II:87)

Aššur-nasir-apli II (883–859)

(KUR) aḫ-la-me-e	*KUR ar-a-ma-ia*	*MEŠ*	(ARI II:163)

In short, Assyrian documents from the end of the twelfth to the middle of the ninth centuries evince an Aramaean ethnicity. Such written evidence, however, does not suggest these populations ever had a propensity for a unifying pan-Aramaean superpower. As Schniedewind avers, "...the Arameans were not so much an ethnic group as a social group. The often-posed question of ethnicity of Arameans must now be dismissed."[57]

53 Klaas R. Veenhof, *Grundrisse zum Alten Testament* (ATD Ergänzungsband 11; Göttingen: Vandenhoeck & Ruprecht, 2001), 210.

54 Gotthard G.G. Reinhold, *EHS.T* 368 1989, 35–36. As for the term aḫlamû, Michael Herles defines its referent as an "amalgamation of people from various tribes," not a distinct ethnicity (idem, "Zur geographischen Einordnung der aḫlamû–eine Bestandsaufnahme" *AltorF* 34, no. 2 [2007]: 322, see further 319–341).

55 See Ernst Weidner, Book Review Arno Poebel, The Second Dynastie of Isin according to a New King List Tablet VIII (Assyriological Studies, No. 15), Chicago: Chicago Press, 155, *AfO* 17 1954–1956, 383–385.

56 A. R. Millard, Fragments of Historical Texts from Niniveh: Middle Assyrian and Later Kings, *Iraq* 32 1970, 167–176, esp. 168–169.

57 William M. Schniedewind, *The Rise of the Aramean States*, 283.

Only in the eleventh century, during the reign of Ashur-bel-kala (1074–1057), did the Aramaeans receive a designation distinct from the term Aḫlamû: "He attacked a contingent of Arameans in GN" or "He undertook a campaign against the Arameans in GN" (*ḫarrâna ša KUR Arimi ina GN imtaḫas*).[58] More explicitly, the cuneiform fragment BM 134497 refers to a certain "Land of the Arameans" (Tablet 33, ln. 4): *mât meš 6 kam ([ar]ki) a-ri-mi ša šatti (1ᵏᵃᵐ 2-[šu...])*, best translated "(after) the Land of the Arameans which in the (first year twice [...]).*"[59]

Although Schniedewind rejects the previous formulaic parameters for designation of ethnic groups in this particular instance and prefers instead to translate *mât a-ri-mi meš* as "Region of Aram," the implication of an ethnic group seems evident here, since the text employs *mât* in place of the expected *KUR*.[60]

58 Rykle Borger, *Einleitung in die assyrischen Königsinschriften I: Das zweite Jahrtausend v. Chr.* (HO I Ergänzungsband V/1; Leiden, Köln: E. J. Brill, 1961), 139 f.; A. K. Grayson, *Assyrian Royal Inscriptions II*, Wiesbaden: Otto Harrassowitz, 1976, esp. 52–54, 58, 62 and *Assyrian Rulers of the Early First Millennium I (1114– 859 BC)*, The Royal Inscriptions of Mesopotamia. Assyrian Periods 2, Toronto., Buffalo, London: University of Toronto Press), 1991, 93–94, 100–103.

59 A. R. Millard, "Fragments of Historical Texts from Nineveh: Middle Assyrian and Later Kings" *Iraq* 32 (1970): 167–176, esp. 168–169.

60 See Richard Caplice, *Introduction to Akkadian* (Studia Pohl: Series Maior 9; Rome: Pontifical Institute, 1983), 87, where *KUR* = mâtum "land."

3 Toward the Origin of the Aramaeans in the Hebrew Bible

As indicated in the oldest extrabiblical sources (2), Aramaean segments of the population resided in the desert region of western Mesopotamia up until the end of Middle Bronze Age II. Based on ceramic analysis from regional surveys, Glen M. Schwartz posits an initial population growth in the middle of the Ḥabur region during the Late Bronze and Early Iron Age.[61] Such information supports the proposal of Amihai Mazar, who concludes that ancient traditions underlie the patriarchal narratives—passed on from generation to generation and circulated in some written form already during the Israelite-Judahite monarchy.[62] Kenneth A. Kitchen likewise dates the patriarchal narratives to the early second millennium according to the socioeconomic milieu manifoldly reflected in the oldest written evidence.[63] However, other scholars of Hebrew Bible like Van Seters, argue for a much later writing of these narratives: i.e., during the late monarchy, when deported Israelites of the Ḥabur region, Aramaeans relocated to Palestine, and Aramaean settlers of the Harran region all practiced similar ways of

---

61 Glenn M. Schwartz, "The Origins of the Arameans in Syria and Northern Mesopotamia: Research Problems and Potential Strategies," in *To the Euphrates and Beyond* (ed. O.M.C. Haex, H.H. Curvers, and P.M.M. Akkermans, Rotterdam, Brookfield: VT A.A. Balkema, 1989), 275–291, esp. 285; in particular, see those statistics for the "number of sites through the time (North Eastern Syria)" and "hectares occupied through the time: Ḥabur and Biqʿ surveys" as set forth in Thomas C. McClellan, "Twelfth Century B.C. Syria: Comments on H. Sader's Paper" in *The Crisis Years: The 12th Century B.C. From Beyond the Danube to the Tigris* (Dubuque, IA: Kendall/Hunt Pub., 1992), 164–173.

62 Amihai Mazar, *Archaeology of the Land of the Bible, 10.000–586 B.C.E.* (New York: Doubleday – Anchor, 1990), 225–226.

63 See Kenneth A. Kitchen (1995, 56 ff. ; 2003, 313 ff.). For the problem of establishing the historicity of the patriarchal narratives, B.S.J. Isserlin (1998, 42 ff.). To the age of the patriarchs see already before: Thomas L. Thompson (1974, 315 ff.), William H. Stiebing (1975, 16–24 and John J. Bimson (1980, 59 ff.). For recent literature on the patriarchal period, see n. 5.

life and adapted themselves ethno-nationally.[64] The question then arises as to whether or not already after the fall of the southern kingdom and the subsequent deportation of the greater social strata—and even into the reign of Nabunaid (556–539)—the basic trajectory of ancient Israel's thought would have centred on the nation itself, the return to native soil, and the restoration of land and city alike, particularly Jerusalem and the temple. Within this framework, literary compositions would have set in the foreground no longer the theme of "the departure of ancient Israel's forefathers from Mesopotamia" but much more "the return of myriad deported Israelites to that home of theirs which was once acquired but was now destroyed by mighty Babylon."[65] To establish these "Aramaean relationships," W.T. Pitard enumerates various traditions:[66]

1. First, he cites the descendants of Nahor (Gen 22:20–24, esp. v. 21), where Aram appears as the eponym of the Aramaeans and grandson of Abraham's brother, Nahor, whose sons include both Buz and Kemuel, the father of Aram.[67] As for Uz (Job 1:1,3), C. Westermann proposes a region northeast of Edom, Buz (Job 31:1–3; Jer 25:23) localizable near Edom and further attested in the inscription from Sefire (COS 2.82, IB: 2, 9).[68] While Chesed rests within the vicinity of Uz and Buz (2 Kgs 24:12; Job 1:17), Hazo certainly designates the highlands northeast of Ba-a-zu. Finally, Tebaḥ along with the cities Tubiḫi (= *[Du]b-bi-ḫi*) and Maacah (Deut 3:13; 2 Sam 10:5; 20:14 f.; Josh 13:11,13) most likely refer to established Aramaean territory.

2. Second, Pitard references the priestly genealogy, the so-called "Table of Nations" (Gen 10:22), in which Aram appears alongside Elam, Asshur, Arpachschad, and Lud as one of the sons of Shem, the sons of Aram then including Uz, Hul, Gether, and Mash (v.23). Although Aram represents the Aramaeans as ethnic groups of Syria and Mesopotamia, the relationship with Hul and Gether remains unknown. For this reason, Mash reportedly

---

64 John Van Seters, Abraham in History and Tradition, New Haven, London: Yale University Press 1975, 34.

65 Gotthard G.G. Reinhold, *EHS.T* 368 1989, 66.

66 Wayne T. Pitard, *Arameans: People of the Old Testament World* (Cambridge: The Lutherworth Press, Grand Rapids, Michigan: Baker Books, 1996), 207 f.

67 C. Vandersleyen, *L'Euphrat, Aram Naharaim et la Bible*, 8/9.

68 Claus Westerman, *Genesis I:1–11* (BKAT 1/1; Neukirchen-Vluyn: Neukirchener Verlag, 1974), 662–665, 685.

lies with Mons Masius northeast of Nusaybin and Uz (cf. Gen 22:21 J) and in the Safa region east of Hauran.[69]

3. Pitard finds a third tradition for the origins of Aram in Amos 9:7, where the home of the Arameans appears in conjunction with Kir, although the prophet Amos speaks of Aram's banishment to Kir already in the oracles against the nations (1:5, final section), which thereby accords with 9:7(!).[70] The passage centres broadly on "the turn of holiness" (9:7–15), specifically on the so-called "judgment of purification."[71] Crucial for this connection, a thirteenth-century cuneiform document from Emar on the Euphrates refers to dPil-su-Dagan (*KUR*), the king of URUEmar (*E-mar*), who was also king of the land of Qi-ri (gen.).[72] Amos could thus have aroused in the Israelite-Judahite monarchic period ancient oral memories of early Aramaean history. This postulate does maintain a certain feasibility.

4. Aramaean kinship may also receive allusion in connection to Bethuel and Laban (Gen 25:20;31:20), with particular mention emerging from the story of Esau and Jacob's birth (Gen 25:19–28), whereby v.20 describes Rebecca as the daughter of Bethuel the Aramaean from Paddan-Aram and the sister of Laban the Aramaean.[73] Genesis 31:20 contrasts this genealogical portrayal, however, in Jacob's flight from Laban the Aramaean.

5. For the final tradition concerning the kinship of ancient Israel with the Aramaeans, Pitard cites the well known verse from Deuteronomic law, Deut. 26:5 f.: *'ă r a m m î 'ô b e d 'â b î.*

As Gerhard von Rad has demonstrated, this passage stands as a credo "which bears all the marks of great antiquity [i.e., from the early monarchic

---

69 See G. Fohrer, "Uz" in *BL Calwer*, Sp. 1378.
70 Jörg Jeremias, *Der Prophet Amos* (ATD 24/2; Göttingen: Vanbdenhoeck & Ruprecht, 1995), 11, 13–14; Hans Walter Wolf, *Dodekapropheton 2: Joel und Amos* (BKAT XIV/2; Neukirchen-Vluyn: Neukirchener Verlag, 1969), 189–191.
71 Jörg Jeremias, *Amos*, 128, 130–131; Hans Walter Wolf, *Dodekapropheten*, 398–400; see further Bruce E. Willoughby, "Amos" in *The Anchor Bible Dictionary*, vol. I (New York, London, Toronto, Sydney, Auckland: Doubleday, 1992), 203–212, esp. 209.
72 See Daniel Arnaud, *Textes sumériens et accadiens*, vol. 3 (Recherches au pays d'Aštata, Emar VI/3., Paris: Editions Recherche sur les Civilisations, 1986, 42: 8–9.
73 Claus Westermann, *Genesis 2:12–36* (BKAT 1/2; Neukirchen:-Vluyn: Neukirchener Verlag, 1981), 501, 503, 594.

period]."[74] Secondary Deuteronomic reworking expanded earlier material (vv.5–11) that originally consisted of an old cultic tradition regarding provisions for the first fruits harvest and the liturgical ceremony for their presentation (vv.4,10). Analysis from R.P. Merendino has further revealed how already the Deuteronomic redactor possessed a "creed in expanded form," thereby evincing a pre-Deuteronomic redactor.[75] In contrast, both B.S. Childs and W. Richter consider the stage of this cultic confession Deuteronomistic.[76]

Crucial for the understanding of this passage is the background chosen for precise translation of these three components. With some fantasy of the negative sort, the term *'ărammî* has been rendered à la M.A. Beek in the sense of "sheeperder," which merits little serious consideration.[77] W.F. Albright's translation "wandering trader"—which comports with his broader "donkey caravan" theory—moves in the same questionable direction: "Since 'RMY meant 'travelling trader' in early South Arabic (Qatabanian), the phrase may simply have meant 'wandering trader.'"[78] Rather, this phraseology most likely suggests the ancient Israelites felt themselves akin to the Aramaeans and even had knowledge of their forefathers' ancestry. Proper understanding of *'âb* (v.5a) proves similarly problematic.

Based on the frequency with which *âbad* appears in the Qal with the meaning of "to perish" (78 times), H. Seebaß imagines a "downfall of

---

74 Here I refer to Leonhard Rost (1965, 11), Gerhard von Rad (1969 (Nachdruck), 135/36). See also E. W. Nicholson (1973, 20 ff.), Horst Seebass (1978, 110) and William McKane (1979, 116).

75 Rosario Pius Merendino, *Das Deuteronomische Gesetz–Eine literarkritische, gattungs- und überlieferungsgeschichtliche Untersuchung zu Dr. 12–26* (BBB 31; Bonn: Hanstein, 1969), 362.

76 B. S. Childs, "Deuteronomic Formulae of the Exodus Tradition," in *Hebräische Wortforschung. FS W. Baumgärtner,* SVT 16; Leiden: Brill, 1967), 30–39, spec. 39; W. Richter, "Beobachtungen zur theologischen Systembildung in der alttestamentlichen Literatur anhand des 'kleinen geschichtlichen Credo'" in *Wahrheit und Verkündigung. FS für M. Schmaus zum 70. Geburtstag* (München, Paderborn, Wien: Verlag Ferdinand Schöningh, 1967), 175–212, esp. 210–212.

77 Martinus Adrianus Beek, "Das Problem des aramäischen Stammvaters (Deut XXVI 5)," *OTS VIII* (1950): 197–212, esp. 203.

78 William Foxwell Albright, "Emergence of the Arameans" *CAH³* 2/2 (1975), 529–536, esp. 531.

threatened Arameans."[79] The lexeme also denotes "to vanish" (21 times) or "to go astray" (six times), which led von Rad to speak of "Wandern der Väter" (in sense of) "Umherirren verlaufener Herdentiere."[80]

R.P. Merendino prefers the third option since it preserves contextual continuity with not only the wandering of the forefather—who possessed no land of his own at the beginning (v.5 'ôbêd)—but also the phrases "I have entered" (v.3 bâ'tî) and "I bring (progeny)" (v.10 hêbê'tî).[81] Such a statement, however, requires some refinement: the forebear did not so much "wander" erratically as much as "run away." To borrow from Schniedewind, Abraham was actually a "fugitive Aramean"![82] Yet this description, applies more to Jacob than Abraham, for he had to abandon Laban's family and economy in secret, fleeing to the Transjordan and ultimately moving to Egypt on account of famine.[83] As for the fundamental significance of this 'ărammî ôbêd, the phrase finds considerable analogue in the social status of the *munnabtu*, an individual who found himself on the run and sought political asylum at a secure locality where he could not rightly be seized.[84]

In conclusion, two cuneiform texts prove relevant. The first refers to the "land of the Arameans" and describes the Sutu as inhabitants of tents,

---

79 H. Seebaß, *Der Erzvater Israel und die Einführung der Jahweverehrung in Kanaan* (BZAW 98; Berlin: Alfred Töpelmann, 1966), 4.

80 Gerhard von Rad, *Das fünfte Buch Mose Deuteronomium* (ATD. Neues Göttinger Bibelwerk, Teilbd. 8, Berlin: Evangelische Verlagsanstalt, 1965), 114.

81 R. P. Merendino, 1969, 352.

82 W. M. Schniedewind, *The Rise of the Aramean States*, 282–283.

83 Ibid. Although he recognises the problematic, Schniedewind attempts to relate this passage directly to Abraham: "Certainly, the gentilic nominal formation of 'Aramean' ('rmy) allows such an interpretation. It might then reflect the region of Abraham's origin, that is Harran on the Middle Euphrates, as well as the semi-nomadic pastoralist setting that we see in the patriarchal narratives." He concludes: "This socioanthropological background, unfortunately, does not aid in dating the origins of the Patriarchal narratives since seminomadic pastoralism was and is a staple of these regions until the present day. [...] On the other hand, the use of the term Aramean in Abraham's confession might suggest that the confession 'My father was a wandering/fugitive Aramean' arose *before* the crystallization of the Aramean states as the arch-enemies of Israel."

84 Giorgio Buccellati, "'Apirû and Munnabtûtu—The Stateless of the First Cosmopolitan Age," *JNES* 36 (1977), 145–147.

refugees, and a "treacherous, marauding race:" *i-na mati ma-ad-bar šá-a-t-ú (amel)a-ra-me (amel) su-ti-í a-ši-bu-ut kuš-ta-ri mu-nab-tu sa-ar-ru mâr ḫab-ba-ti* (Nimrud Prism of Sargon II [721–05], Col VII. 57–59).[85] The second comes from the annals of Sennacherib in connection to the governor of the city of 'La-ḫi-ri and alludes to Shuzubu, a Chaldean (*[m]Šú-zu-bu [am]Kal-dà-ai*), portraying him as an Aramaean refugee, runaway, murderer, and plunderer:[86] (22) *'La-ḫi-ri [am]A-ra-me ḫal-ḳu mun-nab-tú[1] a-mir da-me* (23) *ḫab-bi-lu și-ru-uš-šu ip-ḫu-ru-ma ki-rib 'a-gam-me* .... While the former witness employs the terms *a-ra-me... mu-nab-tu... mâr ḫab-ba-ti*, the latter uses *a-ra-me ḫal-ḳu mun-ab-tú*. If indeed the usage of such terminology, which appears in connection to the Sutu, Aramaeans, and other nomadic ethnic groups from the desert, did not fundamentally change within the cuneiform sources over several centuries, then these particular texts may well express the conception evident in older texts of the second millennium. Thus, Millard correctly interprets the diction of Deut 26:5, "which asserts a shift to a higher status, reflects the same traditions, and can be understood well in the light of 2nd. millennium B.C. society."[87]

---

85 C. J. Gadd, "Inscribed Prism of Sargon II from Nimrud" *Iraq* 16 (1954): 173–201, esp. 192–193 and Plate L.

86 Daniel David Luckenbill, *The Annals of Sanherib* (OIP II; Chicago, Illinois: The University Press, 1924), 42, Col. V.:22; see also idem, "The Wandering Arameans," *AJSL* 36 (1920): 244–245; Alan R. Millard, "A Wandering Aramean,"*JNES* 39 (1980); 153–155.

87 Alan R. Millard, "Arameans" in *The Anchor Bible Dictionary*, vol. 1 (New York, London, Toronto, Sydney, Auckland: Doubleday, 1992), 345–350, esp. 348.

4 Aram's Ascent to Power at the End of the 2nd and Beginning of the 1st Millennium BCE until the End of its Rule

4.1 Aram's Development in Northern Syria and Upper Mesopotamian from the 11th to 8th Centuries BCE

As already mentioned in Section 2, the Aramaeans crossed the Euphrates and withdrew into the environs of the Bishri mountains after their defeat by Tiglath-Pileser I (1114–1076). The Assyrian king, however, continued pursuit, destroying six Aramaean cities in the region and campaigning successfully.[88] Understandably, Tiglath-Pileser's military goals converged with concerns for control of trade routes spanning from the Mediterranean and Anatolia to Babylon, with nomadic shepherds of the Middle Euphrates and Ḫabur Region implicated in recurrent attacks on caravans. Tiglath-Pileser continually traversed the Euphrates, even twice in one year, to drive back the Aḫlamu-Aramaeans.[89] But at the end of his reign—and during one especially severe drought—he was unable to emerge victorious from a large-scale Aramaean invasion into Assyria. After the capture of Ninevah, flight remained the only option for him and his army. Tiglath-Pileser's son and successor, Ashur-bel-kala (1073–1056) also led campaigns against Aramaean groups in northwestern Assyria, the Ḫabur Triangle, and the western Euphrates.[90]

In contrast to this period of Assyrian rule when the Aramaeans had not yet developed any significant political power but migrated as shepherds and inhabited smaller settlements, the situation changed in the late 11th and 10th centuries. A number of states crystallized within Syria and Upper Mesopo-

---

88 ANET 275b. Albert Kirk Grayson, *Assyrian Royal Inscriptions Part 2: Records of the Ancient Near East* (ed. Hans Goedecke; Wiesbaden: Otto Harrassowitz, 1976), 23; E. Lipiński, "Aramäer und Israel," *TRE III* (1978): 591; *TUAT* I/4 (1984): 357; W. T. Pitard, *Arameans*, 210–211; Schniedewind, *Rise of the Arameas States*, 277.
89 Horst Klengel, *Syria 3000–300 B.C.* (Berlin: Akademie Verlag, 1992), 185.
90 Ibid.

tamia under Aramaean control, the ruling classes showing a strong cultural affinity to the old Hittite empire. These Neo-Hittite states emerged with such names as Patina, Hamath, Que, and Gurgum. Likewise, such states material-ized in Upper Mesopotamia, established on tribal systems and named after the dynasties' founders in the form bît-PN (i.e., "house of PN"), as with Bît Zamâni, Bît Baḫiâni, Bît-Ḫalupê (or Ḫadippe), and Laqê. These polities ran north-south along the Upper Tigris and Ḫabur River up to its connec-tion with the Euphrates.[91] To the west, at the great bend of the Euphrates, Bît-Adini arose as a dangerous opponent to Assyria during the early ninth century. Yaḫan, later called Bît-Agusi, extended north of the Euphrates, and northwest of Bît Agusi lay the important state of Hamath, whose rulers bore Anatolian names during the tenth and ninth centuries, Aramaean ones in the eight.[92] The rulers of Aram-Zobah controlled the region south of Hamath. One of the most powerful Aramaean states, Aram-Zobah dominated the land northeast of Anti-Lebanon and into the Syrian-Arabian desert toward Tad-mor (Palmyra), continuing as far as Aram-Damascus (4.2), which succeeded Aram-Zobah politically and became the strongest and most important of the Aramaean states.[93] Smaller territories consisted of the following: (a) Aram-(Bît-)Reḥob—previously several distinct localities—with its centre located perhaps at Tell el-Muʿallaqa[94] of Wâdi er-Raḥûb, east of Irbid at Khirbet

---

91 For these Aramaean states in particular, see Glenn M. Schwartz, "Origins of the Arameans," 278–289. To the historical topography, the ancient Neo-Hitite states and the Aramaean dynasties in Mesopotamia see the following maps in: Horst Klengel (1992, 263 ff. (Syria, 2 and 1 millennium); André Lemaire, Jean-Marie Durand (1984, 62/63), Joachim Voos (1988, 348 Abb. 1) and P. E. Dion (1997, Carte 1–2).

92 Regarding the rulers of Hamat, see Hélène S. Sader, *Les états araméens de Syrie depuis leur fondation jusqu'à leur transformation en provinces assyriennes* (BTSt 35; ed. Orient-Institut der Deutschend Morgenländischen Gesellschaft; Wies-baden: Franz Steiner, 1987), 287–288: To'i and Joram/Hadoram (ca. 1004–965), Paratas (ca. 880–60), Urhilinas (ca. 860–30), and Uratamis (ca. 830–10), as well as Zakkur (ca. 810–775), Eni-ilu (ca. 750–30), and Yaubi'di (ca. 730–20).

93 See Stefania Mazzoni, Syria and the Chronology of the Iron Age, (2015, 124).

94 See Höhne, Ernst. Red., Hermann Wahle, Kart., Palästina. Historisch-Archäologische Karte, Göttingen: Vandenhoeck & Ruprecht, 1981, Blatt Nord, 81, 95 (= G 5).

er-Raḥûb (Cavea Roob), or Riḥâb, in the western landscape of El-Mefraq[95], but more probably either in the area of the southern Biqâ', north of Dan, as already suggested by R.T. O'Callaghan, A. Dupont-Sommer, M. F. Unger, and others[96] or as a still unknown Aramaean Bît Rhb located south of Aram-Zoba[97]; (b) Aram-Maacah with the region west of the Galilean Sea, Jordan River, and Mount Hermon; and (c) Geshur with the quarters east of the Galileean Sea and Bashan. Undoubtedly, these boundaries continually shifted according to political circumstance, the larger territories ultimately incorporated into the great Aramaean empire of Aram-Damascus. Even into the tenth century however, the Aramaean states along the Ḥabur River lay within the dominion of Ashur-dan II (934–912), Adad-niraris II (911–891), and Tukulti-ninurta II (890–884)[98]. The Aramaean states of Bît-Zamâni, Bît-Baḫiâni, Bît-Ḥalûpe, and the region of Laqê all fell to subjugation under Ashur-dan II.[99]

---

95 So Ibid., 15, 81 (= H 6).
96 Ibid., 15 (= D 4); Wayne T. Pitard, 1987, 89; Edward Lipinski, LAOS 3 2013, 126.
97 See also T. C. Mitchell, Rehob, in: GBL, Wuppertal, Giessen, Bd. 3 1989, Sp. 1279. On the other side Tel Rehov (arab. Tell es-Sarem), meaning "broad," "wide place," was occupied in the Bronze and Iron Age, five km south el Beth-Shean (arab. Tell el-Ḥöṣn), three km west of the Jordan river, (http://en.wikipedia.org/wiki/Rehov) is already in the Pharao Seti I. - Stele from Beth Shean described as "city-state Rehov," was under Davids control, when he smote Hadad-ezer, king of Aram-Zoba, a native of Aram-Rehob (see Horst Klengel, 1992, 193) and is also listed as one of the cities from Pharao Shishak, which he has captured. In the Iron Age II a (1000–925 BC) the lower and upper cities of Tel Rehov, a large city for that time (!) – until to the destruction of the lower city 830 BC – have demonstrated a large occupation. The situation of Stratum IV is connected with Hazaels conquest and with the settlement-gap and Stratum III with Jeroboam's rebuilding and the destruction of the city by Tiglath-pileser III's campaign in 732 BC. See: Tel eth-Shean: http://www.rehov.org/project/tel_beth_shean.htm; TelRehov: http://rehov.org/Rehov/Results.htm; Tel Rechov, Beit-She'an Valley: http://www.biblewalks.Com/sites/Rechov.html and at all: Othmar Keel and Amihai Mazar, (2009, 57* ff.), Amihai Mazar (2014).
98 Horst Klengel, 1992, 194.
99 See further Hrayr Avetisyan, "On the Role of Aramean Principalities in the History of Northern Mesopotamia," in Šulmu IV: Everyday Life in the Ancient Near East: Papers Presented at the International Conference Poznan, 19–22 Sept. 1989 (ed. Julia Zablocka and Stefan Zawadzki; Universytet im Adama Mickiewiczca w Poznaniu; Seria Historia 182, Poznan: Adam Mickiewicza Universytet, 1993), 21–26.

At this time, Bît-Adini implicated itself in anti-Assyrian machinations and supported a rebellion in Bît-Ḫalupê, where the pro-Assyrian governor was murdered and subsequently replaced with a loyalist of Bît-Adini. The years 877 and 867 then saw Bît-Adini's auxiliary efforts in a revolt consisting of Laqê, Ḫindânu, and Sûḫu. As vengeance, Ashurnasirpal desolated a number of cities, though Bît-Adini never fully capitulated.

During the time of Shalmaneser III (858–24), Assyria expanded its domain further west (COS 2.113A).[100] Four years of bitter conflict ensued until Bît-Adini finally succumbed to Assyria's provincial system, thereby granting the Assyrians full control over the Euphrates. Still farther westward, Shalmaneser successfully relegated various states to Assyrian vassals, including Bît-Agusi (still Yaḫan at the time of Ashurnasirpal), Sam'al, and the Neo-Hittite states of Karkemish, Patina, Kummuḫ, Gurgum, and Que, among others. In the middle of the ninth century, he then concentrated his expansion efforts on central and south Syria.

Shalmaneser marched his troops southward to Hamath and encountered a tremendous and powerful coalition[101] of Syro-Palestinian states, which he fought at Qarqar in the vicinity of Hamath, the royal city (cf. section 4.2). After 853, he found himself embroiled predominantly in northern Syria and Upper Mesopotamia. With the final years of his reign and the incumbency of Shamshi-Adad V (823–811) came increased resistance from the north Syrian states, which sought to escape Assyrian control more and more. Yet Adad-nirari III (810–783) found himself in good position to stabilize the political situation.[102] Following the campaign of 808, which brought about the conquest of the Ghouta in Bît-Baḫiâni, he spent the years 805 and 804 fighting a coalition led King Attar-shumki of Bît-Agusi. Adad-nirari crushed the rebellion and returned to northern Syria to solidify control in the region.[103]

---

100 Cf. Horst Klengel, 1992, 196 ff.

101 See also Nadav Na'aman, The Northern Kingdom in the Late Tenth-Ninth Centuries BCE., in: Understanding the History of Ancient Israel, (Proceedings of the British Academy 143), Oxford/New York: Oxford University Press 2007, 399–418, esp. 408.

102 A. R. Millard and Hayim Tadmor, "Adad-nirari III in Syria: Another Stela Fragment and the Dates of His Campaigns" *Iraq* 35 (1973): 61.

103 Ibid., 58–62.

Assyrian power in northern Syria dwindled during the 8th century. Despite a few campaigns, Shamshi-ilu had to show his true mettle, for Arpad and other western states had distanced themselves from Assyria.[104] All in all, the complete political portrait of 760–750 remains obscure. This unfortunate state of affairs also pertains to the specification of rulers set forth in the so-called Sefire treaties, which include a concord of Mati'el, son of Attar-shumki and king of Arpad, and Bar-ga'yah, king of Ktk—the latter kingdom an enigma.[105] Indeed, the identification of Ktk continues to receive divergent identifications, thereby obfuscating the political landscape of north Syrian history during this period.[106] The vassal treaty between Mati'el and Ashur-nirari V of Assyria proves similarly hazy.[107] Nevertheless, although the ascent of Tiglath-Pileser III to the throne brought about quick control over northern Syria, Assyria still continued to face a menacing opponent: Mati'el of Arpad, the vassal of the Sefire treaties. With support from Urartu and the states of Melid, Gurgum, and Kummuḫ, Mati'el chal-

---

104 J. D. Hawkins, "The Neo-Hittite States in Syria and Anatolia" in *CAH III/I* (1982): 372–441, esp. 404–405.

105 Otto Rössler, "Die Verträge des Königs Bar-Ga'yah von Ktk mit König Matti'-II von Arpad (Stela von Sefire)," *TUAT* I/2 (1983), 178–89; Hélène S. Sader, 1987, 120 ff.; E. Puech, VII Les Traités de Sfiré 19. Traités de BarGayah, roi de KTK, avec Mati'el, roi d'Arpad. Traites et serments dans le Proche-Orient Ancien 88n 107 (Supplement au Cahier Evangile 81, Paris: Editions du Cerf., 1992), 88–107, esp. 106/107; Peter Kyle McCarter, Ancient Inscriptions. Voices from the Biblical World, Washington, D.C.: Biblical Archaeology Society, 1996, 94/95.

106 See especially the following well-known and recent studies: Joseph A. Fitzmyer (1967), Gershon Galil (2000, 39), William Morrow (2001, 83 ff.), Steven Grosby (2002), 125 ff.), Dan'el Kahn (2007, 66 ff.). For a revised examination of the Stelae inscriptions from Sefire (or as – Safirah), approximately 23 km south-east of the Aleppo citadel/ ca. 7 km west of the Ǧabbūl Lake, see Reinhold (2000, 2004), also presented to Prof. Dr. Wolfgang Zwickel, Johannes Gutenberg-Universität Mainz (2008) and Dr. Izaak J. de Hulster, Georg August-Universität Göttingen (2011). Cf.. also R. Lamprichs (1993, 109 ff.) and as summary (L. Lamprichs, 1995, 209 ff.).

107 Rykle Borger, "Der Vertrag Assur-Niraris mit Mati'ilu von Arpad," *TUAT* I/2 (1983), 155–177 and Simo Parpola and Kazuko Watanabe, Neo-Assyrian Treaties and Loyalty Oaths (SAA II, Helsinki: Helsinki University Press, 1988), 8–13, esp. XXVII–XXVIII and recently Roswitha Del Fabro, A New Archaeological Look at Sefire, FO Vol. 51 2014, 177–188, esp. 181, 185.

lenged Tiglath-Pileser III but to no avail in the end. Besieged for three years, Arpad ultimately fell in 743, and Bît-Agusi followed suit. The year 738 then brought about the defeat of Unqi and Hamath, all of northern Syria finally succumbing to the Assyrian provincial system by 737.[108]

4.2 Aram's Development in Central and Southern Syria and Its Adversary Israel: Confrontation and Alliance in the First Millennium BCE until the End of Aram-Damascus' Dominance in 732, According to Biblical and Extrabiblical Sources

4.2.1 The Aramaean States in Central and Southern Syria during the Davidic and Solomonic Dynasty

For the development of relations between the Aramaean states of central and southern Syria, we begin in the time of David, king of Judah. The marriage of Maacah (Heb. מעכה) daughter of Talmai, the Aramaean king of Geshur at the northern end of the Golan, with the military leader and regent of the Davidic kingdom was not without purpose: it placed the Eshbaal kingdom in a precarious political position between Geshur and Judah. Geshur, however, remained neutral in that military conflict between David and Israel, which thereby deterred any armed confrontation with Israel's northern neighbour. With the final phase of David's reign came an increased bellicosity between his own monarchy and the strengthened Aramaeans to the north of Palestine. Israel's territorial expansion northward precipitated this hostile climate, and ultimately resulted in its victory over Aram-Zobah despite the latter's predominance in Syria itself.

For the Davidic monarchy's consolidation of power and concomitant confrontation with the Aramaeans, Ammon played no small role. Indeed, when Hanun son of Nahash (2 Sam 10:2 f.) ascended to the Ammonite throne[109] and subsequently accused an Israelite delegation of espionage, relations between the two polities—once amicable—descended into ani-

---

108 J. D. Hawkins, *CAH III/I* (1982): 410–413.
109 For a recent chronology of the Ammonite kings see already Gotthard G. G. Reinhold (2003, 101–118, esp. 105, 111, 113) and the following precise chronology from Pieter Gert van der Veen (2005, 155 ff.; 2013, esp. 185–186).

mosity. Having humiliated the Israelite messengers, Ammon then feared war with their Cisjordanian neighbours, prompting them to seek alliance with the Aramaeans to the north, Aram (Bet-)Reḥob and Hadadezer, son of Reḥob and king of Zobah.[110] Not only Ammon but also the Aramaean coalition of (Bet-)Reḥob and Aram-Zobah considered themselves threatened. Now activated, the military support of the Aramaeans—further buttressed by troops from Maacah and Tob—fortified the buffer state of Ammon, which was to serve as a sort of defensive bloc against an Israelite invasion against its eastern and northeastern peripheries. Aramaean military contribution to Ammon, however, proceeded from Aram's own objectives: a military expedition into the Transjordan to take control of the King's Highway, which was the essential caravan route for international trade, running from Damascus along the eastern Transjordan down to Eilat and Arabia.

Lying in the fertile plane of Ghouta (section 2), Damascus was an early centre for caravans and trade by donkey, as indicated in the original toponym *Ša-imêrê-^{meš}-šu* (Donkey-Town or Donkey-Stallion).[111] Considerable dispute notwithstanding, the possibility still remains that Hadadezer was implicated in not only the political events of those states south of his territory but also the state formation of those political entities north of his territory up to the borderlands of the Upper Euphrates. Nevertheless attempts to reestablish erstwhile spheres of influence could prove calamitous. Accordingly, the annals of Ashur-dan II (934–912) report Aramaean conquest of various districts at the time of Aššur-rabi II (1012–972), though the precise cause for such aggression receives no mention. The annals of Shalmaneser III offer more information recording that *šar₄ KUR a-ru-mu* (i.e., "the king of Arumu") carried away the cities of Ana-Aššur-utîr-asbat (Pitru) and Mutkinu, 20 km south of Karkemish, which Tiglath-Pileser I had conquered around 1100 (ARAB I §603).[112] Although Pitard locates a

---

110 Gotthard G.G. Reinhold (2003, 101–118, esp. 103).

111 See S. Hafthórsson, *A Passing Power: An Examination of the Sources for the History of Aram-Damascus in the Second Half of the Ninth Century B.C.* (CBOT 54; Stockholm: Almquist & Wiksell, 2006), 16: 'the land /country of the donkey driver' or 'the land/country "Donkey driver".

112 See also R. Zadok, The Aramean Infiltration and Diffusion in the Upper Jazira 1150–930 B.C., 579, and the important contribution from Grant Frame, The Political History and Historical Geography of the Aramean, Chaldean,

KUR A-ri-mi only in Upper Ḫabur (based on eleventh-century sources) and
KUR a-ru-mu in the province of Ḫanigalbat (according to tenth-century
sources), he nonetheless adheres to 2 Sam 8:3 f. in positing Hadadezer
sought to quell a revolt by his vassals in the region.[113]

Yet such Aramaean influence in the northern quarters of the Syrian-
Arabian desert—that is, on the fringe of the Upper Euphrates—could have
materialized only under certain conditions. Hadadezer likely sought to
consolidate control over the caravan routes north of Damascus and east
of Hamath up into the Euphrates region, an effort facilitated by the weak
political position of Ashur-rabi II. At the same time, he probably gathered
allies useful for his political and military objectives. Routs in the south
would not have prevented this Aramaean ruler—warring with Maacah,
Tob, and Ammon against Israel—from continuing to deploy his military
forces. Having underestimated David's strategic and tactical faculties, the
Aramaeans must have ultimately accepted defeat by Hadadezer. With David's death and Solomon's succession, a chief aim then emerged for Israel:
to strengthen the kingdom both economically and politically, internally and
externally alike, and to bolster military strategy all for the preservation of
the international power and prestige recently won. Solomon thus sought to
create a counterweight to that northern Aramaean state which began to in-
crease its combative capacities anew during the time of Solomon's reign. To
this end, he expanded a calculated fortification system. Among the most important of these outposts stood Hazor, the bridgehead at the state's northern
limit. A garrison and stockpile of considerable strategic significance, this
city underwent continued assault by Aramaeans from Aram-Damascus, as
evinced in the destruction layers of Strata VIII (Hazael of Aram-Damascus)
and VII (Aramaeans at the time of the Israelite kings Jeroboam II and

---

and Arab Tribes in Babylonia in the Neo-Assyrian Period*, LAOS 13 2013,
87–121, esp. 90–92.

113   Wayne T. Pitard, *Ancient Damascus: A Historical Study of the Syrian City-
State from Earliest Temple Times Until its Fall to the Assyrians in 732 B.C.E.*
(Winona Lake, Ind.: Eisenbrauns, 1987), 91–92; see already Eckhard Un-
ger, "Die Aramäer auf der Höhe ihrer Macht," *FuF* 22/23 (1928): 226–228;
E. Forrer, "Aramu" *RLA I* (1932): 131–139, esp. 135.

Jehoash).[114] Solomon advanced his economic and military objectives even further through the buildout of border towns, which served as strongholds for Israel and thus targets for the Aramaeans, Moabites, and Assyrians.[115] Such citadels include Kedesh in Naphtali—one of the three Canaanite cities of refuge, the other two being Shechem and Kiryat-Arba/Hebron—as well as Bezer (Umm el-'Amad), Ramoth-Gilead (Tell er-Rumeith/Ramit; Ramtha [Er-Remtā]), and Golan in the Transjordan. Concerning Solomon's economic and political activities, these border towns north and south alike spared no effort to decouple themselves in advantageous political situations, as with the escape of Rezon ben-Eliada from Hadadezer and subsequent coup d'état in Damascus before 955, where he apparently availed himself of a band of insurgents who were able to conquer the Aramaean state and secure its rule along with the help of his own supporters (1 Kgs 11:24).[116] Undoubtedly, he himself founded a royal dynasty in Aram-Damascus.[117] The conquest of Edom by Hadad the Edomite also proves relevant in this regard (1 Kgs 11:14–22, 25b). Nevertheless, the reason for Rezon's revolt arose from largely internal differences—particularly his opposition to Hadadezer's careless war efforts by campaigning northward in response to the growing threat along the southern border of the "Aramaean coalition" and by undertaking military activities in the Transjordan, which resulted in Aramaean defeat. During this period of military and general political crisis, the Israelites stood as the principal opponent. Rezon would have endeavoured to cut off connections between Israel and the north to upset if not paralyse the flow of goods into Syria-Palestine. Escalated invasions on north-south arteries may have inflicted considerable damage on caravans to and from

---

114 See Israel Finkelstein, "Hazor and the North in the Iron Age: A Low Chronology Perspective," *BASOR* 14 (1999): 55–70, spec. 65 Table 1.

115 Significantly, such border towns include cultic and asylum cities that lay on important traffic arteries.

116 Even if in using older researches see Ziva Shavitsky, *The Mystery of the Ten Lost Tribes: A Critical Survey of Historical and Archeological Records relating to the People of Israel in Exile in Syria, Mesopotamia and Persia up to ca. 300 B.C.E.*, Newcastle upon Tyne: Cambridge Scholars Pulishing 2012, p. 8: "Rezon was a military functionary in the militia of Hadadezer....".

117 Samuel Abramski, The Resurrection of the Kingdom of Damascus and its Historiographic Record, (SBANE, Presented to S.E. Loewenstamm, Jerusalem: Rubinstein, 1978), 183–184.

Asia Minor—and on the Anatolian horse trade in particular—thereby necessitating increased sea commerce along the Levantine coast. According to 1 Kgs 11:25a, Rezon may have opposed Israel until the end of Solomon's reign in 931/930 (or perhaps even longer, until 925). His connection to Aramaean royal succession—namely, that of kings Hezion, Tabrimmon, and Ben-Hadad I (1 Kgs 15:18)—remains uncertain. For M. Noth, Kitchen, and Pitard, chronology may have divided Rezon and Hezion, though other scholars have sought to associate the names and identities of the two rulers.[118] Only new finds can advance this debate.

4.2.2 Aram and Israel before and after Qarqar in the Ninth Century BCE

As for political development after Rezon Ben-Eliada's uprising in Damascus, already during the final years of Solomon's reign a political shift loomed with Egypt's return to prominence under Pharaoh Shishak (conventionally Shoshenq I)[119]—an ascent that benefited Israel in Syria-Palestine, as described in the history of ancient Israel. Aramaean gains came from increased confrontation with Judah and Israel, and these clashes ultimately led to the collapse of the Solomonic kingdom. Consequently, Aram-Damascus witnessed a growth in autonomy vis-à-vis that of its political predecessors to the south and thus the opportunity for greater sovereignty in its pursuits. While the Aramaeans confronted considerable threats from the north following Assyria's rise under Adad-nerari II (911/909–889), they used to their advantage the auspicious political circumstances in the south that emerged from the Israelite-Judahite border conflict of 886 (1 Kgs 15:16–22), where-

---

118 M. Noth, *Könige I* (BK IX/I, Neukirchen: Neukirchener Verlag, 1968), 254–55, 338; Kenneth A. Kitchen, "Aram, Arameans" in *NBD* (ed. T.D. Douglas; Grand Rapids: Eerdmans, 1967), 57; W.T. Pitard, 1987, 100–04, 144.

119 See as before: Erika Schott (1989, 48). To the present chronological debate of Shischak (conv. Shoshenq I, but presently late 9th century B.C.E. !) in publications see: John J. Bimson (1992/93, 19 ff.); Peter van der Veen & Uwe Zerbst (2002, 113 ff.), Peter van der Veen (2005, 8, 42; 2009, 2015); R. Chapman, (2009, 4 ff.) and above all: Peter James and Peter van der Veen (2015, 127).

by Aram-Damascus under Ben-Hadad I was able to augment its influence over Palestine.[120]

This conflict between Judah and Israel precipitated from two central concerns: 1) Judah annexed a portion of Benjaminite territory, pushed the border with Israel further north, and won additional land for Jerusalem, while 2) Israel's ruler Baasha (908–886) wanted to secure economic advantage with states to the north by securing his southern border with Judah, as indicated in the buildout of the border city of Ramah and the restriction of access roads to Jerusalem. The political landscape changed with the appeal Asa of Judah made to Ben-Hadad I of Aram-Damascus, which included a considerable payment from the temple and palace treasuries in Jerusalem to the Aramaeans for the termination of certain economic alliances between Ben-Hadad I and Baasha of Israel. In this way, Israel lay exposed on two potential fronts, against Judah to the south, which pushed the border back even further north with the fortification of Geba and Mizpah (Tell en-Nasbeh), and against Aram-Damascus to the north, which forced Israel to relocate its greatest military force northward where onslaught by the Aramaeans threatened most. Though once preserved through friendly relations with Aram, a northern border sentineled and protected insufficiently now subjected Israel to significant population loss and destruction of its most significant political, economic, and strategic centers. From archaeological excavations and the textual evidence of 1 Kgs 15:20, Ijon (Tell Dibbin), Dan (Tell el-Qadi), Abel-

---

120   In the current view from Israel Finkelstein, The Great Wall of Tell en-Nasbeh (Mizpah), The First Fortification in Judah, and 1 Kings 15:16–22*, VT 62 2012, 14–28 based on his suggestion for a different Great Wall-dating of Tell en-Nasbeh, which he dates to the late Iron Age A, the story is transferred to "the main construction activity of Mizpa in the reign of Jehoash" and the Damascene king Ben-Hadad probably referred to the historical Ben-Hadad, son of Hazael!

beth-Maacah (Tell Ābel el-Qamh)[121] and Chinneroth (Tell el-'Oreme)[122] on the northwestern shore of the Galilean Sea, along with the entire land of Naphtali—including Qadas/Kedesh, the Hula Valley, Safed, and 'En Gev—all suffered Aramaean invasion.[123]

Only extrabiblical sources can determine whether Ben-Hadad I had, in fact, developed an interest in integrating the trade policy and economic arrangements of Israel before the reign of Omri (1 Kgs 20:34). Indeed, such evidence would have to establish the same Aramaean Ben-Hadad of this particular biblical passage as the son of Ben-Hadad I, the ruler who strengthened trade relationships through the construction of royal trading stations in Samaria, whether accommodations or storage facilities.[124] Confirmation does not emerge before the first construction period (i.e., 870–842), Aram's commercial undertakings in Samaria (1 Kgs 20:26–34) receiving considerably more attestation in the time of King Jehoash of Israel. Apart from 1 Kgs 20:34, no additional sources from the time of Omri suggest political and military loss for the Aramaeans; in fact, Omri likely had

---

121 Here I refer to the lesson from Nava Panitz-Cohen, Aram-Maacah? Arameans and Israelites on the Border: Excavations at Tel Abil el Qameh (Abel Beth Maacah) in northern Israel, IHW Colloqium Heidelberg, 1.Sept. 2014, to Tel Abel Beth Maacah Excavations, http://www.abel-beth-maacah.org/index.php/aqbout and to Excursus II.

122 A special archaeological overview to Kinneret supplies Stefan Münger, Early Iron Age Kinneret – Early Aramean or Just Late Canaanite? Remarks on the Material Culture of a Border Site in Northern Palestine at the Turn of an Era, LAOS 3 2013, 149–182 and ibid., Who, When and Why – Investigating Cultural Footprints at Early Iron Age Tel Kinrot, lesson at the IWH Symposium Heidelberg, 1. Sept. 2014.

123 See Angelika Berlejung, Nachbarn, Verwandte, Feinde und Gefährten: „Die Aramäer im Alten Testament, LAOS 3 2013, 57–86, esp. 72: "Nach Lipinski und Hafþórsson, die Kön. 15, 16–22 für eine verlässliche historische Information halten, war es schon Bar/Ben-Hadad I. (900–880), der Dan bis Kinneret auf seinem Weg zur Küste eroberte".

124 See also Rami Arav, Geshur: The Southwesternmost Aramean Kingdom, LAOS 13 2013, 1–29, spec. 11: "Undoubtedly, this plaza is the biblical *Hutzot,* the extra-mural city market. This biblical term indicates a structure aiming to house local and long distance trade, sometimes carried out by official merchants. The Bible provides an illustration for this institution."

a robust foreign policy, as the Mesha inscription confirms for this Israelite ruler (KAI 181: 4,7; TUAT I/6, 646 f.: l. 4.7).

With these considerations of conflict the examination now turns to the history of research on successors of the dynasty in Aram-Damascus. Precise identification and description of Ben-Hadad I has proven quite difficult. A majority of researchers now reject the extension of his reign into the time of the Israelite king Ahab, dating his rule from 900/890 to 874/840. According to E.R. Thiele's chronology, Ahab reigned from 874 to 853.[125] Already before but especially since the discovery of the Zakkur stela from Aleppo/Tell Afis (1903) and the Melqart or Bir/Bar-Hadad stela from Bureij/Aleppo (1939) as well as the publication of inscriptions from Pazarcik, Turkey, by Veysel Donbaz (1990) along with that of the Têl Dan inscription (1993/94), various lists of rulers from Aram-Damascus have proliferated and thus created divergent historical portraits.[126]

4.2.2.1 Before Discovery of the Zakkur Stela from Tell Afis (Hazrak)[127]

Already Albert Šanda (1902) distinguished King Rezon of 1 Kgs 11:23 from Ben-Hadad I (ca. 900), Ben-Hadad II (877–44; written Bir-'Idri in cuneiform), Hazael, Ben-Hadad III (804–774; referred to as Mari', "Lord"), and Rezin (List A), though 1 Kgs 15:18 does not mention all these kings in precisely this way. At the same time, Šanda did not exclude the possibility

---

125 Edwin T. Thiele, A Chronology of the Hebrew Kings (Contemporary Evangelical Perspectives, Grand Rapids: Zondervan Publishing House, 1977), 75.

126 For a more elaborate history of scholarship pertaining to these competing proposals, though not without gaps, see Gotthard G.G. Reinhold, EHS.T 368 1989, 139 ff., 221 ff.. There is also a detailed bibliography.

127 See Stefania Mazzoni, Tell Afis and Lu'ash in the Aramean Period, in: The World of the Arameans II, Studies in History and Archaeology in Honour of Paul-Eugènie Dion (JSOT. SS 325, Sheffield: Sheffield Academie Press., 2001, 99–114 and her lesson 'Identity and multiculturality in the Northern Levant of the 9th–7th century' at the IWH Symposium Heidelberg, 2014, as well as to the king of Hamat and Lu'ash, Zakkur (zkr): A. R. Millard, The Homeland of Zakkur, Semitica 39 1990, 47–52.

of extending the range of Ben-Hadad I's rule, thereby reckoning the two Ben-Hadads (I and II) as a single ruler (List B), Tab. 1.

Tab. 1: The Aramaean King List (A and B) by Šanda (1902)

List A	List B
Rezon	Rezon
[Hezion]	[Hezion]
[Tabrimmon]	[Tabrimmon]
Ben-Hadad I (ca. 900)	Ben-Hadad I (ca. 900–844 B.C.E.) (Cuneiform: Bir-ʻIdri)
Ben Hadad II (ca. 870–844) (Cuneiform: Bir-ʻIdri)	
Hazael	Hazael
Ben-Hadad III (Mariʼ, "Lord")	Ben-Hadad II (Mariʼ, Lord)
Rezin	Rezin

4.2.2.2 After Discovery of the Zakkur Stele from Tell Afis (Hazrak)

Based on the Zakkur inscription (KAI 202), Heinrich Zimmern (1909) identified Hazael's son (2 Kgs 13:24 f.) as Ben-Hadad III. Given the epigraphic uncertainty of reading either *brhdd* or *brhdr*, he understood Ben-Hadad II as Bir-ʻIdri through the cuneiform inscription's (ilu)IM-ʻIdri, which thus placed him in line with Šanda's List A. Dhorme (1910), for his part, equated Rezon (1 Kgs 11:23) with Hezion (1 Kgs 15:18) and distinguished between three Ben-Hadad kings following Tabrimmon (1 Kgs 15:18): Ben Hadad I (1 Kgs 15:16 ff.), who was contemporary with Asa and Baasha; a second Aramaean king from the time of Ahab (also named Ben-Hadad), whom he understood as the Adad-ʻIdri of the cuneiform inscription (Heb. *hddʼzr*)[128] and who was murdered sometime between 845 and 842; and finally the Ben-Hadad who succeeded his usurper father, Hazael (2 Kgs 13:24). Already in 1910, then, Adad-ʻIdri stood over and against the Ben-Hadad kings of the Masoretic text, even if no specific differentiation emerged. Although

---

128 Cf. Sina Schiffer, Leipzig: J.C. Hinrichs'sche Buchhandlung, 1911:34.

Dhorme stood in the camp of Šanda's List A, he modified the precise progression, including only Ben-Hadad I and Ben-Hadad II in the dynastic list of Aram-Damascus (Tab. 2).

Tab. 2: The Aramaean King List and the Books of Kings by Dhorme (1910)

Rezon	1 Kgs 11:23
Hezion	1 Kgs 15:18
Tabrimmon	1 Kgs 15:18
Ben-Hadad I	1 Kgs 15:16 ff.
Adad-'Idri (= *hdd'zr*)	(death 845/842) Biblical Ben-Hadad, contemporary with Shalmaneser and Ahab
Hazael	Usurper
Ben-Hadad II	2 Kgs 13:24 Contemporary of King Jehoash of Israel
[Rezin]	

The first to work intensively on the succession of Aramaean kings in Aram-Damascus, Daniel David Luckenbill (1910/11) came to a number of conclusions that diverged from previous studies. Accordingly, Tabrimmon and then Ben-Hadad I (contemporary with Asa and Baasha, ca. 900–890) followed Hezion (= Rezon) (1 Kgs 11:23; 15:18). He located the unnamed father of Ben-Hadad II to the time of Omri (ca. 885) based on 1 Kgs 20:34. Finally, Luckenbill divided Ahab's reign into two parts: the first (1 Kgs 20 = MT) saw the rule of Ben-Hadad II (ca. 875), the second that of Adad-'Idri (Heb. *hdd'zr*), who featured in the Battle of Qarqar (854) and at Ramoth-Gilead (1 Kgs 22). Leading further war efforts from 849 to 842, Adad-'Idri was deposed sometime between 846 and 842 and subsequently pursued by Hazael. Only much later did Rezin (Akk. Raṣunnu) appear as Ben-Hadad III (2 Kgs 14:37 ff.). While Luckenbill followed the general trajectory of the list set forth by Šanda and Dhorme, he also departed from hypotheses of doubled names and identified persons, thus postulating at least two Ben-Hadads before Adad-'Idri (Tab. 3).

Tab. 3: The Aramaean King List and the Books of Kings by Luckenbill (1910/11)

Hezion (=Rezon)	1 Kgs 11:23; 15:18
Tabrimmon	
Ben-Hadad I	900 1 Kgs 15:18 f.
Father of Ben-Hadad II	885 1 Kgs 20:34 (unnamed)
Ben-Hadad II	875 Early period of Ahab's reign (1 Kgs 20)
Adad-'Idri (= *hdd'zr*)	854–846/42 (Later period of Ahab's reign) At Qarqar in 854 At Ramoth-Gilead (1 Kgs 22)
Hazael	844/42
Ben-Hadad III	2 Kgs 14:37 f.
Rezin (= Akk. Raşunnu)	

Emil G. H. Kraeling (1918) continued the inquiry of his predecessor Luckenbill and further modified the list of rulers from Aram-Damascus. Consequently, after Hezion (1 Kgs 11:23) came Tabrimmon followed by Ben-Hadad I, who reigned during the time of Asa of Judah and Baasha of Israel (2 Kgs 15:18 f.). Similar to Luckenbill, he inserted two Aramaean kings before Adad-'Idri (= *hdd'zr*)—namely, the father of Ben-Hadad II (perhaps identical to Rezon) and Ben-Hadad II (death 858)—based on evidence from 1 Kgs 20:34. Kraeling further associated Adad-'Idri with that "king of Aram" mentioned in 1 Kgs 22 and the battle at Ramoth-Gilead. Even more, he maintained Hazael followed Adad-'Idri and considered as a gloss the king Ben-Hadad whom Hazael murdered (2 Kgs 8:7–15). Ben-Hadad III (= Mari') came to power after Hazael sometime between 804 and 773/772. As for the insertion of two Ben-Hadads before Adad-'Idri, Kraeling believed the only possibility for identifying Ben-Hadad with Adad-'Idri (Heb. *hdd'zr*) lay in postulating a full name "Ben-Hadadezer," whereby the Assyrians would have omitted the first element, the Hebrews the second (Tab. 4).

Tab. 4: The Aramaean King List and the Books of Kings by Kraeling (1918)

Hezion (= Ḫaziânu)	1 Kgs 11:23
Tabrimmon	
Ben-Hadad I	1 Kgs 15:18 f.
Father of Ben-Hadad II (perhaps Rezon)	1 Kgs 20:34
Ben-Hadad II	Death 858
Adad-ʿIdri (= hddʾzr)	Battle of Qarqar Ramoth-Gilead 1 Kgs 22 "king of Aram"
Hazael	
[Ben-Hadad]	[Gloss in 2 Kgs 8:7 f.]
Ben-Hadad III (= Mariʾ)	804–773/772
Rezin	

In contrast to Kraeling, Anton Jirku (1928) identified Ben-Hadad II (contemporary with Ahab of Israel) with Bir-ʿIdri (cf. already Šanda 1902) while Heinrich Zimmern (1909), further connected him to the battle of Qarqar in 854, when Shalmaneser III finally defeated this ruler between 846 and 842 to install Hazael as his replacement. E. Forrer (1932) proposed three kings named Ben-Hadad as well, but like Jirku, he equated the names and identities of Ben-Hadad II and Adad-ʿIdri of Aram-Damascus. While Tabrimmon followed Rezon (=Hezion, Hezrom?) (1 Kgs 11:23), the successors Ben-Hadad I (1 Kgs 15:18 f.) and Ben-Hadad II (1 Kgs 20:1 ff.; 2 Kgs 8:7, 9) remained distinct. Equated with Adad-ʿIdri (= hddʾzr), Ben-Hadad II spearheaded the battle against Shal-maneser III in 853 (Qarqar), 849, 848, and 845, but ultimately suffered defeat in 845, resulting in the kingship of Hazael (Hazaʾilu) over Aram-Damascus. The next generation then saw Ben-Hadad III on the Damascus throne (so the Zakkur inscription). While Adad-nirari III immured King Mariʾ in Damascus, Tiglath-Pileser III utterly desolated the city after a number of battles against Raṣunnu/Rezin.

Tab. 5: The Aramaean King List and the Books of Kings by Anton Jirku (1928) and Roland de Vaux (1934)

Rezon (= Hezion, Hezrom?)	1 Kgs 11:23
Tabrimmon	
Ben-Hadad I	1 Kgs 15:18 f.
Ben-Hadad II (= Adad-'Idri = *hdd'zr*)	853–845 1 Kgs 20:1 ff.; 2 Kgs 8:7,9; 2 Kgs 8:15
Hazael (= Haza'ilu)	845/41–800
Ben-Hadad III	
Mari'	
Rezin (= Akk. Rasunnu)	

Even before discovery of the Melqart or Bir/Bar-Hadad inscription from Bureij/Aleppo (1939), Roland de Vaux (1934) explained the line of succession in Aram-Damascus during the second half of the ninth century in such a way that the usurper Hazael (845/41–800) followed Adad-'Idri (= *hdd'zr*)—identified with the King Ben-Hadad of 2 Kgs 8:15—after which Hazael's son Ben-Hadad III succeeded his father to the throne.[129] Like Kraeling, de Vaux interpreted the name Ma-ri-' from the Adad-nirari III inscription as an official title (Tab. 5).

4.2.2.3 Subsequent to Discovery of the Melqart /Bar-Hadad Stela

Divergent readings of that extraordinarily corrupt second line of the Melqart or Bir/Bar Hadad inscription—and the associated succession list of Aramaean kings in Aram Damascus—have had serious consequences for the historical portrait of the Aramaeans and Israel.[130] Despite acceptance of several different graphemes, Maurice Dunand (1939) was the first to read

---

129 Roland de Vaux, La Chronologie de Hazael et de Benhadad III. Roi de Damas, *RB* 43/4 1934, 512–518 and already Anton Jirku, Der assyrische Name des Königs Benhadad III. Von Damascus, *OLZ* 1918; 279; Zakkur Stela: Lidzbarski, Ephem. III, 3 Z.4; 2 Kgs 13:3.

130 See the overview in Gotthard G.G. Reinhold, *EHS.T* 368 1989, 221 ff..

the line as follows, though he inclined towards < ' > rather than < T > in a second publication (1942/43): *dd.br t'b.pš ...b*(?). Without postulating *t'b*, A. Herdner (1946–48) later followed him in this reading. Albright (1942), however, amended the inscription's second line to br.T(br)(m)n (b) (r). (Hzyn)(n) and then identified the Bir-Hadad of the Melqart stela with the Ben-Hadad I of the Hebrew Bible. Although Albright's conclusions carried significant influence in the scholarship that ensued, de Vaux (1941) and Dunand (1942/43) had already emphasized that the monument's poor condition prevented any reconstruction of the genealogical succession of Aramaean kings from Aram-Damascus. If Ben-Hadad I ruled over Aram-Damascus contemporaneously with Asa of Judah and Baasha of Israel, such a long reign would permit identification with both Adad-'Idri (Qarqar in 853) and the Ben-Hadad of the Elisha narratives (2 Kings). This kind of calculation therefore brought about the "double name hypothesis," whereby Ben-Hadad I corresponds to Adad-'Idri and Hazael's son Ben-Hadad (2 Kgs 13:3, 24, 25) stands as the second among those Aramaean kings named Ben-Hadad, i.e., Ben-Hadad II[131] One of the most common interpretations equates Bir-Hadad of the eponymous inscription not only with Ben-Hadad II of the biblical text (1 Kgs 20) but also Adad-'Idri of the Assyrian sources listing him as contemporary with Ahab of Israel—this figure ruling Aram-Damascus until about 842.[132]

As for the Melqart or Bir/Bar-Hadad inscription, other reconstructions of the second line as well as literary-critical investigations of biblical texts have dated that Aramaean king mentioned in the stela to the time of Haz-

---

131 Those scholars of the Hebrew Bible and ancient Near East who advocate for this lengthy reign of Ben-Hadad I consist of the following: W.F. Albright (1942), G.L. Della Vida/W.F. Albright (1943), P.K. Hitti (1951, 1957), M.F. Unger (1957), M. Black (1958), R.A. Bowman (1962), A.S. Kapelrud (1966), H.-CH. Schmitt (1972), Conn Grayson Davis (1979). To this older literature (notes 126–128) I refer to Gotthard G.G. Reinhold, *EHS.T* 368 1989, 112 ff.

132 Champions of this position include A. Jirku (1928, 1932, 1963), M. Dunand (1939, 1942/43), A. Dupont-Sommer (1949), A. Malamat (1954a, 1973), A. Parrot (1957), F. M. Tocci (1960), W. W. Hallo (1960), B. Mazar (1962), H. Bardtke (1962), R.D. Barnett (1963), K. A. Kitchen (1967, 1987b), M. Noth (1968b), A. van den Born (1969), J. A. Soggin (1971), M. Elat (1975), Ch. Herzog/M. Gichon (1978).

ael and/or his son Ben-Hadad. E. Lipinski (1971a) represents the greatest proponent of this theory. He first considered Ben-Hadad the "son" or, better yet, "descendant, offspring" of *'tr hpš*, the purported grandfather of Bir-Hadad. Since Hazael receives no mention in the inscription, Lipinski postulated a *damnatio memoriae*, locating such condemnation in the surrender of Damascus at the end of his reign in 803, much to the chagrin of Aram. Lipinski later attempted another reconstruction, reading the inscription's second line as *dd.br 'zr[š]mš z*[y]. *'b*. On this explanation, 'Idri-Šamaš became Hazael's father, Bir-Hadad Hazael's brother.

Tab. 6: *The Reading of the Melqart or Bir/Bar-Hadad Stela inscription (l. 2) and the Aramaean King List from Ben-Hadad I to II by Eduard Lipinski (1971a, 1975, 1979)*

Lipinski (1971a)	Lipinski (1975, 1979)
Ben-Hadad I	Ben-Hadad I
Adad-'Idri	Adad-'Idri
[Hazael] 'tr hpš (Melqart stela)	Hazael – Bir-Hadad – 'Idri-Šamaš (Melqart stela)
Ben-Hadad II	Ben-Hadad II. (Hebrew Bible, Zakkur stela)

Ben-Hadad son of Hazael is thus the third—or, absent the possibility of equating in name and identity Adad-'Idri with the biblical Ben-Hadad of Ahab's time, the second—king by the name of Ben-Hadad. Already long before Lipinski, however, though, such a reduced list of Aramaean kings from Aram-Damascus received considerable support from a number of different scholars.[133]

One of the few scholars to Albright's proposal for some time, S. H. Horn eventually accepted a new reconstruction by F. M. Cross (1972).[134] Reading

---

133   E.g., R. P.P. Dhorme (1910), E. Forrer (1932), G. Garbini (1958), J. Miller (1966, 1969, 1983), S. Hermann (1981), G. Begrich (1975), J.C.L. Gibson (1975), A. Lemaire (1984), and H.S. Sader (1987).

134   S. H. Horn, Relics of the Past: The world's most important Biblical artifacts, Washington D.C. (Ministerial Association of the General Conference of SDA, n.d.), 1–16. To the printed paper see also Leona Glidden Running, Beverly U. Currie, Selected Bibliography of Siegfried H. Horn to 1985, in:

the stela's second line as *dd.br'zr[.]mśqy' b*[r], Cross considered Bir-Hadad the son of Adad-'Idri of Damascus. Furthermore, he related the Melqart inscription to the Assyrian campaigns of 849, 848, and 845 and deemed the campaign of 845 the likeliest political situation for memorial's construction, i.e., shortly before the end of Ben-Hadad II's reign. Erection of the stela could thus commemorate either a victory over Assyria or (in the case of the Aramaeans' own defeat) a successful escape, if not organized rescue, from certain death and subsequent recovery from serious injury received in battle—all supposing Bir-Hadad son of Adad-'Idri led his father's troops, that is. The following list of Aramaean kings from Aram-Damascus corresponds to this reconstruction of the inscription (Tab. 7):

Tab. 7: The Reading of the Melqart or Bir/Bar-Hadad Stela inscription (l. 2) and the Aramaean King List from Ben-Hadad I to IV by F. M. Cross (1972)

Ben-Hadad I	Son of Tabrimmon ca. 885–ca. 870
Ben-Hadad II	Adad-'Idri 870–842
Ben-Hadad III	Son of Adad-'Idri, Co-regent? 845(?)–842
Hazael	"Son of Nobody" 841–ca. 806(?)
Ben-Hadad IV	Mari' ca. 806(?)–?

Detailed study of the inscription by W. H. Shea (1978/1979) carried the discussion even further. Reconstructing the stela's second line as *dd.br'zr dmsq brmn*, Shea identified Bir-Hadad with Ben-Hadad II (= Adad-'Idri II) and his father, 'Idr, with Ben-Hadad I (thus Adad-'Idri I); he then adjudged brmn ("son of Rimmon" = [Tab-]Rimmon) the father of 'Idr (= Ben-Hadad I). In contrast to Cross, Shea believed the stela referred to the campaign of 853, when the Aramaeans fought the Assyrians at Qarqar. A rather obscure

The Archaeology of Jordan and Other Studies, ed. by Lawrence T. Geraty and Larry G. Herr, Berrien Springs, Michigan: Andrews University Press, 1986, 641–691, esp. 645.

event therefore merited the erection of a stela by Bir-Hadad (= Ben-Hadad II = Adad-'Idri II).

Yet another minimal list of Aramaean kings from Aram-Damascus (Tab. 8) came from E. Puech (1981) and J. A. Dearman/J. M. Miller (1983):

Tab. 8: *The Reading of the Melqart or Bir/Bar-Hadad Stela inscription (l. 2) and the Aramaean King List from Ben-Hadad I to III by E. Puech (1981) and J.A. Dearman/ J. M. Miller (1983)*

E. Puech (1981)		J.A. Dearman / J.M. Miller (1983)	
Ben-Hadad I (=son of Tabrimmon)	(ca. 900–875)	Ben-Hadad I	(ca. 885–865)
Ben-Hadad II	(ca. 875–843)	Adad-'Idri (son of Ben-Hadad I)	(ca. 865–843)
Hazael	(ca. 843–806)	Hazael	(ca. 842–806)
Ben-Hadad III (=Mari',son of Hazael)	(ca. 806–775)	Ben-Hadad III (son of Hazael)	(ca. 806–?)

Considerably different from the later work of André Lemaire (1984) and Pitard (1987), P. Bordreuil and J. Teixidor (1983) offered their own reconstruction of the inscription: *dd.br 'zr' mlk. br rhb*. This reading suggested two separate lines of Aramaean royal succession, one from Aram Bît-Rehob and one from Aram-Damascus, the king of the Melqart stela belonging to the line of Bît-Rehob. While Ezra stood as the son of Hadadezer (2 Sam 8:3), the Aramaean royal line began with Hezion (1 Kgs 15:18). Quite contrary to this proposal, particularly with the dating of the stela itself, Lemaire (1984) attempted a new reconstruction with the reading *dd.br hzyn br [HZ'L]*, judging Bir-Hadad the son of Hzyn and Hzyn the son of Hazael, which made Hazael not the father but rather the grandfather of Bir-Hadad. In this analysis, the Melqart stela reflects the precise series of kings, not the Zakkur inscription (A.4).

Tab. 9: *The Reading of the Zakkur Stela (A 1.4) and the Melqart- or Bir/Bar-Hadad*
Stele inscription (l. 2) by A.Lemaire (1984)

Zakkur stela	Melqart or Bir/Bar-Hadad stela
br.hdd br ḥz'l mlk 'rm	*br hdd. br hzyn br.ḥz'l*

E. Lipinski (1979) also included a certain Hyzn in his king list but only after
Bir-Hadad son of Hazael. This ruler he designated Hadyân, a figure who appears in the stela from Pazarcik, which the museum in Kahramanmaraş (or
Maraş) has preserved. As for Pitard's (1985, 1987) reconstruction, it largely
parallels that of Lipinski (1971), but the consonantal series consists of *hmk*
rather than *hpš* and reads *dd. br'tr hmk* accordingly. With names of rulers
similar to those from Arpad, this stela corresponds more closely to northern
Syria. Pitard (1987) catalogs the kings of Aram-Damascus as follows:

Tab. 10: *The Aramaean King List and Chronology by W. T. Pitard (1987)*

Rezon	(mid 10th cent.)
Hazyān (Hezion)	(late 10th cent.)
Tab-Ramman	(late 10th/early 9th cent.)
Bir-Hadad I	(early 9th cent.)
Hadad-'Idr	(mid 9th cent.– ca. 844)
(Bir-Hadad II?)	(ca. 844/842)
Hazael	(ca. 844/842– ca. 800)
Bir-Hadad III	(early 8th cent.)
Hadianu	(second quarter of the 8th cent.)
Radyān	(mid 8th cent.–732)

4.2.2.4 The Bar-Hadad of the Melqart or Bir-/Bar-Hadad Stela: King of Aram-Damascus or King of Arpad?

Before analysis turns to these subsequent finds, the "double name hypothesis" requires a few additional comments. After Ben-Hadad I, either
Ben-Hadad II ruled followed by Adad-'Idri I (so already Luckenbill), or
Adad-'Idri alone succeeded him to the throne (identical with Ben-Hadad II
according to, e.g., Cross), later initiating the anti-Assyrian coalition at Qar-

qar in 853.[135] The question remains, however, as to whether Adad-'Idri (i.e., Hadadezer according to the Hebrew Bible[136]) ever designated a biblical king with the name Ben-Hadad.[137]

My 1989 dissertation compared qualitative and quantitative descriptions of Aram's forces from biblical texts (i.e., 1 Kgs 20; 22 and 2 Kgs 3; 6–7) and other reports of the battle at Qarqar.[138] Linguistic correspondences still need investigation, however. While Kraeling understood (ilu)IM in Akkadian PNN as the equivalent of Adad and denied any equation of *br hdd* with *hdd 'zr*, Cross averred a possible identification based on his reconstruction of the Melqart inscription's second line, which purportedly reads *br 'zr* after *br hdd* and therefore led him to postulate *br 'zr* and *br hdd 'zr* as parallel, whereby the Assyrians would have decoupled the name's former element, the Hebrews the latter (Kraeling's only alternative).[139] According to the author's own 1986 palaeographic analysis of the Melqart stela in Aleppo as well as further studies continuing into the present, Bir-Hadad was the son of a certain *'zr*, the patronym of *br hdd*, in which case the element *'zr/idr* functions as a diminutive or hypocoristic—to wit, *hdd 'zr*. As a result, that epigraphic

135 Daniel David Luckenbill, "Benhadad and Hadadezer" *AJSL* 27 (1910/1911): 267–284, esp. 272–273; F. M. Cross, "The stela Dedicated to Melcarth by Ben-Hadad of Damascus" *BASOR* 205 (1972): 36–42; cf. Gotthard G.G.Reinhold, *EHS.T* 368, 1989, 114.

136 This is noted also in: Georg Hentschel, Die Elija-Erzählungen. Zum Verhältnis von historischem Geschehen und geschichtlicher Erfahrung, (EThSt Bd. 33, Leipzig: St. Benno-Verlag, 1977), 34.

137 To the different views of OT-scholars see here also K. Lawson Younger, Neo-Assyrian and Israelite history in the Ninth Century: The Role of Shalmaneser, in: Understanding the History of Ancient Israel, ed. by H.G. M Williamson, (Proceedings of the British Academy 143), Oxford/New York: Oxford University Press 2007, 243– 277, esp. 258

138 See Gotthard G.G. Reinhold, *EHS.T* 368, 1989, §§ 2.3.4–2.3.6.

139 Emil G.H. Kraeling, *Aram and Israel or the Arameans in Syria and Mesopotamia* (CUOS XIII; New York: Columbia University Press, 1918), 75–76; F. M. Cross, "The stela Dedicated to Melcarth," 40. For his part, Lawrence J. Mykytiuk asserts, "I find no ancient reference to any Hadadezer as Bar-/Bir-/Ben-hadad, nor vice versa." ("Corrections and Updates to 'Identifying Biblical Persons in Northwest Semitic Inscriptions of 1200–539 B.C.E.,'" *Maarav* 16.1 [2009]: 79). For various transcriptions and translations of the inscription, see Hafthórsson, 2006, 33–39, esp. 39 Table 1.

quandary consists of ...*br* [.] *h* (2) *dd . br ʽzr. dmśqy*[ʼ] *br* (3)*mlk ʼrm*....[140] The Bir-Hadad of the Melqart inscription—most likely erected after 850—is therefore the son and possible successor to Adad-ʽIdri of Damascus.

As for the similar readings Pitard (1988) and Puech (1992) advanced— *brh*[d] (2) *dd.br ʽtrhmk. vac* (Pitard) and <*h*> (2) *dd . brʼtr smk. br hdrm*[?] (Puech)—they resonate strongly with materials from northern Syria, and such results have had considerable influence on historical description of Arpad's monarchy, finding support from any number of other scholars, although the dynasty of Arpad knows no line of Bir-Hadad-kings like Aram-Damascus (Amos 1: 3–5)![141]

Dan'el Kahn in particular has operated within this framework and opined that the Bir-Hadad of the Melqart stela followed Attarshumki sometime between 800 and 754, although palaeographic considerations would de-mand a date closer to 850, since the *ʽayin* grapheme of *ʽzr* contains a dot within the circle.[142] The interpretations of Pitard and Puech, prove highly dubious on palaeographic grounds, however. In consequence, they alone cannot undermine the existence of Adad-ʽIdri's son.[143] In fact, Lawrence

---

140 Gotthard G.G. Reinhold, 1985, 1986; 1989, 2003a; note 1 (see the lectures 2005, 2008)

141 W. T. Pitard, "The Identity of Bir-Hadad of the Melqart Stela," *BASOR* 272 (1988): 3–21; idem, "The Melqart Stela (2.33)," *COS* (2000): II:152–153; E. Puech, "La Stela de Bar-Hadad à Melqart et les Rois d'Arpad" *RB* 99, no. 2(1992): 311–334, esp. 315. In reviews of W. T. Pitard's *Ancient Da-mascus*, both Paul E. Dion and Bob Becking accepted W. T. Pitard's reading of the inscription's second line without undertaking palaeographic analyses themselves (Paul E. Dion, *BASOR* 270 [May 1988]: 97–99; Bob Becking, *BO* XLVI [Jan-Mar 1989]: 146–150).

142 Dan'el Kahn, "The Kingdom of Arpad," esp 82–83; see further "Bit Agusi" in *Religionen in der Umwelt des Alten Testaments II: Phönizier, Punier, Ara-mäer* (ed. Corinne Bonnet and Herbert Niehr; Kohlhammer Studienbücher Theologie 4/2; Stuttgart: W. Kohlhammer, 2010), 243–244.

143 Such issues consist of the following:
(1) Though heavily damaged, the stela gives no indication that the inscription stopped midway through the second half of the line; rather, the present state of the text suggests a line originally complete.
(2) High quality photos reveal certain consonants visible to the naked eye, conso-nants W.T. Pitard apparently did not see, as with a *dalet* following the *resh* in an image by both Wahid Khayata and the present author as well as a "decapitated"or

J. Mykytiuk has confirmed the present author's epigraphic reading through computer enhancement of high-resolution photos.[144] Although the proposal of such a figure—first conjectured by Alfred Jepsen in 1944 and 1952—may finally receive confirmation, only further archaeological discovery of written materials from Syria could ultimately put these questions to rest.[145]

"open" *koph* in the third position following the *dalet*, visible once more in the photograph by Wahid Khayata and those by R.A. Bowman and Horst Klengel. (3) Through computer enhancement of these high-quality photos, the author was able to examine anew the consonants of line two—the transcribed results published in 1984, 1989 (dissertation), and 2003 and further discussed at a 2005 conference: Such analysis established an *'ayin* following the consonants *dd.br*, the dividing mark previously overlooked. After this *'ayin* comes a clearly engraved *zayin* traversed by a fine scratch that does not, in fact, belong to the grapheme itself. Computer enhancement of the images precludes the possibility of a long *taw*, though W.T. Pitard interpreted the secondary score as a "downstroke" and disregarded the upper parallel line of the *zayin*; therefore, technological analysis establishes the *zayin*'s upper horizontal line beyond the realm of dubiety. Such important palaeographic findings, however, receive no attention from Brent Strawn, S. Hafthórsson, or Stefan Beyerle (see bibliography). Even further, photographs from Wahid Khayata and the author reveal a small word divider following *'zr*, left beneath the *resh* and before the (now) clear, full-formed *dalet*. The proportions of these strokes are quite important. What E. Lipinski sees as the long right side of a *waw* proves nothing other than a fine incision for a word divider that cannot possibly belong to the *dalet* based on substantially incommensurate lengths. While the lower stroke of the *dalet* slightly traverses the middle of the right side, no such extension appears at the top of the grapheme that could necessitate the reading of an *aleph*. Neither *shin* nor *aleph* nor *he* occurs here: the grapheme is a clear *dalet*, as computer enhancement firmly establishes. Both the naked eye and computer enhancement also verify a "decapitated" or "open" *koph*. Accordingly, line two of this inscription can no longer undergo analysis without full description of its second part.

144 See Lawrence J. Mykytiuk, "Corrections and Updates," esp. 69 ff. and Lawrence J. Mykytiuk, Sixteen Strong Identifications of Biblical Persons (Plus Nine Other Ids) in Authentic Nortwest Semitic Inscriptions from before 539 B.C.E., in: SBL Archaeology and Biblical Studies, Atlanta 2012, 47/48. Mykytiuk, however, seems to be the only one to comment on these findings both plainly and decidedly! Historical overviews suffer all too often from overlooking the current research of specific disciplines, as with Aramaean studies; cf. F. Gonzáles de Canales, L. Serrano, and J. Llompart, "Tarshish and the United Monarchy of Israel," ANES 47 (2010): 137–164, esp. 146.

145 Alfred Jepsen, "Israel und Damaskus," AfO 14 (1944): 153–72; idem, "Zur Melqart-stela Barhadads," AfO 16 (1952): 315–317.

4.2.2.5 The Books of Kings, Chronology and the Têl Dan Stela Fragments

Regarding the history set forth in the Hebrew Bible, events organised according to the narrative portrayal of 1 Kgs 20 and 22 (Chronology A) contrast considerably with the portrait that emerges after careful analysis of the texts' literary strata (Chronology B). The Têl Dan inscription complicates this picture all the more.[146] Nonetheless, two distinct historical trajectories emerge based on the specific priority assigned to the data.

1. The proposal concentrates on those historical events of 855–841 in which Israel found itself particularly involved, especially the circumstances of 853. That chronology follows:

Tab. 11: *Portrayed events according to the narratives of the Books of Kings (Chronology A)*

Chronology A	
858	Ascent of Shalmaneser III to the throne
857–856	Siege and fall of Til Barsip (Bît Adini)
855	Arameans invade Samaria (1 Kgs 20)
854	Battle of Aphek between Aram and Israel (1 Kgs 20); first alliance with Aram during early reign of Ahab (father of partner in treaty), Ben-Hadad II as "father" of the patron (Tel Dan ln. 4,5)
853	From spring until summer: anti-Assyrian alliance[147]; Battle at Qarqar; beginning of Moabite revolt Before autumn: battle at Ramoth-Gilead; death of Ahab in the battle (1 Kgs 22)[148]; Ahaziah king of northern kingdom

---

146 See Gotthard G.G. Reinhold, dissertation excursus ii.

147 K. Lawson Younger (2007), esp. 255/256, 259 pointed out the indication of Assyrian overall failure, that the opposition against Assyrian increased after the 853 campaign at Qarqar, in both 849 and 848 – despite of tributs 853 – (Carchemish and Arpad), but disintegrated 841 BCE, "partly the result of the repeated Assyrian campaigns, and partly the result of changes in ruler in two of the most powerful states, Damascus (the usurpation of Hazael) and Israel (the usurpation of Jehu)."

148 See Gotthard G.G. Reinhold (1989, 127/128): Chronology A: Here Ahab was seriously wounded in the battle, leaded – from the struggle – to Jezreel and transported his body to Samaria (1. Kgs 22.36).

Chronology A	
852	Joram; second treaty with Aram post-853 (Tel Dan ln. 1); Joram (852–841) as partner in treaty; Adad-'Idri (ante-853–845/41), called "father," the patron of the stela's author
849	Campaign of Shalmaneser III (10th palû); Moabite campaign against Joram (2 Kgs 3)
848	Campaign of Shalmaneser III (11th palû)
847–843	Aramean raid at time of Joram (Dothan); siege of Samaria (2 Kgs 6)
845	Campaign of Shalmaneser III (14th palû); Battle of Adad-'Idri and son Bir-Hadad (i.e., Ben-Hadad III) against Assyria; death of Adad-'Idri in the battle[149] or serious injury, sickness, and death in 842/841 (Tel Dan ln. 3); serious injury but fortunate recovery of Bir-Hadad son of Adad-'Idri after extended sickness in Damascus (2 Kgs 8:78 f.); erection of Melqart stela post 845
842/841	Death of Adad-'Idri (842/41); Bir-Hadad's sickness/relapse from unhealed wounds; crisis in Damascene palace
841	Bir-Hadad III's murder (2 Kgs 8,15,28) by Hazael, an usurper called Mari' (842/41–805); battle of Joram against Hazael at Ramoth-Gilead (2 Kgs 9:14,15; Tel Dan ln. 3–8, 11); death of Joram/Ahaziah[150]; Jehu's ascent to the throne; Jehu's defection to Hazael; withdrawal from Ramoth-Gilead and movement of Aramaean military northward; battle against Assyria (18th palû)
post-838	War with Israel (21st palû) and break between Jehu and Hazael (2 Kgs 10:32 ff.); conquest of Dan
835/30	Erection of Tel Dan stela by Hazael (author)
+/- 800	Destruction of Tel Dan stela (fragments A, B1, B2) during time of Bir-Hadad IV son of Hazael, called Mari' (805–773/72); King Jehoahaz (814–798) and King Jehoash (798–782) (2 Kgs 13:1–9, 22–25)

---

149 For this hypothesis, see, e.g., J.A. Soggin, who translates the Akkadian expression šadâšu êmid of the Assyrian Basalt stela (*KAH* 1, 30; *ANET* 280b; *TUAT* I/4, 365) as "in einer Feldschlacht zu Tode kommen," in contrast to other scholars (idem, "Amos VI:13–14 und I:3 auf dem Hintergrund der Beziehungen zwischen Israel und Damaskus im 9. und 8. Jahrhundert" in *Near Eastern Studies in Honor of W.F. Albright* (ed. Hans Goedicke; Baltimore: John Hopkins Press, 1971), 433–441, esp. 438 and currently also S. Hasegawa, Aram and Israel during the Jehudite Dynasty, BZAW Bd. 434, Berlin/Boston 2012, 77 to the expression šadâšu êmid ("to pass away"), what "not necessarily imply a violent death." But see also the final result from Excursus I!

150 See Edward Lipinski, The Aramaeans in the West (13th-8th centuries), LAOS 3 2013, 123–147, esp. 134: "In the same year (Lipinski dates these events

Fig. 1: Ivory of a royal ruler, possibly Hazael (?), Arslan Tash (Ḥadatu), Louvre Paris: AO11488, RMN No. 70137511

already to 842 B.C.), as it seems, Hazael waged a war against Israel, which was assisted by its Judean vassal state. Hazael won a great victory at Ramoth-Gilead, killing Jehoram, king of Israel, and Ahaziahu, his son, king of Judah. This victory is recorded in the Tell al-Qadi (Têl Dan) inscription, in 2. Kings 8, 28, and possibly on the Tell al-Afis stele."

According to Chronology A, Israel either broke from the anti-Assyrian coalition with Aram or maintained such a fragile alliance that fighting erupted between the Israelites and Aramaeans apart from the Assyrian campaigns. The Têl Dan inscription provides a fundamentally different perspective, however. Dated palaeographically between 839 and 835, the stela suggests Hazael of Damascus (842/41–805) as its author—indicated through the textual contents themselves. More specifically, the monument refers not only to the fall of Joram of Israel (852–41) and Ahaziah of Judah (841) in battle—the latter entity boastfully designated *bytdwd* (ln.9)—though certainly not without the help of Hazael himself, but also to Jehu's (841–14) subsequent rise to the throne (ln.11). The beginning of the text probably references two important agreements: one between the patron of the stela's author and his ally, Joram of Israel, towards the end of Ahab's reign (853) and an earlier one between the patron's father and his own ally. If Hazael were the author, then his "father" (i.e., the patron who had procured him his high position at the Damascene court) would be the Aramaean king Adad-ʿIdri (ante-853–845/842/41). Given the Assyrian threat, Adad-ʿIdri then crusaded with Ahab of Israel (874–53) against Shalmaneser III at the battle of Qarqar in 853. Adad-ʿIdris own father—Ben-Hadad II (from the early reign of Ahab, post 874–ante 853), who succeeded Ben-Hadad I (900–870)—had also allied with Israel only a year after the siege of Samaria in 855, following the 854 battle of Aphek.[151] The Assyrian threat continued even after 850,

---

151 The localisation of the biblical Aphek (hebr. âfik, strength, fortress), which is mentioned in 1 Kgs 20: 26–34, is currently a decisive question, if there is assumed some historical background. In the Old Testament four places for Aphek are stated: 1) a locality north-east of Beirut (Coord. 231.382), identified with the byz. Aphaka, arab. Afaqâ (Jos. 13, 4); 2) a locality in the territory of Asher, the Apqu of the Amarna-letters, known from the Old Testament in Jos.19.30 and Jud. 1.31, which could be identified with Tell el-Kerdâne in the plain of Acco (Coord. 160.250); 3) a locality Afek in the Philistine coastal area, the Afek-Antipatris in the Sharon, identified with Râs el-ʿÊn (Coord 143, 168) and special with the Tel Afek, which is also represented in the Iron Age. See the following contributions: Aphek, NIDB, Pictorial Edition, J.D. Douglas/ Merilll C. Tenney, ed., Grand Rapids, MI: Zondervan Publishing house/Basingstoke, Hants, U.K.: Marshall-Pickering 1987, 66–67; Yuval Gadot (2006); W. Ewing, (2013), Jacqueline Schaalje (2013), Yuval Gadot, Esther Yadin (2013). To Aphek, "situated on the strategically significant Via Maris" see

as reported in Assyrian annals describing the campaigns of Shalmaneser III in 849 (10th palû), 848 (11th palû), and 845 (14th palû). According to a new interpretation of the Bir-Hadad stela, Adad-'Idri almost certainly

---

P. G. van der Veen (2013, 167) and Peter James/Peter van der Veen (2015, 132, 134); 4) a locality in a plateau (mîšôr) of the Golan, in the borderland between Aram-Damascus and Israel.

Against earlier times of biblical exegesis with the traditional localisations of Aphek a) a village called Afeka beyond the Jordan, the territory of the Ruben-tribe (Eusebius, Onomasticon 22,19–21) b) a castellum Afeka near Hippos (Hieronymus), later identified with the Arabian locality Fiq (Coord. 2164.2425) two proposals of localisations based on archaeological researches were assumed, 'En Gev, Khirbet el-Ašeq (Coord 210.243) at the shore of the Sea of Galilee and the Tel Soreg/q, a smaller Iron Age locality near Fiq. To the present the proposal of the Iron Age II-remains of 'En Gev/Khirbet el-Ašeq, as a better candidate for the Aphek in the Book of the Kings, seemed to be certain, although the Iron Age Tel Soreg/q (only a small fort) not represented an ancient city in its proportions. But from the sight of a Geshurite defensive war and of an Aramaean support of the borderland to Israel a battle between the Aramaean army of the king Benhadad with a basis camp (Upper Afek) near Fiq and an advanced Israelite army under Ahab in the north-east direction through the Afek-comb contained the possibility of a considered strategy, if the Israelite troops could use the higher position of the mountains to push the Aramaeans in a surprised attack in the comb, so that they were put to flight and march down to Aphek ('En Gev) at the shore, which had capitulate at last by collapse of the defense system.

See Yigael Yadin (1963, 309), Gotthard G.G. Reinhold (1989, 127), Moshe Kochavi, Timothy Renner, Ira Spar, Ester Yadin (1992, 44), Chaim Herzog/ Mordechai Gichon (1998, 173 ff.) and Moshe Kochavi, Akio Tsukimoto (2008, 1726). But this identification of Aphek (Tel 'En Gev) is not accepted by all OT- and BA-scholars: See currently Shuichi Hasegawa (2012, 71 [a], 71; 2012, [b]).

Meanwhile Wolfgang Zwickel (2010, 322/323) wants to move off from the present position of Afek and the Aramaean interventions in the poor settled region of the Golan, which were more concentrated in the region of Ramoth-Gilead (Tell er-Ramta or better Tell er-Râmît). He votes for an Iron Age Aphek at the headwaters and the side valleys of the Yarmuk river. But such option – contrary to 'En Gev – would open new roads of the researches in BA- and OT-studies!

To the Iron Age in the Jordan Valley and the northern Jordanian plateau of generell interest see the following contributions: Wolfgang Zwickel (1990), Ji. Chang-Ho (1995, 1997), J.A. Sauer, Larry G. Herr (1997), Larry G. Herr (2012), Abdel-Nasser Hindawi (2013).

fought against the Assyrians in 845 together with his son, called *br hdd br ʿzr* (ln.2). His son, Bar-Hadad III, was either a co-regent and young king (845–42/41) or only a potential crown prince who never came to power; regardless, he sustained severe injury in this conflict but survived through a special rescue operation, perhaps from a Tyrian detachment. After 845, the Bir-Hadad stela was then dedicated to Melqart, who received the insignia of a war deity. Himself ill and weakened by injury, Bir-Hadad remained in Damascus through the sickness and natural death of his father (ln. 3). With this precarious political situation in the Damascene palace—which Siegfried Mittmann sought to designate an interregnal period—Joram of Israel had the opportunity to place the Gilead (above all Ramoth-Gilead)[152] and the Haurân in a certain strategic position. Although Israel's southern neighbour may have also found themselves in the temporal and geographic location to advance immediately into the territory of Damascus, an initial attempt to seise control of the eastern Transjordan before a final assault on Ramoth-Gilead proves more likely (5).

Concerning events in Aram-Damascus, Assyrian sources record the death of Adad-ʿIdri and succession of Hazael, "son of nobody" (*^{ID}IM–id-ri KUR–šu e-mi id ^{l}ḫa-za-ʾ i- DINGIR DU-MU la ma-ma-na ^{GIŠ}GU-ZA iṣ-bat*).[153] As recounted in 2 Kgs 8:15, Hazael murdered the vulnerable successor Bir-Hadad and succeeded Adad-ʿIdri to the throne. Hazael then sallied forth to war after a mere seven days (Tel Dan ln. 5 f.), undoubtedly southward through the Haurân and from its south-eastern part on the central road to Tell er-Rumeith/Ramith and the town of Ramta (Er-Remtā), where he dispatched his enemies from Israel (Jehoram) and Judah (Ahaziah) (ln. 7–9). Admittedly, though, this narrative does come from a propagandistic perspective. He continued to operate behind his ally Jehu for a time, a turncoat

---

152 Siegfried Mittmann, "Zwei 'Rätsel' der Mêšaʾ-Inschrift. Mit einem Beitrag zur aramäischen Stelainschrift von Dan (Tell el-Qâdï)" *ZDPV* 118, no.1 (2002): 33–65, spec. 50–51 and Gershon Galil, Shalmaneser III in the West, *RB* T. 109/1 (2002), 40–56, esp. 50/1.

153 COS 2.113A. See Joseph Blenkinsopp, "Ahab and Israel and Jehosaphat of Juda: The Syro-Palestinian Corridor in the Ninth Century", in: CANE II, New York: Charles Scribners Sons: 1309–1319.

also mentioned in the cuneiform texts.[154] With Jehu on the Israelite throne (ln. 11–22), Hazael was forced to withdraw from Ramoth-Gilead already in 841 and moved the majority of his troops northward to defend against a menacing Assyria. When a rupture came between Jehu and Hazael, the latter conquered the city of Dan and subjugated much of Israel (2 Kgs 10:32 f.). Between 835 and 830, Hazael probably had some necessity to justify his course of action against Israel with the erection of the Têl Dan stela, which was ultimately destroyed by Jehoahaz 814–798) or Jehoash (798–782) around 800, long before the Assyrian destruction of Aram under Tiglath-Pileser III in 733/32.

2. Based on the division of sources into their various strata, the second proposal shifts those events centred chronologically, around 853 by the first proposal—such as the Israelite-Aramaean confrontations in Samaria (855) and Aphek (854) (1 Kgs 20) as well as other events set in Samaria according to 2 Kgs 6 (847–ca. 843)—back to the end of the second half of the ninth century, that is, to the years 803 (1 Kgs 20, 2 Kgs 6) and 802 (1 Kgs 20, at Aphek) during the time of Ben-Hadad son of Hazael, which accords with the kings list of Aram-Damascus set forth by Ben-Hadad IV. For the Omride period, Chronology B maintains only two historical events: (a) Ahab's participation in the battle of Qarqar (853) and (b) the conflict at Ramoth-Gilead against the usurper Hazael at the end of Joram's reign, recorded in 2 Kgs 9:14 f. (841). No evidence suggests a final stage of Israelite resistance in this view. Moreover, Aram-Damascus first initiated confrontation on peripheral fronts, the commanders Ahaziah and Joram preserving the integrity of an Israelite-Aramaean alliance against Assyria even after the natural death of Ahab in 853, i.e., through the years 849, 848, and 845. A dissolution of the coalition ultimately did occur, however, even if the Aramaeans did later seek to incorporate their former allies into an anti-Assyrian uprising. The death of Adad-'Idri in 845/844[155] or 842/841, the murder of Bir-Hadad

---

154 See Tammi J. Schneider, "Rethinking Jehu," *Biblica* 77, no.1 (1996): 100–107, esp. 106.

155 See Stuart A Irvine, Critical Note. The Last Battle of Hadadezer, *JBL* 124/2 (2005), 341–347, esp. 345: "Apparently, with Hadadezer's death in 845 or 844 B.C.E. The anti-Assyrian coalition collapsed and only Damascus continued to oppose Assyrian."

son of Adad-ʿIdri, and the usurpation of the Damascene throne by Hazael would have all contributed to such disbandment. For his part, Stefan Beyerle has situated this power shift in the year 843, when Hazael first appears in ancient Near Eastern sources as well as the so-called booty inscriptions[156], which include an Aramaic inscription on a horse's trapezoidal bronze nose piece discovered in the temple of Hera (Heraion) at Samos (ninth cent.) and a partially identical inscription on a horse's bronze cheek piece found at the temple of Apollo Daphnephoros at Eretria, Euboea. While W. Röllig deciphers the inscription from Samos as *zy ntn hdr lmr'n ḥz'l mn 'mq bšn t'rh mr'n nhr*, A. Charbonnet reads the relevant epigraphic portion from Eretria as *š ntn hrb k[m]tnṭ l'lmn 'tmq bšnt b'rhgmr 'mn hr*.[157] Israel Eph'al and Joseph Naveh have analysed the same inscriptions but offered different interpretations: *zy ntn hdd lmr'n ḥz'l mn 'mq bšnt 'dh mr'n nhr*, thus translating, "That which Hadad gave our lord Hazael from ʿUmqi in the year that our lord crossed the river."[158] Had such spoils come from Amqi/Amuq (cf. also the Neo-Hittite Zakkur stela, KAI 202:6), Hazael would have certainly crossed the Orontes River.[159] Yet many ancient Near Eastern texts consistently and formulaically designate the Euphrates with *nhr*. Furthermore, Aramaean challenges to hegemony in this region only began toward the end of the ninth century.[160] The first interpretation therefore

---

156 Stefan Beyerle, "Aram und Israel im 9./8. Jh. v. Chr. aus der Perspektive der aramäischen und assyrischen Inschriften" in *Israel zwischen den Mächten. FS Stefan Timm*, (ed. Michael Pietsch, Friedhelm Hartenstein; Münster:Ugarit-Verlag, 2009), 47–76, esp. 53–55.

157 W. Röllig translates the text as "(Das ist es,) was HDR gab unserem Herrn Haza'el von der Ebene von Basan, 'Stirnbedeckung' unseres erhabenen Herrn' (idem, "Die aramäische Inschrift für Haza'el und ihr Duplikat," *MDAIA* 103 [1988]: 62–75). In contrast, A. Charbonnet offers "Ce qu'a donnè HRB en don(?) aux Dieux Bons ...en l'année 10(?). (la perfection d'Amon Hor?)" (idem, "Le dieu aux lions d'Eritrie," *Ann A Stor Ant* 8 (1986): 117–156).

158 Israel Eph'al and Joseph Naveh, "Hazael's Booty Inscriptions," *IEJ* 39 (1989): 192–200.

159 See Y. Aharoni, "The Land of 'Amqi" *IEJ* 3 (1953): 153–161; Nadav Na'aman, "Hazael of 'Amqi and Hadezer of Beth-rehob" Ugarit-Forschungen Bd. 27 (1995): 381–394.

160 Cf. also Wayne T. Pitard, "Arameans" in *Peoples of the Old Testament World* (ed. Alfred J. Hoerth, Gerald L. Mattingly, and Edwin M. Yamauchi; Cambridge: The Lutherword Press, Baker Books, 1996): 207–230, esp. 220–221.

proves much more likely. Still, only intensive palaeographic analysis of these inscriptions with particular emphasis on dating, if even possible, could locate the evidence in its precise historical context.[161] As for the second historical trajectory more generally, significant difficulties arise for situating those battles recorded in 1 Kgs 20 (Samaria, Aphek) and 2 Kgs 6 (Samaria)—not to mention other events like those of 803 and 802—into their exact chronological frameworks, which must also account for an Assyrian campaign and a movement of Aramaean troops to Samaria, as indicated in the Eponym Canon Cb I and three additional cuneiform monuments dating from 806 to 796, namely, the Nimrud orthostat (COS 2114G) and the inscriptions from Saba'a and Tell-al-Rimaḥ (COS 2.114E, 2.114F, respectively).[162]

Tab. 12: *The Expansionism of Assur in campaigns (Eponym Canon Cb I) against the Aramaean supremacy in Northern and Southern Syria from 806 to 773*

Eponym Canon Cb 1	
806	
805	Campaign circuit of Adad-nerari III; Damascus
804	Northern Syria
803	Rás en-Nâqûra (Mt. Carmel), Ba'albeck, or Ba'ali-sapuna; not Damascus![163]

---

161 To this discussion see also S. Hasegawa, BZAW 434, Berlin/Boston 2012, 62: "Following Eph'al and Naveh, I interpret עמק as the provenance of the object, which was brought Hazael either as tribute or as booty." and "Interpreting נהר as indicating the the Orontes River cannot be excluded due to its proximity to 'Umqi/ Patina." and "Similarly, נהר in the Hebrew Bible refers either to the Jordan ... or to the Euphrates...." and "Hazael's crossing of the Euphrates must be dated after Shalmaneser III stopped crossing the Euphrates after 829 BCE, his campaign to Unqi. More precisely, it would have been after 826 BCE when the Eponym Chronicles no longer mention Assyrian military campaigns. Thus, the campaign of Hazael beyond the Euphrates can be dated between 826 BCE and 805 BCE, when Adad-nerârî III resumed the campaign to ther west of the Euprates."

162 See already H. Chazelles, Une nouvelle stèle d'Araméens d'Assyrie et Joas d'Israel, CRAIBL 113/1, 1969, 106–117, esp. 108–110. An overview to the campaigns of Adad-nerari III. see in: Manfred Weippert, Die Feldzüge Adad-nararis III. nach Syrien. Voraussetzungen, Verlauf, Folgen*, ZDPV 108/1 (1992), 42–67, 49 ff.

163 Cf. S. Hasegawa, BZAW Bd. 434, Berlin/Boston 2012, 47/48, 90.

Eponym Canon Cb 1	
802	Mediterranean or southern Mesopotamian "sea land:" not Damascus !
796	Northern Biqa', southern er-Rable (Riblah), or Masyad, 45 km west/southwest of Hamâ at Jebel Ansariya
773	Damascus, time of Salmanesser IV

Lipinski, for example, proposed Samaria could have defended itself against an Aramaean onslaught given the Assyrian intervention in Aram-Damascus under Adad-nerari III and the siege of Damascus in 803, whereby the Israelites under King Jehoash would have seized the opportunity to campaign against the Aramaeans at Aphek in retaliation.[164]

Tab. 13: *Portrait of the Events According to Textual Analysis of Literary Strata in the Books of Kings (Chronology B)*

Chronology B	
858	Ascent of Shalmanesar III to the throne
853	Battle of Qarqar; Ahab and Adad-'Idri war together against Assyria; natural death of Ahab[165]; Ahaziah king of the northern kingdom
	Joram over the northern kingdom
849	Campaign of Shalmaneser III (10th palû)

---

164 E. Lipinski, "Le Benhadad II de la Bible et l'histoire" in: *Proceedings of the Fifth World Congress of Jewsh Studies* T.1, *Jerusalem: R. H. Hacohen, 1969*, 157–173.

165 Nadav Na'aman, The Northern Kingdom in the Late Tenth-Ninth Centuries BCE, in: H.G.M. Williamson, Understanding the History of Ancient Israel, Proceedings of the British Academy Vol. 143, Oxford/New York: Oxford University Press Inc. 2007, 399–418, esp. 409/410, explained, that – contrary to commonly accepted view that the narrative of Ahab's death in the battle (1 Kgs 22) is legendary (see Gotthard G.G. Reinhold (1989, 136 ff.): Chronology B) – the kernel of the story must be historical and an authentic memory of this king's unusual death, more likely, when he was killed by an arrow in the battle of Qarqar 853 BCE. See already before Na'aman (2005, 466, 470).

Chronology B	
848	Campaign of Shalmaneser III (11th palû)
845	Campaign of Shalmaneser III (14th palû) Adad-'Idri and son, Birhadad, war against Assyria; death of Adad-'Idri or illness and death in 842/41 (Tel Dan ln. 3–4); wounding of Bir-Hadad and sickness in Damascus until 842/41
842	Murder of Ben-Hadad III; Haza'els usurpation; Joram's battle against Hazael at Ramoth-Gilead; revolution of Jehu; campaign of Shalmaneser III (18 th palû)
841	Revolt of Mesha
803	Campaign of Aram under Ben-Hadad, son Hazaels, against King Jehoash of Israel in Samaria (1 Kgs 20*; 2 Kgs 6*)
802	Campaign of Aram under Ben-Hadad, son Hazaels, against Jeohoash of Israel at Apek (1. Kgs 20)

The greatest challenge for this second outline lies in establishing a historical context for the biblical texts employed as evidence, for literary-critical analyses can produce divergent results for the events' chronological placement. Such difficulty may manifest itself most patently for the battle at Ramoth-Gilead (1 Kgs 22), which could date to the time of Joram, Jehoahaz, or Jehoash of Israel. Nevertheless, some kind of conflict did transpire around Ramoth-Gilead in the year 841, as indicated by the annalistic notice of 2 Kgs 9:14–15. Indeed, this confrontation between Joram/Ahaziah and Aram—after Arams campaign to Haurân and Israels retreat from QDM (east of Gilead)—concentrated on a point of great strategic significance, the fort Tell er-Rumeith/Ramith, and the town Ramtha (Er-Remtā). The ivory from Arslan Tash (Ḥadatu) provides valuable collaborative evidence in this regard (Fig. 2).[166] Reconstructed by Puech[167], the inscription reads as follows: ['rs' . zy . q]rb . 'm' . lmr'n . ḥzl.

---

166   Louvre, Paris AO 11489.
167   See È. Puech, "L'ivorie inscrit d'Arslan Tash et les rois de Damas," *RB* 88, no. 4 (1981): 544–562, esp. 561; Francois Bron, André Lemaire, Les inscriptions araméennes de Hazael, *RA* 83 (1989):35–44, esp. 37; cf. also

bšnt[. 'h]zt.[168] *ḥwrn]* ("The bed which the people offered to our lord Hazael in the year of the [annex]ion of Ḥawran"). Early in his reign, Hazael would have then forayed into Ḥaurân to challenge Israel's control of the region (Tel Dan l. 3–5). As for chronological setting, M. Heltzer has dated the inscription to 841.[169] Not only this epigraphic attestation but also later evidence in Assyrian cuneiform texts from the time of Adad-nerari III reflect widespread usage of the Aramaic royal title *mr'* ("lord") as a formulaic form of address within northern Syria during the ninth and eighth centuries. Already in 1934 de Vaux postulated an "excellente transposition dans le *Ma-ri-' šarru ša MÂTDimâšqi*" for a conjectural *mry' mlk dmśq* (cf. Bar-Rakib *mr' . mlk . 'śwr*).[170] As of now, most of the scholars have decided on the Aramaic royal title.[171]

S. Hafthórsson, 2006, 40–43 and Stefan Beyerle, 2009, 47–76, esp. 55–56, who evaluates Puech's reconstruction of "Ḥaurân" as "highly speculative," though such a proposition converges quite well historically with the Tël Dan inscription, (idem, 2009, 70), where he equates qdm with "Ostland," the Ḥaurân, beyond the Jordan and north of the Yarmuk (OT Bashan).

For the inscriptions from Arslan Tas and Nimrud, see already before: KAI II:282, 232; Millard, "Alphabetic Inscriptions on Ivories from Nimrud," *Iraq* 24, no.1 (1962):41–51; M.E.L. Mallowan, *Nimrud and Its Remains*, vol. 2 (London: Collins, 1966), 598–599, no. 582 (ND 11310); Wolfgang Röllig, "Alte und neue Elfenbeininschriften" NESE 2 (1974):37–64, esp. 38 ff., see the additional ivory inscription from Nimrud (ND, 11310), 48; Irene J. Winter, "Is There a South Syrian Style of Ivory Carving in the Early First Millennium B.C.?" *Iraq* 43 (1981): 101–130, esp. 103–109; André Lemaire, Hazaël de Damas, roi d'Aram, in: D. Charpin, E. Joannès, ed., *Marchands diplomates et empereurs*, 1991, 91/92.

168 Otherwise S. Hasegawa, BZAW 434, Berlin/Boston 2012, 59/60 decribes also the translation as "[cap]ture of" as "highly speculative," but wants to put off the event in later times: "At any rate, such or a similar remarkable achievement of Hazael could be dated to the period after Shalmaneser III stopped campaigning to Syria-Palestine (after 837 BCE)."

169 Michael Heltzer, "An Old-Aramean-Seal-Impression and Some Problems of the History of the Kingdom of Damascus" in *Arameans, Aramaic, and the Aramaic Literary Tradition* (ed. M. Sokoloff; Ramat Gan: Bar Ilan, 983), 9–13; André Lemaire, "Joas de Samarie, Barhadad de Damas, Zakkur de Hamat. La Syrie-Palestine vers 800 av. J.-C." *Eretz Israel* 24 (1994): 148–157, esp. 149; Hafthórsson, 2006, 69–70; for detailed discussion, see also Beyerle, 2009, 58–60.

170 Roland de Vaux, "La Chronologie de Hazael et de Benhadad III. Rois de Damas," *RB* 43, no.4 (1934):512–518, esp. 512

171 To this dicussion see S. Hasegawa, BZAW Bd. 434, Berlin/Boston 2012, 119: "The old suggestion of identifying Mari' the sucessor of Benhadad cannot

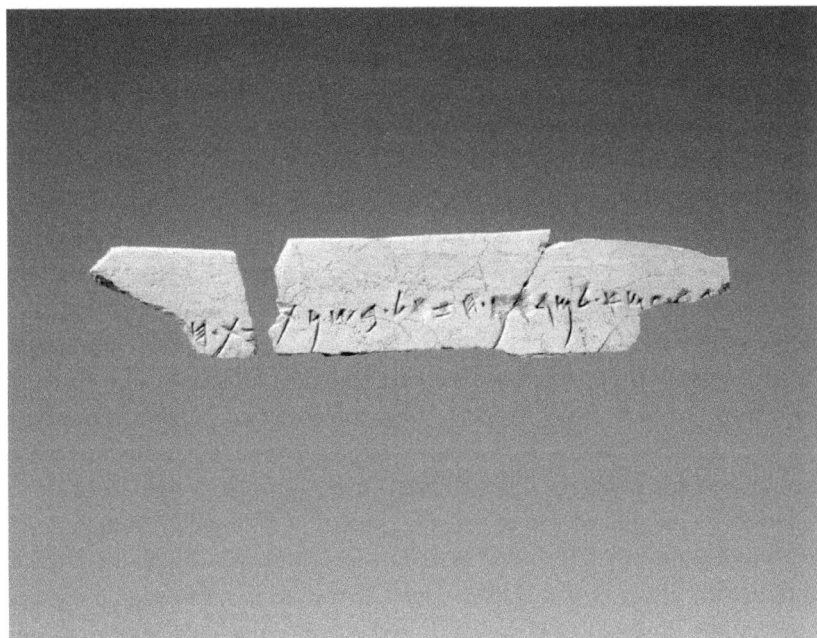

4.2.3 The Historical Background of the Elija and Elisha Narratives: A Short Review

As a result of repeated Assyrian campaigns under Shalmaneser III in the years 849, 848, and 845 after Hazael's usurpation of the Aramaean throne and continued confrontations in 841 and 838, on the one hand, and of the relentless advance of Aramaeans southward (2 Kgs 10:32 ff.: Gilead, Bashan, Haurân) and into the western regions of Israel down to the time of Ben Hadad son of Hazael (2 Kgs 12:18 ff.) more specifically, Tell es Safi/

---

be exluded, but more plausible is to regard Mariʿ as a hypocoristicon of the king's real name, and Ben-Hadad as the throne name, Mariʿ meaning "my Lord" in West Semitic, probably forms a part of the real name Ben-Hadad, son of Hazael."

71

Gath[172] and Jerusalem[173]—on the other, the northern kingdom of Israel was forced to muster substantial economic resources for its defense, creating a protracted, almost inevitable economic crisis on top of that political dilemma already in place. Ravaged by years of war, the land suffered further devastation from extended drought, which exacerbated widespread famine, increased poverty, continued unrest, and socio-political decline. Popular resistance, fueled by circles of Yahwistic prophets from the northern kingdom, also rose in response to the propagation and advancement of the Canaanite cultic apparatus. More concretely, preference for Canaanite deities, especially Baal, widespread polytheism, and syncretistic religious practice along with ostensible contempt for traditional forms of law during the Omride dynasty—escalating under the Sidonian princess Jezebeel, Ahab's wife—all provoked the Israelite prophets to action. The northern kingdom sought to bring its social, political, and legal policies in line with those of the Canaanites, as evident in Phoenician land transactions vis-à-vis unalienable property rights in Israel (e.g., Naboth, 1 Kgs 21 MT). As opposed to the older form of prophecy manifest in Samuel, Nathan, Gad, Ahijah of Shilo, and Jehu son of Hanani, the narratives of Elijah the Tishbite indicate the creation of a certain gentry that lived in a so-called prophetic circle under Elisha of Abel-meholah—who associated himself more closely with these young prophets—and eventually grew into a "powerful revolutionary movement."[174]

---

172 Cf. also the Zakkur inscription. See Aren M. Meir, "The Historical Background and Dating of Amos VI 2: An Archaeological Perspective from Tell es-Safi/Gath" *VT* LIV, no. 3 (2004): 321–334; Aren M. Maier and Carl S. Ehrlich, "Excavating Philistine Gath: Have We Found Goliath's Hometown?" *BARev* 27, no.6 (2001): 22–31, ibid., 'The Aramean Involvement in the Southern Levant: Case Studies for Identifying the Archaeological Evidence, lecture at the IWH Symposium Heidelberg, 2. Sept. 2014 and S. Hasegawa, BZAW Bd. 434, Berlin/Boston 2012, 74.

173 So Nadav Na'aman, "Royal Inscriptions and the Histories of Joash and Ahaz, Kings of Judah", *VT* XLVIII, no. 3 (1998): 333–49. According to Na'aman does not permit the 'âz in the text (vv 15–17 and 18–19), to date Hazaels campaign to Jerusalem in the 23. year of king Joash.

174 A. S. Kapelrud, *Israel—From Earliest Time to the Birth of Christ* (transl. J.M. Moe; Oxford: Blackwell, 1966), 62.

The Elijah and Elisha cycles present themselves as contemporaneous with the end of the Omride dynasty. Without source division, these narratives would stem from the last days of the dynasty's final ruler, Joram (ca. 845), as W.W. Hallo has argued.[175] Such events would include the stories of Naaman (2 Kgs 5), the Aramaean's bewilderment (2 Kgs 6:8 f.), and Elisha's designation of Hazael (2 Kgs 8:7–15—with the report of Elisha's death falling in the time of King Jehoash (2 Kgs 13:14). However H. Chr. Schmitt, has undertaken extensive analysis of the narratives' literary strata and postulated the successive development of individual chapters, revealing the historical contexts of these literary constructions:[176]

Tab. 14: The Elija and Elisha narratives in the Books of Kings and Chronology by H. Chr. Schmitt (1972)

Narrative	Chronology
Naaman	Jehoahaz of Israel (814–798 B.C.E.)
Elisha's final days	Jehoash of Israel (798–82)
Designation of Hazael	Jeroboam II (793–53)
Aramaean Bewilderment	Jeroboam II (793–53)
Elijah at Horeb/combination with Elisha cycle (1 Kgs 19:15b-17)	Terminus a quo 587

Since these traditions themselves provide quite little in terms of historical particularity, reconstructing an exact chronological trajectory for their production proves considerably problematic, so other serialization and periodization remains not only possible but also necessary. According to Schmitt, however, the story of Naaman presupposes peaceful relations and political accord between Aram and Israel, correspondent to the reign of Jehoahaz. Yet such circumstances may have obtained at an even earlier point in time. A secondary connection of Elisha to Carmel (2 Kgs 2:25; 4:25), Dothan (6:8,23), and Damascus (8:7,15) has enjoyed considerable support. Closely

---

175 W.W. Hallo, "From Qarqar to Carchemish," *BA* 23, no. 2 (1960): 34–61, esp. 40.
176 H. Chr. Schmitt, *Elisa. Traditionsgeschichtliche Untersuchungen zur vorklassichen nordisraelitischen Prophetie* (Gütersloh: Gerd Mohn, 1972): 137–138.

associated with the usurpation of Hazael (842/41)[177] and new analyses of epigraphic material—namely, the Ashur basalt statue (COS 2.113G), the bull inscription of Shalmaneser III (COS 2.113C), the black obelisk from Nimrud (COS 2.113F), the Melqart inscription from Aleppo (COS 2.32), and the Têl Dan inscription (COS 2.39)—the coronation of Hazael could have transpired within a timeframe close to the Damascus coup d'état. The story of Elisha's final days, in contrast, could date to the Jehoash's reign, as suggested by Schmitt. But questions remain as to whether the narrative of Aramaean confusion reflects historical events at the city of Dothan, which would then correlate with the tradition's development in the second half of the ninth century. Excavations at Tell Dôtān[178] have established the strong possibility of an Aramaean invasion for Strata IV (Area L) and III of the Iron II period, that is, during the ninth century.[179]

Against H. Chr. Schmitt (1972) some years ago O.H. Steck (1968) had attributed the story of Elisha at Horeb, especially the passage in 1 Kgs 19:15b-17, to the end of the ninth century, when the Elisha tradition "had essentially been finalized."[180]

Concerning literary criticism of the Elijah and Elisha narratives, Manfred Oeming[181] has provided a survey of scholarship, from Hugo Greß-

---

177   K. Lawson Younger (2007), 265 has advanced this date: "In 2 Kings 8.7–15, Hazael murders Ben-Hadad and seizes the throne. While it is impossible to confirm the historicity of the murder, the Assyrian text asserts that Hazael was not the legitimate heir to the throne of Damascus. Thus sometime in 844 or 843 Hazael became king in Damascus." and N. Na'aman, (2007), 414 one year later, "about 43/42 BCE."

178   See J. P. Free, The Excavations of Dothan, BA 19 1956, 43–48, esp. 48 and The Seventh Season at Dothan, BASOR 160 1960, 6–15.

179   Assaf Kleiman, in his lesson 'Dating the Aramean Campaigns to the Northern Levant: Gradual Process of Destructions or Regionalism in the Pottery Assemblages?', at the IWH Symposium Heidelberg, 2. Sept. 2014, associates late Iron Age II A destruction layers, dated to the second half of the ninth century, with the aggressive politics of Aram-Damascus.

180   O. H. Steck, Überlieferung und Zeitgeschichte in den Elia-Erzählungen (WMANT 26; Neukirchen-Vluyn: Neukirchner Verlag, 1968), 95.

181   See especially Manfred Oeming,, "And the King of Aram was at War with Israel" – The Construction of the Aramean as an Enemy in the Elisa Cycle 2 Kings 2–13., in: Heidelberg Colloquium, Aram and Israel: Cultural Interac-

mann (1921)[182] to R. Sauerwein (2014)[183] and W. Brueggeman/D. Hankins (2014).[184]

4.2.4 Toward Hazael's Dominance in Syria-Palestine and the Political Events of His Son, Ben-Hadad IV

Despite the campaigns of Shalmaneser III that attenuated Aramaean hegemony in 841 and 843, the collapse of the anti-Assyrian coalition among western states, and the fall of Hamath from predominance in that coalition, Aram-Damascus ultimately reestablished control over the Aramaean territory of northern Syria along with regions in the Euphrates valley once Assyrian influence waned under Shamshi-Adad V (823–10). Its reach extended into the Israelite territories of the Transjordan up to Arnon (2 Kgs 10:32–33) and even into western Palestine itself. Moreover, Aram-Damascus consolidated its control over those areas in Palestine dominated by the Philistines. At this point in time, Jehoash of Judah took the opportunity to bribe Hazael with tribute from palace and temple alike in order to spare Jerusalem from conquest (2 Kgs 12:18, 19). Only under Adad-nerari III (809–782) did the Aramaeans suffer another perilous decline—he most likely being that long-desired messiah mentioned in 2 Kgs 13:5, though Jeroboam II might also be a possible contender in this regard. But newer research by Peter James and Peter G. van der Veen[185] has suggested Shoshenq I, whose campaign probably proceeded along the coastal route in the final third of the ninth, could have been the savior of Israel.

Thereafter, Israel and Judah enjoyed political and economic ascent. Significant textual evidence—namely, the Eponym Canon Cb I, the Saba'a and Rimah stelae (COS 2.114E-F), the orthostat from Nimrud (COS 2.114G), the Tell

---

tion, Political Borders and Construction of Identity during the Early Iron Age (12 th – 8th Centuries BCE), Sept. 1–4 2014, 16–17.

182 Hugo Greßmann, Die älteste Geschichtsschreibung und Prophetie Israels: von Samuel bis Amos und Hosea, Göttingen: Vandenhoeck & Ruprecht, 1921

183 R. Sauerwein, *Elischa. Eine redaktions- und religionsgeschichtliche Studie* (BZAW 465; Berlin: de Gruyter, 2014)

184 W. Brueggemann – W.D. Hankins, "The Affirmation of Prophetic Power and Deconstruction of Royal Authority in the Elisha Narratives, *CBQ* 76 2014, 58–76

185 BAR International Series 2732 2015, 129.

Sheikh Hammad stela (COS 2.114D), and a fragmented stone slab of unknown provenance (COS 2.114C), which alludes to events recounted in the basalt stela[186]—indicates that Hazael's son successfully led his father's troops already before 805 and even warred in the Cisjordan before the end of King Jehoahaz' reign (2 Kgs 13:24, 25), all while Hazael continued to sit on the throne in Damascus. However, during the campaign circuit of Adad-nerari III—which went to Arpad (Cb I: a-na [mât] ar-pa-da)[187], pro-Assyrian Hamath, Damascus, and then back northward—both Jehoash of Israel and a certain Mari' (probably Hazael) paid tribute to Adad-nerari III, as reported in cuneiform texts. The first set of Samaritan ostraca, dated to years nine and ten (thus 806 and 805, respectively), almost certainly comes from this period, that is, during the reign of Jehoahaz. The northern kingdom thereby forced to replenish the royal stores with funds, cereals, oil, and wine, Jehoahaz's regime underwent severe hardship from Hazael and his son. As for the second group of ostraca, associated with years 15 (800) and 17 (798), they provide some insight into conscription organization, mentioning particular officers to whom recruits reported. These finds correspond to Israel's political rise under King Jehoash (805–798), which began as early as his co-regency Jehoash defeated Aram-Damascus and its new ruler, Ben-Hadad IV, on numerous occasions (2 Kgs 13:25).[188]

The question of potential sources concerning Hazael's activities now emerges. A fragment of a large Aramaic stela inscription with one reconstructed name] LḤZ'[L surfaced at Tell Afis (Hazrak or Hadrak) in temple A I (Fig. 4).[189] But without added fragments, this question must remain open.

---

186 Here I refer to my special sections in: Gotthard G.G. Reinhold (1989, 180 ff., 194/195) and to the numerous publications of the stelae, the orthostat, the stone slab and the inscriptions: V. Scheil, "Notules," *RA* 14 (1917): 159 ff.); Stephanie Page (1968, 139 ff.); idem (1969, 483 ff. [a]; 1969, 457 ff. [b]; H. Tadmor (1969, 46 ff.); Aelred Cody (1970, 325 ff.); Alan Millard and H. Tadmor (1973, 57 ff.); H. Tadmor (1973, 141 ff.); A.R. Millard (1973, 161 ff.); W.H. Shea (1978, 101 ff.); Brad E. Kelle (2002, esp. 651 f.) and Karen Radner (2012, 265 ff.). To all these inscriptions see also S.Hasegawa, BZAW Bd. 434, Berlin/Boston 2012, 92–96.

187 S. Hasegawa, ibid., 90/91.

188 See already W. H. Shea, Israelite Chronology and the Samaria Ostraca, *ZDPV* 101/1 1985, 9–20.

189 See the full-page photography by M. Necci, Afis Expedition Archives (Fig. 4). A recently new discovered fragment (24 cm high, about 8 cm broad, 5.2 cm

Aram-Damascus suffered further rout according to the Zakkur inscription. Having mustered Bar-Gush king of Arpad, the kings of Que, 'Amuq, Gurgum, Sam'al,[190] Meliz, likely Karkemish, seven Phoenician city-states and two other states in addition—hence sixteen political entities *in toto* (ln. 4–8)—Ben-Hadad IV, called Bir-Hadad (IV), spearheaded a joint venture to besiege the city of Hazrak and force Zakkur, the king of Hamath and Lu'ash,[191] and successor of Irḫuleni, into an anti-Assyrian coalition, harassing him and seizing his territory to this end. Yet Zakkur emerged victorious. While the stela simply ascribes salvation and succor to Ba'lshamayn (ln. 13 f.), Lipinski attributes such success to intervention from a king allied with Hamath: Adad-nerari III himself.[192] For Lipinski, this advance came after his 796 campaign against *a-na (uru) man-su-a-te*. Pitard has also called

---

thick) of a large Aramaic stela from Tell Afis (Hadrak) and dated to the last third of the ninth century BCE could have a possible reference to Hazael and his activities. Not certain is the preserved portion of the text] YHW (?)[.
Maria Giula Amadasi Guzzo prefers to derive the three letters YHW from the root HYH, "to be" (imperfect, third person plural?).
The preserved text reads as follows:

    ]'[
    ]''(?)[
    ]Q ' 'D/R[
    ]SL' KL[
    ]LḪZ'[L
    ]YHW(?)[
    M]LK[

See Maria Giula Amadasi Guzzo, TELL AFIS IN THE IRON AGE: The Aramaic Inscriptions, ASOR NEA 77/1 2014, 54–57, spec. 54/55; K. Lawson Younger, Some of What's New in Old Aramaic Epigraphy, ASOR NEA 70/3 2007, 139–146, spec. 139; Aren M. Maeir, Review of Jonathan Miles Robker, The Jehu Revolution: A Royal Tradition oft he Northern Kingdom and Its Ramifications, RBL [www.bookreviews.org] (2015).

190 For development of the Aramaean city-states in Sam'al, see in particular Ralf-B. Wartke, *SAM'AL. Ein aramäischer Stadtstaat des 10. bis 8. Jhs. v.Chr. und die Geschichte seiner Erforschung* (Mainz: Philipp von Zabern, 2005), esp. 57–90.

191 See Efrem Yildez, "Los Arameos de Lu'aš y Hamat" Arabismo.com ano 2001, 1–10.

192 E. Lipinski, „The Assyrian Campaign to Masuate in 796 B.C. And the Zakir stela,", *AION* 31 1971: 393–399, esp. 397 ff.

additional attention to the problematic of B ln.2–3 on the stela, for even here alongside his charioteers, the king has no mention by name.[193]

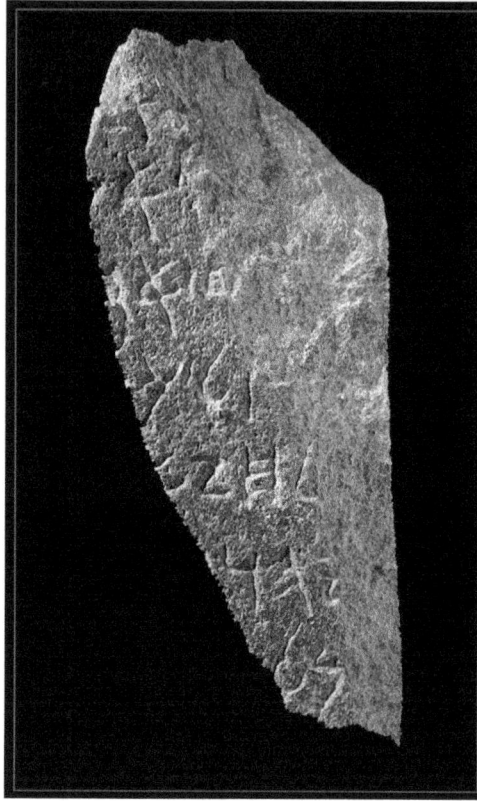

---

193 W. T. Pitard, 1987, 174; S. Hafthórsson, 2006, 65–66. E. Lipinski is dating the events, which are recording about the siege of Hazrak, to the year 796 B.C.! See E. Lipinki, LAOS 3 2013: 139: "The purpose of the Assyrian campaign to Mansuate in 796 was to rescue Zakkur, besieged in Hadrk/Hatarikka (Tell al-Afis) by a coalition led by Bar-Hadad II of Damascus and by the king of Arpad, who may now be securely identified with Bar Hadad, son of Attarsumki I." But here it's evidently, that E.Lipinski is not involved in the new researches to the Bar Hadad stela from Bureij/Aleppo! See L.J. Mykytiuk (2009, 2012, 2015) and G.G.G. Reinhold (Excursus II)!

The dating of these events must therefore be adjusted to give the coalition time to assemble, prepare for battle, and force Hamath to their side. Hence, the timeframe would converge with Assyria's strained political and military circumstances beyond those states in northern and southern Syria—Assyria's confrontations with Urartu under Menua (ca. 810–781) and Argišti I (ca. 780–756) serving as serious contenders in the regard.[194] The campaigns enumerated in the Eponym Canon Cb I assert quite clearly that "the force of Urartu grew larger and larger, the scope of Assyria's military activity smaller and smaller."[195] Indeed, over the course of his ten-year reign, Shalmaneser IV (783/81–774/72) undertook six campaigns against Urartu alone.

As for the chronology of the events described in the Zakkur inscription (Fig. 4: front A), the Assyrian campaigns of 773 against Damascus and 772 against Hazrak, Zakkur's capital, remain strong possibilities.[196] Hazael's son Bir-Hadad likely fell in the battle against Zakkur, for already during the reign of Shalmaneser IV in 773, the military commander turtânu Shamshi-ilu undertook a campaign against a certain Ḥaziânu/Ḥadiânu (Ḥazyân II) of Imērišu (i.e., Aram), as recorded in the inscription from

---

194   Stefan Beyerle also considers the strengthening of Urartu and military involvement of Assyria; See Beyerle, 2009, 56/57.

195   So Marcus Wäfler, "Zum assyrisch-urartäischen Westkonflikt," *APA* 11, no.12 (1980): 79–97.

196   See already Gotthard G.G. Reinhold, Diss. 196 and 249–265 (Zakkur Stela-inscription). S. Hasegawa, BZAW Bd. 434, Berlin/Boston 2012, 63 leaves open a defined chronology of these events: "The siege took place either at the end of the ninth or at the beginning of the eight century BCE." But, he favours the date 804/03 BCE., ibid, 102/103: "Adad-nerari III's 804/3 BCE campaign forced this coalition to hurry northwards in order to defend their homeland and thus Hamath was saved." "This dating seems the most probable because it produces no conflict with the descriptions in the Assyrian inscriptions" and: "Provided that the siege of Hadrach took place in 804/3 BCE, the absence of Joahaz from among the besieging troops in the Zakkur Inscription may indicate the the Kingdom of Israel did not take part in the siege. It might show that Joahaz had already attempted to throw off the Damascene yoke, by refusing to participate in the anti-Assyrian coalition."

Pazarcik, Turkey (COS 2.114B).[197] Unfortunately, no extant evidence can determine whether this Aramaean ruler, perhaps a descendent of Hazael, continued to function as co-regent with Bir-Hadad after 773, whether he began his own rule in 772, how long such a reign might have lasted,[198] and when he would have ultimately met his demise. Regardless, the dates 773 and 772 establish a clear limitation for the reign of Bir-Hadad IV.[199] After these events, Aramaean power declined substantially, and Israel's political and economic significance then escalated considerably under the rule of Jeroboam (793–53). Israelite penetration into Aramaean territory probably did not begin until the end of his reign, though—and thus at the time of Ashur-dan III (772/71–754) or Aššur-nerari V (753–45)—for the Assyrians continued to undertake Syrian campaigns against Hazrach and Arpad in 755 and 754, respectively. With the triumph of Zakkur of Hamath came the failure of Bir-Hadad IV, son of Hazael, to coordinate an anti-Assyrian coalition among the states of northern Syria and Anatolia, yet northern Syria managed to form a series of alliances for the fight against Assyria, as stated in the Sefire inscription from Suğīn (1.3 km northeast of Sefîre), a treaty between Mati'el of Arpad and Barga'yah king of Ktk.[200] The localization of Ktk has proven difficult. While Jongwon Choi[201] has proposed the city of Kittika—known from the late Roman period (fifth century CE) and identified with Yel Baba, a "mound on the eastern outskirts of the modern village of Šayḫ Ri'aḥ, 11 km east

---

197 See V. Donbaz (1990, 8 ff., 14 ff.) and Nili Wazzana (2001, 696 ff.). For the political situation I refer to Gershon Galil (1992, 55 ff.), Carlo Zaccagnini (1993, 53 ff.), Stefan Beyerle (2009, 61 ff.) and S. Hasegawa(2012, 97 ff., 101, 135: Eponym Chronicles).

198 To this insecurity of this king's reign see also Gunnar Lehmann (2008, 148).

199 See especially Stefan Timm, *König Hesion II. von Damascus* (WdO; Göttingen:Vandenhoeck & Ruprecht, 1993): 55–84, esp. 81–83.

200 See already note 90 and the work of Ran Zadok, "On the Historical Background of the Sefire Treaty," *AION* 44 (1984): 529–538.

201 Jongwon Choi, Zur Bedeutung der Zahl Sieben. Eine literar- und kompositionskritische Studie zu den Vorstellungen von Fluch und Strafe im Alten Orient und im alten Testament (Kleine Arbeiten zum Alten und Neuen Testament 11; Kamen: Hartmut Spenner, 2011), 21.

of 'Azâz"—J.C.L. Gibson has posited an Urartian vassal state east of the Euphrates near the Balikh River since the equation of *tl'ym* (Sefire III:23) with the city of *Ta-al-ḫa-yi-im(ki)*, frequently mentioned in Mari texts, seems quite certain.[202] For his part, A. Malamat connects Ktk with the fragmentary *Ki-(x) qa* of the Kurkh monolith inscription of Salamanasser III, which recounts an Assyrian campaign against Bît-'Adini in 858 (COS 2.113A).[203] While Yutuka Ikeda[204] has argued "KTK/Ki[..]qa should be interpreted as the name of Til Barsip, used by her indigenous Luwian population," both a fragment in hieroglyphic Luwian ("Louvre fragment")[205] and a published stela from the Eli Borowski collection[206], now establish the Neo-Hittite equivalent of Til-Barsip was *ma-su-wa/i-ra/i-na* (URBS), that is, (the city) Masuwari.

202 J. C. L. Gibson, *TSSI* II:22–23 and Frederick Mario Fales, Istituzioni a confronto tra mondo semitico occidentale e Assyria nel I Millenio a.C.: Il tratto di Sefire, in: L. Canfera, M. Liverani, C. Zaccagnini, eds., *I tratti nel mondo antico. Forma, ideologia, funzione* (Saggi di Storia Antica 2: Roma: L ' Erma di Bretschneider, 1990), 149–173, esp. 169/70.

203 A. Malamat, "A New Proposal for the Identification of Ktk in the Sefire Inscription" (Hebrew) in mifkâdîm u-m'gillot-jahas u-mašmâ' ûtâm ha-historiît l-îmê ša'ûl we-dâwîd (ed. M. Razin; Ornamin: Haifa University, 1976), VII–IX; ANET, 277 and especially Ran Zadok, On the Historical Background of the Sefire Treaty*, *AION* 44 1984, 529–538, esp. 529 f., 532, 534.

204 Yutuku Ikeda, Once again KTK in the Sefire Inscriptions, EI 23 1993, 104*– 108*, esp. 104* ; André Lemaire & Jean-Marie Durand, *Les inscriptions araméennes de Sfiré et l' Assyrie de Shamshi-ilu*, (= École Pratique des Hautes Études II, Hautes Études Orientales 20), Genève-Paris: Librarie Droz, 1984 pp. 47 ff. (part III "Roi DE *KTK*").

205 J. D. Hawkins, ,The Hittite Name of Til Barsip: Evidence from a New Hiero-glyhic Fragment from Tell Ahmar', *AnSt* 33 1983, 131–136, esp. 132.

206 I. Singer, A New Stela of Hamiyatas, King of Masuwari, *Tel Aviv* 15/16, 1988/89, 184 ff.

4.2.5 The Rise and Fall of Damascene Hegemony under Rezin (ca. 750–732 BCE)

With the death of Jeroboam II (793–53), the weakness of Assyria under Ashur-nerari V (754–45), the rise of Urartu under Sardur II (ca. 765–33), and the considerable dependence of north Syrian states on the political objectives of Urartu came a period of general détente for south Syria. This context permitted Rezin's Aram-Damascus to regain its political and economic significance.[207] During the mighty rule of Tiglath-Pileser III, however, a significant reversal ensued that benefitted the states with Sardur II of Urartu, namely, Arpad, Meliz, Gurgum, and Kummuḫ, though they themselves suffered defeat by the Assyrian king in 743. Contemporaneous with payments of tribute to Assyria in 740, 739, and 738—discharged by the majority of states in Syria-Palestine (Israel and Aram-Damascus), Phoenicia (Tyre and Byblos), northern Syria (Arpad, Amqi/Amuq, Karkemish, Sam'al[208]), and southern and eastern Anatolia (Que, Gurgum, Kummuḫ, Meliz), among others—certain political entities from northern Syria and the Levantine coast were able to form an anti-Assyrian resistance movement under Azriyau.[209] Although the insurrection's theater lay along the coast of northern Phoenician, encompassing the states of Usnu, Siannu, Simirra, and Kashpuna and stretching as far as the environs of Tripoli and the mountain of Amanus (Jebel el-Ansarien) in Anti-Lebanon, the precise territory in which Azriyau began the conflict remains uncertain. Such dubiety derives from Na'aman's new analysis and correction of the Assyrian cuneiform fragment K 6205, which suits the time of Sennacherib (705–681) much more than that of Tiglath-Pileser III.[210] Nonetheless, Assyria's increased demands for tribute led to a decline in Israel's economic and social conditions. Under King Pekah, an anti-Assyrian party then formed that sided with the political ambitions of Rezin of Damascus, a

---

207 See also S. Hasegawa, BZAW Bd. 434, Berlin/Boston 2012, 149: "The rise of Urartu unter Sarduri II (764–734) brought about the decline of the Assyrian Empire in the last years of Jeroboam II., which reduced Assyria's political influence in the Syro-Palestinian arena. It opened the way for the rise of Rezin who ascended the Damascene throne in the mid-eight century BCE. Damascus under Rezin exerted considerable influence on the political situation in the kingdoms of Israel and Judah."

208 Here I refer to Herbert Niehr, The Religion of the Arameans in the West. The Case of Sam'al, LAOS 3 2013, 183– 221.

209 So B. Oded, The Historical Background of the Syro-Ephraimite War Reconsidered *, CBQ 34 1972, 153–165, esp. 160: "In the annals of Tiglathpileser III, lines 102–133, there is an account of an anti-Assyrian coalition led by Azriyau from the Land of Yaūdi (i.e. Uzziah-Azariah king of Judah)."

210 Nadav Na'aman, "Sennacherib's 'Letter to God' on His Campaign to Judah" BASOR 214 (1974): 25–39; so also Carl S. Ehrlich, Coalition Politics in Eight Century B. C.E., Palestine: The Philistines and the Syro-Ephraimite War*, ZDPV 107 1991, no. 1–2, 48–58, esp. 53; Gershon Galil, "A New Look at the Inscriptions of Tiglath-Pileser III" Biblica 81 (2000): 511–520.

figure M. Weippert has called the "motor of the secession movement"[211]—his regime becoming the most formidable Aramaean state after the neutralization of Urartu and its auxiliary powers (Arpad and greater Hamat) during the first phase of Tiglath-Pileser III's westward expansion. Following the failed attempts of Aram-Damascus and Tyre to achieve their political and military ambitions, Assyria saw the opportunity to seize control of the entire trade industry along the Mediterranean coast in the Levant and to secure Palestine's southern border with Egypt. The withdrawal of Assyrian forces in 734 provided Aram and Israel along with Judah one last chance to build an anti-Assyrian coalition. To effect such an alliance, Aram and Israel sought to overthrow the Davidic dynasty to the south with an usurper who would support the cause, the "son of Tabeel" (Isa 7:6). Precisely how legitimate this figure's successional claims were remains unknown, but he almost certainly promised Damascus and Israel loyalty in their endeavors against Assyria.[212] The duress of the Judean monarch to accede to the coalition and engage in the subsequent Syro-Ephraimite war, did not come without consequences, however. When Ahaz implored the Assyrian king for help, Tiglath-Pileser III returned to south Syria in 733 and undertook a comprehensive invasion of Syria and Palestine as far as the Egyptian border. With a devastating campaign in Trans- and Cisjordan as well as a successful foray deep into Palestine in 733, Assyrian troops saved their worst enemy for last: Aram-Damascus.[213]

---

211 Manfred Weippert, "Zur Syrienpolitik Tiglatpilesers III.," *BBVO* 1, no. 2 (1982): 395–408, esp. 396/97

212 For this political situation, see, Gershon Galil (1992, esp. 60 ff.) and Nadav Na'aman, "Rezin of Damascus and the Land of Gilead," *ZDPV* 111, no.2 (1995): 105–117.

213 According to 2 Kgs 15:29, the cities and regions of Ijjon, Abel-Bet-Maacah, Janoach, Kedesh, Hazor, Gilead, Galilee, and Naphtali were conquered, the people deported. A similar portrait emerges from archaeological research for the regions of Golad, Gilead, and Galilee as well as the cities of Dan, Hazor, Kinneret, Bethsaida, Tel Hadar, 'Ēn Gev, Bet-Shean, Kedesh, Megiddo, Jokneam, Qiri, Akko, Keisam, Schiqnoa, and Dor.
See most importantly Hanan Eshel (1990, 104 ff.), Paul Garelli (1991, 46 ff.), Gershon Galil (2000, 511 ff.), Peter Dubovský (2006, 153 ff., 165, Table 1) and also Rami Arav (2009, 328 * ff.).

They besieged Rezin's Damascus[214] in 733, the city fully capitulating in 732. The history of the Aramaeans is indeed complex, and only new archaeological finds, particularly textual materials, can illuminate this historical portrait further. For the time being, two trajectories for the royal succession of Aram-Damascus come to the fore:

Tab. 15: The Royal Line of Succession in Aram-Damascus and the Extrabiblical Sources in the Researches from Gotthard G.G. Reinhold (1986 to 2008), Lawrence J. Mykytiuk (2009 to 2015) and W. T. Pitard (1987 to 1988)

The Royal Line of Succession in Aram-Damascus		
Gotthard G.G. Reinhold (1986 to 2008) Lawrence J. Mykytiuk (2009, 2012, 2015)		W.T. Pitard (1987, 1988)
Rezon		Rezon
Hezion (= Hazyân I)		Hezion (= Hazyân I)
Tabrimmon		Tabrimmon
Ben-Hadad I		Ben-Hadad I
Ben-Hadad II		
Adad-'Idri	Monolith & Bull Inscription, Black Obelisk, Basalt Statue (Kurkh, Calah, Assur) of Shalmaneser III	Adad-'Idri (=Ben-Hadad II)
Ben-Hadad III	Melqart- or Bir/Bar-Hadad Stela, Bureij/Aleppo (Reinhold/ Mykytiuk)	

---

214 The killing of the Aramaean king Rezin occurred after 732 B.C. See M. Christine Tetley, The Date of Samaria's Fall as a Reason for Rejecting the Hypothesis of Two Conquests., *CBQ* 64/1 2002, 59–77, esp. 69: The only years remaining after 732 when Tiglath-pileser could have gone to Damascus, killed Rezin, and installed Hoshea as king are 728 and 727, and the latter only in the time before Shalmaneser succeeded Tiglath-pileser on 25 Tebet.

The Royal Line of Succession in Aram-Damascus		
Hazael (= Mari')	Black Obelisk, Basalt Statue (Calah, Assur), Marble bead inscription of Shalmaneser III and Stone Slab (Calah), Stela Inscription (Saba'a) of Adad-nerari III; Hazaels Ivory Inscriptions (Arslan Tash); Horse Bronze Cheek Piece Inscriptions (Samos) and (Eretria, Euboea); Large Stela Fragment from Temple A I (Tell Afis)	Hazael
Ben-Hadad IV (= Mari')	Zakkur Inscription (Tell Afis)	Ben-Hadad III
Hazyân II	Stele Inscription from Pazarcik, Turkey	Hazyân II
	Melqart- or Bir/Bar-Hadad Stela: Arpad (Pitard)	
Rezin	Annalistic Records (Calah) of Tiglat-pileser III	Rezin

5 Excursus I: The Melqart or Bir/Bar-Hadad Stela[215]

The Aramaic text from a stela at the village of Bureij, just north of Aleppo in Syria, was first published by Maurice Dunand in 1939.[216] With rather standard dedicatory contents, the text reports the stela was erected by a king named Bir-Hadad in honour of the god Melqart, who had heard and answered his petition. Uncertainty surrounds the identity of this Bir-Hadad—the direct equivalent of Ben Hadad in Hebrew—whose name clearly appears at the end of the first line and beginning of the second. Problems arise since there are at last three or possibly four different Aramaean kings mentioned in 1. and 2. Kings who bore this name. The question centers on which erected this stela. Alternatively, this figure may have been yet another, non-biblical king or some other great personality.

If the text were whole and relatively undamaged, identification would have likely been straightforward. The rest of the second line does provide some identifying characteristics or titles, but a crucial juncture, the stone is poorly preserved, the text extremely difficult to read. As a result, a number of different readings[217] have been offered for the rest of the second line, and thus identification of the king mentioned has varied considerably—

---

215 To the Melqart or Bir/Bar-Hadad stela see Wahid Khayyata, Guide to the Museum of Aleppo. Ancient Oriental Department, Aleppo: Arab National Printing House, 1977, Plate 25: The Phoenician God Melqart, Bridg near Aleppo, 9th Cent. [M. No. 5052] and Gotthard G. G. Reinhold (1989, Exkurs I Taf. 5 and 7).

216 Maurice Dunand, Stéle araméenne dê diêe a Melqart du Musêe d' Alep, *BMB* 3 1939, 65–76, Pl. 13; *TUAT* I, Gütersloh 1982/83/84/85, 625; Joseph A. Fitzmyer/Stephen A. Kaufmann, An Aramaic Bibliography Part I, Old Official and Biblical Aramaic, Baltimore, London: The John Hopkins University Press, 1992, 11.

217 See already Scott C. Layton, ed. by Dennis Pardee, Literary Sources for the History of Palestine and Syria. Old Aramaic Inscriptions. *BA* Sept. 1988, 172–189, esp. 176/177; Peter Kyle McCarter, Jr., Ancient Inscriptions Voices from the Biblical World, Biblical Archaeology Society, Washington D.C.: Biblical Archaeology Society, 1996, 94: 74; S. Hafthórsson, A Passing Power: An Examination of the Sources for the History of Aram-Damascus in the Second

presented by a table of different transcriptions, arranged in chronological order:

Tab. 16: The Scholars Literature & Lectures and Their Different Transcriptions of the Melqart or Bir/Bar-Hadad Stela Inscription (l. 2)

Maurice Dunand, BMB 3 1939: 73	brd/dd.br t'b.pš.[　]b /mlk 'rm
W. F. Albright, BASOR 87 1942: 25	brh/dd.br.t br[m]n[b] r.hzy[n]
A. Herdner, Syr 25 1946–1948: 329	brh/dd br t (?)..p(?)...b
E. Lipinski, AION N.S. XXI 1971: 103	'tr hpš
F.M. Cross, BASOR 205 1972: 42	brh/dd. br 'zr[.]ms q 'b[r] /mlk 'rm
E. Lipinski, SAIO I 1975: 15 f.	br.h/dd.br 'zr š mš z[y].'b /mlk 'rm
E. Lipinski, Act Ant Hung 27 1979: 69	Ibid.
W.H. Shea, Maarav 1/2 1979: 166	br h/dd.br 'zr dmsq brmn /mlk 'rm
P. Bordreuil/ Aula Or 1 1983: 271 J.Teixidor	brh/dd. br 'zr' mlk.br rhb /mlk 'rm
A. Lemaire, Or 3 1984: 29	br.h/dd.br hzyn br[hz'l]　/mlk 'rm
G.G.G. Reinhold, AUSS 24/2 1986: 120	br.h/dd.br 'zr.dmsqy ' br /mlk 'rm
W.T. Pitard, Ancient Damascus, 1987: 141	br h/dd.br 'trhmk.　　/mlk 'rm
W. T. Pitard, BASOR 272 1988: 4	br.h/dd br 'trhmk.
G.G.G. Reinhold, EHS.T XXIII Vol. 386 1989: 238	br.h/dd br 'zr. dmsqy' br /mlk 'rm
E. Puech, RB T. 99–2 1992: 315	br h/dd br 'trsmk. br hdrm [?]
W. T. Pitard, COS II 2000: 152–153	See, 1988
K.A. Kitchen, On the Reliability of the Old Testament, 2003, 12	Ibid.
G.G.G. Reinhold, At Sunrise on the Tell, 2003: 129	br.h/dd br 'zr.dmsqy' br/mlk 'rm
G.G.G. Reinhold, paper pres. 2005 Fachtagung ABA Schönblick/ Schwäbisch Gmünd	Ibid.

Half of the Ninth Century B.C (= Coniectanea Biblica Old Testament Series 54), Stockholm: Almquist & Wiksell, 2006, 33–39, esp. 39 Table 1.

G. G. Reinhold paper pres. 2008 ETL, Löwenstein	Ibid.
C. Bonnet/H. Niehr, RUAT II, 2010, 47	See E. Puech, 1992
L. J. Mykytiuk, SBL Nu. 19, Atlanta, 2012: 47/48	See G.G.G. Reinhold, 2003, 2005, 2008
E. Lipinski, LAOS 3 2013: 123–143	See E. Puech, 1992
G. Bunnens, IWH Symposium Heidelberg, 2. Sept. 2014	Ibid.
L. J. Mykytiuk, 50 People in the Bible Confirmed Archaeologically (Internet 2015)	See L. J. Mykytiuk, 2012

5.1 Epigraphy

The following epigraphic reading is synthetic in nature, combining those from photographs by J. Starkey I–III (ST), W. Khayata IV (KH), Reinhold IX–XII (REI) and personal inspection (examination, drawing, new photographs, and computer-enhancement), at the original stela in the National Museum of Aleppo in the summer of 1986.[218] Additional recourse came from two important photographs by R. Bowman[219] and H. Klengel.[220] According to these sources, I propose my epigraphic reconstruction for the second line of the Bir-Hadad stela inscription (Fig. 5–6):

---

218 Gotthard G.G. Reinhold (1989, 234–245).
219 R. A. Bowman. Art. Ben-Hadad, in: IDB, NewYork, Nashville: Abingdon Press, 1962, 381–382, esp. 382, fig. 28.
220 Horst Klengel. Handel und Händler im alten Orient, Wien Köln, Graz: Böhlau, 1979², 139, fig. 55.

Fig. 5: Bir-Hadad Inscription / Epigraphic Analysis of line 2 (Gotthard G.G. Reinhold, 2005, manuscript, Part I)

Transcribed letter/ Word-divider	Photography	Special description	Image
d	LIV, IX, XI, XII	small equilateral triangle rounded with a small tail	
d	Ibid.	Ibid.	
.	I, IV, IX, XII	short word-divider	
b	IV, IX, XI, XII	vertexed stem-Beth, the lower leg of the Beth-triangle extended to the right (in comparision to l. 1)	
r	Ibid.	rounded head to the left middle length of the tail	
'	IV	a circle with a dot in its center	
z	XI, XII	Latin z-form (in comparision to l. 4) in contrast to the Latin H-form (l. 1 and 4); a long thin rent under z; no interpretation as Taw	
r	IV, XII	rounded head to the left, middle length of the tail (something small in comparision to the first r in l. 2)	
.	Ibid.	small stroke below the r-head, left side; word-divider	

Fig. 6: Bir-Hadad Inscription / Epigraphic Analysis of line 2 (Gotthard G.G. Reinhold, Ibd., Part II)

d	IV, XII	triangular head, over-lapping of the right and the lower leg (in com-parision to the r in l. 4)	
m	IX, X	Latin W with a charac-teristic rounded stem on the right side (in comparision with the letters in l. 3)	
s	V, VII	Latin W-form	
q	IV,X,R.Bowman H. Klengel	leftward leaning figu-re, beheaded oval; missing of the upper part	
y	IV, V	long leftward shaped Arabic numeral 2 with a dash in the middle of the vertical spine	
ʾ	I, II, X	parallel-strokes (open angle) in the letter	
b	I, X	small squared form	
r	Ibid.	small figure, falling down to the right side	

5.2 Palaeography

With respect to its script, the Bir-Hadad text resembles the Amman Citadel inscription, studied intensively by Siegfried H. Horn[221] and Cross[222] already in 1969. Both of these inscriptions are specifically less developed palaeographically than that of the Zakkur stela, which belongs to the period between 800 and 770. Like the Amman Citadel inscription (ca. 875–825 B.C. or, more specifically, mid-ninth century), the Bir-Hadad stele shows a mixture of archaic and more developed graphemes, as demonstrated by the following examples.

Daleth:
The short tail is typical for early Aramaic forms. In photo XII (REI), computer-enhancement (Fig. 9) reveals a slight bend to the left stroke of the triangular head.

He:
The *he* in line 5, shows a round shoulder, as in line 5 of the Amman Citadel inscription. This form differs significantly from that in later texts.

Zayin:
The fully developed zayin appears in the Zakkur inscription from the early eighth century. While the more archaic form occurs in two (line 1, 4) of four instances, the later form emerges in line 2 (photo XII (REI) and computer enhancement) (Fig. 8) as well as line 4.

Kaph:
Though identical with those in the Amman Citadel inscription, this form appears primitive over against that of the Zakkur inscription.

'Ayin:
The 'ayin with the dot in its circle represents the earlier form of the grapheme (cf. the Tell Fakhariyeh bilingual inscription, from Syria in the mid-ninth century B.C.)[223] and this particular, form clearly occurs here, in

---

221 S. H. Horn, The Ammân Citadel Inscription, *BASOR* 193 1969, 2–13

222 F. M. Cross, Epigraphic Notes on the Ammân Citadel Inscription, *BASOR* 193 1969, 13–19

223 The 'Ayin with the dot in the circle is also archaising in the description from Benjamin Sass (2006, 41 Tab 3).

line 2: cf. precision photograph IV (KH), photograph IX (REI) and my own computer-enhancement (Fig. 7).

Śin and Open Qoph:

An open qoph—unambiguous in the photographs by Bowman[224] and Klengel,[225] following śin (similar to the Latin w) in line 2—finds further support in photograph IV (KH), photograph X (REI) and my own computer enhancement (Fig. 10).

Taken together, these palaeographic features suggest a date between 850 and 840 or, in any event, sometime after the middle of the ninth century but well before the end of that century.[226] L. J. Mykytiuk.[227] thus dates the Melqart stela of Aleppo to ca. 850 for good reason.

See also P. Kyle McCarter, Jr., *Ancient Inscriptions. Voices from the Biblical Word*, 1996, 84/85. Currently A. Lemaire (2012, 304) referred to the dated inscription in the second half of the ninth century and on foundation of historical reasons the proposed date ca. 850–825, but Klaus Beyer (2013, 14–16) from 850.

224 See note 2.
225 See note 3.
226 A large space of dating, "irgendwann zwischen 850 und 770" and "Abb. 2: Bar Hadad Brêdsch: 850–770 [?]" (Abb. 2)" was shown by Josef Tropper, Eine altaramäische Stelainschrift aus Dan, Ugarit-Forschungen Bd. 25, Kevelaer: Verl. Butzon & Berker, Neukirchen-Vlyn: Neukirchener Verlag, 1993, 395–406, esp. 398–400. See already before Nadav Na'aman, Royal Inscriptions and the Histories of Joash and Ahaz, Kings of Judah, VT XLVIII, 3 1988, 333–349, esp. 335: "second half of the ninth century" and the same dating Herbert Niehr in his lecture 'The age. Language situation and languages politics in Sam'al' at the IWH Symposium Heidelberg, 2. Sept. 2014.
227 Lawrence James Mykytiuk, Identifying Biblical Persons in Hebrew Inscriptions and Two Stelae from before the Perisan Era, Dissertation Ph.D., University of Wisconsin-Madison, 1998. Revised Edition 2001, p. 135; Identifying Biblical Persons in Northwest Semitic Inscriptions of 1200–539 B.C.E. (SBL. Academia Biblica 12, Atlanta: SBL, 2004), 116 and Corrections and Updates to Identifying Biblical Persons in Northwest Semitic Inscriptions of 1200–539 B.C.E., *Maarav* 16.1 (2009), 49–132, esp. 69–85; Sixteen Strong Identifications of Biblical Persons (Plus Nine Other IDs) in Authentic Northwest Semitic Inscriptions from before 539 B.C.E., in: SBL Archaeology and Biblical Studies, Nu. 19, Atlanta, 2012, 35–58, esp. 47/48 and the same: 50 People in the Bible Confirmed Archaeologically, thedailyhatch.org/2015/20/50-people-in-the-bible-confirmed-archaeologically/

Line 2: Enlarged through Computer Enhancement[228]

Fig. 7: 'Ayin IX (REI)

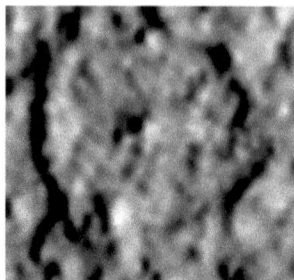

Fig. 8: Zayin XII (REI)

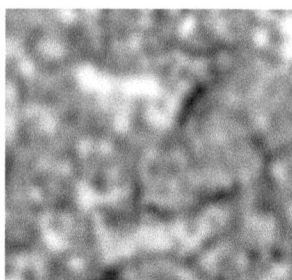

Fig. 9: Word Divider and Daleth XII (REI)   *Fig. 10 Śin and Open Qoph X (REI)*

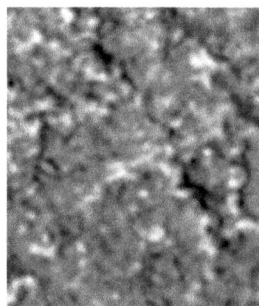

Based on precision photographs and computer enhancement, evidence from the second line of the Melqart stela reveals Pitard's[229] downstroke of the z

---

228 The following photo computer enhancements were produced by the author from photos, when he researched the Melqart stela in the National Museum of Aleppo summer 1986. See Gotthard G.G. Reinhold (1989):
Fig. 7: Excursus I Plate 9: 'Ayin IX (REI)
Fig. 8: Excursus I Plate 12: Zayin XII (REI)
Fig. 9: Excursus I Plate 12: Word Divider and Daleth XII (REI)
Fig. 10: Excursus I Plate 10: Śin and Open Qoph X (REI)

229 Wayne T. Pitard, The Identity of Bir-Hadad of the Melqart Stela, *BASOR* 272 1988, 3–21, esp. 5; idem, The Melqart Stela (2.33), COS II 2000, 152–153 and Gotthard G.G. Reinhold, Bei Sonnenaufgang auf dem Tell. Essays about decades researches in the field on Near Eastern Archaeology, Remshalden: Verlag Bernhard Albert Greiner, 2003, 128, note 498.

(from Ezer[230] in my translation) to be only a tear of the basalt-stone (!), thinner than the ordinary sign and disconnected from the thicker consonant z, which seems much more an inscribing of the word Ezer (XII REI) in line 2. Likewise, computer enhancement of photo XII (REI) clearly confirms a < D > and no other consonant after < R >, which precedes a word-divider (after Ezer: ʿzr.).[231]

The comments from Alan R. Millard (1990, 263), Ingo Kottsieper (1998, 492), Winfried Thiel (1994, 123; 2000, 197 ff.) and from Stuart A. Irvine (2005, 345 note 23) were written on the foundation of W.T. Pitard's earlier researches. And so also K. Lawson Younger (2007, 258, 265), Stefan Beyerle (2009, 47 ff.), Corinne Bonnet, Herbert Niehr (2010, 243) and Shuichi Hasegawa (2012, 505) provide no new specific comments to the second line of the Melqart stela. So the last confirmation we could find only in new Aramaic inscriptions.

230 In the Hebrew Bible "ʿzr (= ʿEzer) is a combination of two roots, one ʿ-z-r meaning "to rescue," "to save," and the other ǵ-z-r meaning "to be strong." See R. David Freedman, Woman, A Power Equal to Man. Translation of Woman as a "Fit Helpmate" for Man is Questioned, *BAR* Jan./Febr. Vol. IX/1 1983, 56 and Patrick D. Miller, Ugaritic ǴZR and Hebrew ʿZR II, UF 2 1970, 159–175.
So ʿzr is very good confirmed on seals of the Iron Age: Robert Deutsch (2003, 83: lmnhm bn ʿzr), on Ostraca K. Yassine/T. Teixidor (1986, 49: gdʾzr) and E. Eshel (2003, 151: ʿzr bn Šaw'), on inscriptions Gotthard G. G. Reinhold (2003, 130) and on new discovered triangular clay tablets in Aramaic, like the tablets, which belong to the archive of Šulmu-šarri, known from Dur-Katlimu documents (Mark J. Geller and Tuviah Kwasman, 2003, 99 ff.), presented by E. Lemaire (2010, 195/196, Fig. 2d), on which were found the names ŠLMN ʿZRY (Verso 11) and ʿZRDD (Verso 13). But ʿzr in PN existed always yet in later times, on a Punic stela (fourth century B.C.) from Sant Rafel, Sant Antoni de Portmany, Ibiza, Spain, seen on my visitation of the Museum Eivissa (Benjamin Costa/Jordi H. Fernández, 1995, 44: MTNT S BʿLʾZR). To the PN Iezer, ʾj compound with ʿzr as ʾj ʿzr see Joel S. Burnett (2005, 225/226).

231 See Lawrence J. Mykytiuk, *Maarav* 16.1 (2009), 74/75: "I find Cross' reading to be not only "sufficiently plausible," but moreover, "the most acceptable" and I, too, have "no better reading to propose." I find it especially so, because it has been confirmed by the independent, truly exhaustive work of Reinhold and also has particular support for the letters ʿzr in line 2 from Lipinski, Shea, Bordreuil, Teixidor, and Sader."
And the same: Sixteen Strong Identifications of Biblical Persons (Plus Nine Other IDs) in Authentic Northwest Semitic Inscriptions from before 539

Finally, as indicated in W. Khayata's precision photograph IV as well as my own computer enhancement of photograph X (REI) (Fig. 10), the second part of line 2 contains an open < Q > in dmśqy['].

5.3 Reconstruction, Transliteration, and Translation (Fig 11)[232]

Fig. 11: Reconstruction, Transliteration, and Translation (Reinhold, 2003, 129)

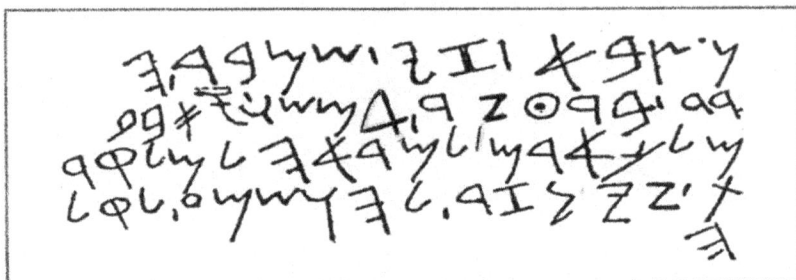

Transliteration

Z 1	nṣb' .zy .ś m br[.] h
Z 2	dd.br'zr.dmś qy [']br
Z 3	mlk 'rm [.]lmr'ḥ lmlqr
Z 4	t. zy nzr [.] lh wšm' .lql
Z 5	h

The Stele which Bir-Hadad, son of Ezer, the Damascene, son of the king of Aram, erected to his Lord Melqart, to whom he made a vow and who heard his voice.

B.C.E., in: SBL Archaeology and Biblical Studies, Nu. 19, Atlanta, 2012, 35–58, esp. 47/48.

232   To Fig. 11 see Gotthard G.G. Reinhold (2003, 129) and Brent A. Strawn, Who's Listening to Whom? A Syntactical Note on the Melqart Inscription*, Ugarit-Forschungen, Band 37, Kavealaer, Neukirchen-Vluyn: Neukirchener Verlag, 2005, 621 641, esp. 626/629, who points out the significance of the syntax, because many scholars leave the question of who is listening to whom in the inscription. He differentiates two options:

5.4 Iconography

One of the most remarkable aspects of the Melqart stele for the northern Syrian context is the strong Phoenician portrayal of the god Melqart himself.[233] Striding barefoot from right to left, he holds an axe with a crescent blade in his left hand, and which extends over his left shoulder. This axe constitutes a popular archaizing feature in Phoenician art. Known mostly among Syrian and Palestinian sites from the early Middle Bronze Age until the second half of the first millennium, it appeared again in Iron Age Phoenician art. As W. Culican[234] and E. Gubel[235] have shown, its presence on seals depicting Melqart indicates it was a common symbol of this deity.[236]

Option 1: Melqart listened to Bir-Hadad; or
Option 2: Bir-Hadad listened to Melqart.
In his opinion the best translation and understanding of the text is in the following way:
"The stela which Bir-Hadad (....) king of Aram set up for his lord, for Melqart, which he (Bir-Hadad) vowed to him (Melqart), and he (Bir-Hadad) listened to his (Melqart's) voice."
In other words, my own translation is similar to Brent A. Strawn's suggestion:
"…erected to his Lord Melqart, to whom (Melqart) he (Bir-Hadad) made a vow and who (Bir-Hadad) heard his (Melqart's) voice."
But Corinne Bonnet, Herbert Niehr (2010, 247), Edward Lipinski (2013, 136, 139) and repeatedly Guy Bunnens (2014) are based on the palaeographic results of E.Puech (1992, 311 ff.) [a]), but not on precisional photos and computer-enhancements. To the transliteration and translation of the Melqart stela see here the clear position of the author!

233   To the deity Melqart see: W. Röllig (1965, 297 ff.), W. T. Pitard (1988 13; 2000, 152 /153), Sergio Ribchini, (1995, 1053 ff.) and (Corinne Bonnet, 2007). Like already Marx S. Smith (1996, 774) has emphasised: "inscriptions outside the mainland call him "Baal of Tyre" (b'l sr)."

234   W. Culican, "Melqart Representations on Phoenician Seals", Abr-n 2 1960–1961, 41–54, esp. 43.

235   Eric Gubel, A Essay on the Axe-bearing Astarte and their Role in a Phoenician Triad Author, *Riv Stu Fen* 8 1980, 1– 17, esp. 6– 9.

236   See otherwise the representations of the weather-god from Aleppo (now museum Instanbul) or from Sam'al (Orthostat, 9. B.C.): Julia Gonella, Wahid Khayata und Kay Kohlmeyer (2005, 14 fig. 9; 15 fig. 10), Ralf-B. Wartke (2005, 71, fig. 64: Vorderasiatisches Museum Berlin, Inv.-Nr. VA 2648), Evelyn Klengel-Brandt (1986, 13 fig. 6), Herbert Niehr (2013, 197 fig. 4) and Izaak J. de Hulster (2014, 239).

Melqart carries another object in his right hand, but its nature is not entirely clear, perhaps the Egyptian *ankh*-sign, also a well-attested Egyptianizing/Phoenician motif.[237] Melqart's head, adorned with a low dome-shaped hat, depicts the contours of the eye, the nose, the mouth, a broad beard with a rounded-off lower point (incised with short parallel lines of irregular length), a small ear (two parallel curved lines), a tuft of hair above the eye (four curved furrows), as well as on the neck (with evenly parallel lines). While the torso is uncovered, the loins are draped in a skirt fastened by a belt.

The right front remains open, however. Parallels for this type of fastened garment have surfaced at 'Amrit (Marathus), Nimrud and Arslan Tash. The skirt is decorated with two striking tassels, depicted in the form of cobras that run almost vertically down the legs but raise their heads in opposing fashion just above the hem. Though a clear Egyptianizing trait, the motif is also well attested in Phoenician iconography.

Melqart could at least have theoretically belonged to the Aramaean pantheon, but no concrete evidence suggests he actually did. As a matter of fact, Melqart does not materialize in any other Aramaic inscription. Pitard[238] has proposed a shrine dedicated to Melqart probably existed in a town inhabited by an enclave of Phoenician traders (e.g. at the Iron Age site Tell Muslimiyyeh, some six km north of Bureij) and further posited Bir-Hadad erected the stela at the local shrine in honor of the Phoenician god. Such a shrine may have been built by foreigners (presumably Tyrians)[239], who wished to worship their patron deity, Melqart. At this time, foreigners customarily made vows and erected stelae to various deities worship when abroad.

As for why, exactly such a stela dedicated to the Lord Melqart would have been erected, Bir-Hadad might have considered himself the recipient of special aid, perhaps during a rescue operation, led by a Tyrian contingent in

---

237 Brent A. Strawn, Who's Listening to Whom? A syntactical Note on the Melqart Inscription *, Ugarit-Forschungen, Bd. 37, 2005, 621–641, esp. 634, 635 (Fig. 1), 636–638.

238 W.T. Pitard, *BASOR* 272 1988, 15–16.

239 See also Corinne Bonnet, Herbert Niehr, *Religionen in der Umwelt des Alten Testaments II. Phönizier, Punier, Aramäer*, (Kohlhammer Studienbücher Theologie Bd. 4,2, Stuttgart: W. Kohlhammer, 2010), 247.

a military clash or with the Assyrians, when he himself had been a member of the Aramaean royal house of Damascus.

5.5 Persons and Deities

Bir-Hadad, son of 'Ezer, the Damascene, son of the king of Aram:

Bir-Hadad of lines 1–2 receives designation as *br 'zr* ("son of 'Idr"), which involves the patronymic *br . hdd . br 'zr*, producing the equivalent of Akkadian Adad-'Idri ('zr simply being the hypocoristicon of *hdd 'zr*). Taken at face value, Bir-Hadad's father would be Adad-'Idri of the cuneiform annals, who fought against the Assyrians at the battle of Qarqar in 853. This connections finds confirmation in Bir-Hadad's explicit denomination as *dmsqy'*, a "Damascene" (line 2). Such a gentilic has an analogue in the Moabite stela, which calls Mešša *hdbny*, "the Daibonite" (see lines 1–2): "I am Mesha' son of Kemosh[yat], king of Moab, the Daibonite."[240]

The Bir-Hadad at hand could be have been a young king, who ruled as co-regent alongside Adad-'Idri between 845 (or somewhat earlier) and 842/41. In this case he would number Bir-Hadad III (in a maximal list) or II. (in a minimal list) as successor to the throne of Aram-Damascus after Bir-Hadad I (900–870), the original name bearer (over against Akkadian Adad-'Idri, the equivalent of the Hebrew "Hadad-Ezer").

Alternatively, Bir-Hadad may only have been a potential crown prince within the royal house of Aram-Damascus, who may have never ascended the throne, perhaps murdered by Hazael after Adad-'Idri's violent ousting (845/842/841) or dying a natural death (842/841). Called *mar la mammana*" ("son of nobody") in the Basalt statue, Hazael would have been the actual successor to this Aramaean ruler, in such a reconstruction.[241]

---

240 See Kent P. Jackson, The Language of the Mesha' Inscription, in: *Studies in the Mesha Inscription and Moab*, ed. by Andrew Dearman, (ASOR. SBL Archaeology and Biblical Studies, Nu. 02, Atlanta, Georgia: Scholars Press, 1998), 96–130, esp. 97. Klaus Beyer, Die Sprache der moabitischen Inschriften, in: *KUSATU* 11 2010, 5–41, esp. 19 translates here "der König von Moab aus Deban," but he knows on the other hand also the translation DYBNY "Debanite" (p. 15).

241 See Lawrence J. Mykytiuk, *Maarav* 16.1 (2009), 77: "Further, the above reading of the Melqart stela informs that Hadadezer, designated by the hypocoristicon Ezer, had a son who called himself Bar-hadad and, as crown prince or

Lord Melqart:
The god of Tyre Melqart (literally "king of the city," with "qrt" usually understood as designation for Tyre) first appears in the Aramaic inscription of the Bir-Hadad stela. On this stela, dedicated by Bir-Hadad, king of Aram, Melqart bears the insignia of a warrior deity.[242]

5.6 History

The following historical outline comes from comparison of this stela's epigraphy, palaeography, and iconography with biblical and extra-biblical sources:

1. The text of the Bir-Hadad inscription belongs to a period that post-dates 850. The political situation during this period seems to suggest a date around 845 (14 th palû: Bull Inscription) or 841 (the 18th palû: fragment of an annalistic text).

2. The second line of this text identifies Bir-Hadad as a son of the Aramaean king Adad-'Idri. This king is known here only by his second element 'Ezer, whereby 'Idri in Akkdian corresponds to 'Ezer in Aramaic and Hebrew. Adad-'Idri spearheaded the western coalition of kings and armies in the 853 battle at Qarqar, in Syria, against Shalmaneser III of Assyria.

3. In the period after the battle of Qarqar, this father and son-duo would have shared the reigns of power on the throne of Damascus. Son Bir-Hadad may possibly have attained leadership over the army at that time. At first he may have been no more than a potential crown prince of the royal house of Damascus, before being elevated to the status of a co-regent and young king in 845 or slightly earlier. 'Adad-Idri is usually identified with Ben-Hadad II

---

coregent, very likely succeeded him. In the absence of other candidates, the Bar-hadad named in the Melqart stela was most likely the one whom Hazael assassinated. Thus the terms used to refer to Damascene kings of Aram in Shalmaneser III's inscriptions, in the books of 1–2 Kings, and in the above reading of the Melqart stela, when placed side by side, reveal a pattern that suggests a king list on which all three ancient sources agree." and p. 85:
"Since there are three identifying marks of an individual for both Ids, that of Hadadezer and that of his son Benhadad in the Melqart Stela, and because they are based on agreement between Aramean, Assyrian, and Hebrew sources, I find both to be reliable grade 3 IDs."

242 S. Ribchini, Melqart, 1995, 1058.

in the sequence of Damascene kings known by this name within the Hebrew Bible. After insertion of his son in that same line of rulers as yet another Ben-Hadad, the Bir-/Ben-Hadad who inscribed this stela should therefore be numbered Ben-Hadad III, the later Ben-Hadad of the biblical texts, i.e. the son of Hazael, then Ben-Hadad IV. Alternatively, Hazael may have actually succeeded 'Adad-Idri, if Bir-Hadad merely remained a potential crown prince and never attained the full status of co-regent or young king.

4. A statement in the Assyrian annals of Shalmaneser III may shed light on the final fate of 'Adad-Idri/Ben-Hadad II (if the two are indeed one and the same figure)[243] against whom the Assyrians fought so frequently. This statement may well indicate 'Adad-Idri died a violent death in the battle of 845 and hence he may not have continued to live on until 842/841, as previously held. If so, it would have been natural for his son, the Bir-Hadad of the stela, to have accompanied his father into that battle. If 'Adad-Idri was killed at that time, Bir-Hadad may himself may have been injured. This Bir-Hadad of the stele, then, would be the same Ben-Hadad whom we encounter in 2 Kings 8, who lay sick, or still recovering from his wounds when the usurper Hazael entered and murdered him in 842/841. The national and personal turns of fortune experienced by this Bir-Hadad (Heb. Ben-Hadad) logically resulted in the takeover by the "son of nobody," Hazael (reported on the Basalt statue).

5. Moreover, Bir-Hadad could have received special aid and rescue by a foreign military contingent during a military operation, when the former was wounded during this war against the Assyrians in 845 (14th pâlu).

The well-known Bull inscription may confirm this interpretation (Bull Inscription = Bull B):

"In the fourteenth year of my rule, I called up the innumerable (inhabitants) of my vast country and crossed the Euphrates, at its flood, with my army of 120.000 (men). At the same time, Hadad-'Ezer of Damascus, Irhuleni from Hamath as well as 12 (other) kings from the shore of the Upper

---

243 See John F. Gates, Ben-Hadad, NIBD, 1987, 134–135. In his view Hadadezer of the Assyrian monuments is Benhadad II of the Bible, the son of Ben-Hadad I and this Aramaean king possibly identified with Rezon, the founder of the kingdom of Aram-Damascus; but see my results to the royal line of the Aramaean kings in Damascus!

and Lower Sea, called up the(i)r innumerably large army and rose against me. I fought with them and defeated them. I did destroy their chariots (and) their cavalry-horses, taking away from them their battle equipment. To save their lives they dispersed."

If 'Adad-Idris died in a final battle against the Assyrians (cf. the meaning of Akkadian phrase *šadašu êmid*, "to be killed in a battle" as with J. Alberto Soggin[244]) or by natural death as late as 842/841[245], Bir-Hadad have remained ill and weak, as he stayed in the king's house. This state of affairs could have caused Hazael to rebel and kill the potential crown prince, thereby usurping the power after 'Adad-Idri. In this way he would have changed the political relations in Aram-Damascus and continued to fight against Assur (18th palû: fragment of an annalistic text). Such an interpretation accords with the conclusion of N. Na'aman[246]:

"The solution that the king in the story (i.e. 2. Kings 8) *was originally anonymous and that the name Ben-Hadad was only later added to the text, when the other Ben-Hadad stories were incorporated in the book of Kings is arbitrary."*

---

244 See J. Alberto Soggin, Amos VI: 13–14 und I: 3 auf dem Hintergrund der Beziehungen zwischen Israel und Damaskus im 9. und 8. Jahrhundert, in: (*Near Eastern Studies in honor of W. F. Albright*, Hans Goedicke (ed.), Baltimore: John Hopkins Press, 1971), 433–441, esp. 438. Currently Shiuchi Hasegawa, Aram and Israel during the Jehudite Dynasty, (= BZAW Bd. 434), Berlin/Boston: Walter de Gruyter 2012, 76/77 is supplying here more a literarical explanation than any kind of special historical background. In his view the historical nucleus of the story 2 Kgs 8: 7–15 is to "confirm by the Assyrian source which attests to Hazael's illegitimacy in occupying the Damascene throne."

245 Angelika Berlejung, Nachbarn, Verwandte, Feinde und Gefährten: Die „Aramäer" im Alten Testament, LAOS 3 2013, 57–86, esp.75 writes about the natural death of Hadad-idri/ezer I, but she seems to be not yet involved in the new researches of the Aramaen King list from Aram-Damascus, because she knows only two kings, called Bar/Ben-Hadad (S. 77). See no comment of her to Lawrence James Mykytiuk, *Maarav* 16.1 2009, 49–132 and SBL, Nu. 19, Atlanta 2012, 35–58.

246 Nadav Na'aman, Hazael of 'Amqi and Hadadezer of Beth-rehob, Ugarit-Forschungen, Bd. 27, Münster: Ugarit-Verlag, 1995, esp. 388 and Gotthard G.G. Reinhold (2003, 148).

6 Excursus II: The Fragments of the Têl Dan Stela (Title Page)[247]

The first fragment of a large monument made of basalt stone, inscribed in early Aramaic, and erected by an Aramaean king was discovered by Gila Cook at Têl Dan (formerly known as Tell el-Qadi) on July 21, 1993. Designated fragment A, this larger piece preserves 13 lines of text and measures 32 cm in height and max. 22 cm in width.[248] Two other smaller fragments were joined together as fragment B—B1 (20 cm in length, 14 cm in width, with 6 lines) discovered on June 20, 1994 by Malka Herschkovitz and B2 (10 cm in length, 9 cm in width, with 4 lines) discovered again by Cook on July 30 1994, each in a different find spot (B2 at the base of a wall eight metres north of where fragment B1 materialized).[249] During the Ba'ja excavations in Jordan (1999)[250] and those of Ramat

---

247 See the Têl Dan Stela fragments on the title page.
248 See here the well known literature to Têl Dan: Avraham Biran (1993, 81 ff.), Rupert L. Chapman (1993, 23 ff.); Avraham Biran, Joseph Naveh (1993, 74 ff.), Avraham Biran (1994, 275 [a]; 1994, 50 ff. [b]). To fragment A see also Baruch Halpern (1994, 64/65), André Lemaire (1994, 87) and Pietro Kaswalder, Massimo Pazzini (1994, 195).
249 See Avraham Biran, Joseph Naveh (1995, 2) and Hans Peter Müller (1995, 122/123).
250 See Katrin Bastert, Hans-Dieter Bienert, Roland Lamprichs, Dieter Vieweger, Ba'ja-Regional Project Report on the First Season, 1999, *Occident & Orient* 5/ 1& 2 Dec. 2000, 39–42; Hans Dieter Bienert, Roland Lamprichs, Dieter Vieweger, et. al., Ba'ja – The Archaeology of a Landscape 9000 Years of Human occupation: A preliminary report on the 1999 Field Season, *ADAJ* XLIV 2000, 119–148; Idem, Ba'ja: Archäologie einer Landschaft in Jordanien-Bericht über archäologische Feldforschungen, in: Ricardo Eichmann (hrsg.). Ausgrabungen und Surveys im Vorderen Orient I (Deutsches Archäologisches Institut Orient-Abteilung. Orient-Archäologie Band 5), Rahden/Westf.: Verlag Marie Leidorf GmbH, 2002, 161–213 and Gotthard G.G. Reinhold (2003, 159 ff., 183/184).
In free work periods here I worked for the first time about the Têl Dan stela-text and the historical background: Gotthard G. G. Reinhold (1999, manuscript). See also the new revised text, idem (2003, 122 ff.).

Rachel in Israel (2005)[251], I had the opportunity to research early Aramaic inscriptions and the new compound fragments of Têl Dan, with not only secondary literature and photographs but also the stela itself in the Israel Museum. Since then, the scholarly literature on the fragments has grown immensely. Much speculation questioned the nature of discovery, whether these fragments belonged to different inscriptions or constituted forgeries, as well as the reading, whether *bytdwd* ("house of David," A line 9) stemmed only from pure imagination. These debates also served to maintain a rather widespread publicity. In light of continued debate as well as the relevance to the study at hand, some comments are necessary concerning 1. arrangement of the fragments, 2. epigraphic and paleographic analysis, 3. persons, toponyms, and deities mentioned in the text, as well as 4. the historical background.

6.1 The Arrangement of the Fragments

When fragments A and B1 + B2 arrived at the Israel Museum, three possible arrangements emerged:

1. Fragment B (= B1 + B2) precedes fragment A. G. Galil[252] identified Bir-Hadad, the son of Hazael with the stela's author and justified chronological arrangement of fragment B (= B1 + B 2) before fragment A. This suggestion proves unlikely since reference to the author's father belongs to the introduction of the stela.

2. Fragment B (B 1 + B 2) has its position beneath fragment A. Both physical positioning and chronological order would argue against this hypothesis.

---

251 See my lecture Gotthard G.G. Reinhold, Investigations into Persons and Deities of the Aleppo Stela/Syria and the Têl Dan Stela Fragment/Israel, Fachtagung für Biblische Archäologie Schönblick/Schwäbisch Gmünd, 4–6 November, 2005, manuscript, and also S. Hafthórsson, *A Passing Power. An Examination of the Sources for the history of Aram-Damascus in the Second Half of the ninth Century B.C.*, Coniectanea Biblica Old Testament Series 54, Stockholm: Almquist & Wiksell, 2006, esp. 49–65.
252 G. Galil, A Re-arrangement on the Fragments of the Tel Dan Inscription and the Relations Between Israel and Aram, *PEQ* 133 2001, 16–21, esp. 17/18 and Table 1. See also Bob Becking, The Second Danite Inscription. Some Remarks, *BN* 81 1996, 21– 29, esp. 22 (2.1 Archaeological Context).

3. Fragment B was originally positioned left of fragment A. Though different from joining B1 + B2, this arrangement still provided a meaningful text, as produced by the restorers Nili Cohen (Hebrew Union College), A. Weiner and Ruth Yekuteli (Israel Museum). This reconstruction differed from that of Ada Yardeni and Israel Eph'al, however. More specifically, fragments A and B (= B 1 + B 2) were reconstructed such that they joined below the surface at line 5, the lines of fragment A thus continuing those of fragment B.[253] More than the small joint itself—a fragmentary break in the basalt slab, whose joining was "tenable" also in the view of S. Yamada[254]— a straight crack running from the upper left edge of fragment B (= B1 + B2) in the direction of the crack on the left side of fragment A also supports connection.

Ingo Kottsieper[255] has thus commented:

"Die von den Erstherausgebern auf Grund eines möglichen Joints unterhalb der Oberfläche in Höhe von Z. 5 vorgeschlagene Zuordnung von B 1–8 mit A 1–8 wird zwar von einer kleinen Gruppe von Gelehrten bezweifelt, aber sie bewährt sich nicht nur durch die Möglichkeit, hieraus einen fortlaufenden Text zu rekonstruieren, sondern auch an der Zeilenlage, sofern man die Tatsache beachtet, daß die Zeilen teilweise gegeneinander geneigt und in sich auch leicht gekrümmt sind."

Arguing against the small join between B (= B1 + B2) and A. Georg Athas[256] contends there are "two clenched fists placed end to end" (p. 177) that show no actual connection. A significant component of his argumentation rested on incongruence of line trends[257] between fragment A and B

---

253 Ibid.
254 S. Yamada, Aram -Israel Relations as Reflected in the Aramaic Inscriptions from Tel Dan, UF, Bd 27, Neukirchen-Vluyn: Butzon & Bercker, Kevelaer, 1995, 611– 625, esp. 612.
255 Ingo Kottsieper, Aramäische und phönizische Texte, *TUAT* Ergbd., Gütersloh: Gütersloher Verlagshaus, 2001: 176–179, esp. 176.
256 Georg Athas, The Tell Dan Inscription, A. Reappraisal and a New Interpretation (JSOT SS 360), Copenhagen International Seminar 12), London, New York: Sheffield Academic Press, 2003, 177.
257 Ibid., 179 Fig. 5.2 Such incongruences of line trends, a falling down or an overlapping of single letters on the line appear also in other inscriptions: In the Nerab-Inscription the first line beneath the head moved away down to the end of the line. See Mark Lidzbarski, II. Part, Plates, Weimar: Emil Felber,

(= B1 + B2). Accordingly, the engraver of fragment B—placed below fragment A and approximately 32 cm in width[258]—first chalked the text, which was laid flat on the ground so he could rest in a more comfortable posture to the left of the slab[259], and worked in an upward direction. His argument also concentrated on the marks of the fragments in their palaeographic distinction. Responsing to Athas, however, Victor Sasson[260] has convincingly shown in detail how the engraver could have worked in a different scenario, namely, from top to bottom without having first chalked the stone. He could have errors as he inscribed the stone, which was placed upright in its display position, by standing in front of the slab against the letters. In his own review of Athas, William A Schniedewind[261] contended a separation of A and B would alter the entire historical interpretation of the early Aramaic inscription.

6.2 The Epigraphy, Palaeography, and Dating of the Early Aramaic Text

The fragments of the Têl Dan inscription present a careful epigraphy, with letters running, to some extent, in a line of consistent height and featuring word dividers as well. Altogether, the text with the fragments B (= B 1 + B 2) to the left and fragment A to the right contain twenty of total twenty-two letters of the early Aramaic alphabet, excepting *têt* and *sâde*. The shapes of the letters correspond best to the following inscrpitions:

1898, Pl. XXV and P. E. Dion, *Les araméens à l'âge du fer: Histoire politique et structures sociales* (É Bib NS No. 34), Paris: Gabalda, 1997, table 10: Stèle funéraire de Sin-zer-ibni (Nêrab). See also the incongruencies to Arslan Tash I, Blane W. Conklin, Arslan Tash I and other Vestiges of a Particular Syrian Incantatory Thread (*), *Biblica* 84/1 2002, 89–101, esp. 100–101 (Arslan Tash I, recto and verso).

258 Ibid, 191 Fig. 5.4 0
259 Ibid, 32 Fig. 3.5
260 Victor Sasson, The Tell Dan Aramaic inscription: The problems of a new minimized reading,. A review article, *JSS* L/1 Spring 2005, 23–34, esp. 25/26.
261 William M. Schniedewind, Review, Athas, George, The Tel Dan Inscription: A Rappraisal and a New Interpretation, *RBL* 10 2003, Society of Biblical Literature 2003.

1. Bir-Hadad stela inscription from Bureij/Aleppo   post 850
2. Kilamuwa inscriptions from Zicirli   825
3. Hazael inscriptions from Eritrea and Samos   post 810–805
4. Zakkur inscription from Afis/Aleppo   773–772

Palaeographic analysis of the stela inscrption yields the following traits.

'Âlef:
This form has a short vertical downstroke similar to the Kilamuwa stela and dissimilar to the longer downstroke of in more developed shapes, as in the Melqart/Bir-Hadad stela, the Mesha stela, the Hazael inscriptions (Arslan Tash) and the Zakkur stela (A line 2–11; B1 line 2, 5 B2 line 6)

Dâlet:
The most distinctive feature of this grapheme shows a clear short downstroke comparable to the Melqart or Bir-Hadad stela (line 2: beginning dd with short downstrokes) and in contrast to the triangular head slightly rounded on the left, which overlaps with the right and lower leg, as in dmsqy['] and the Kilamuwa stela (A line 5, 9, B1 line 4).

Wâw:
In the present stela, *wâw* exhibits a vertical stem with a "hook" branching off to the left, shaped like a lying "v" at the stem, as in the Kilamuwa inscription (A line 8. 3, 5 – 9, 12; B1 line 1, 3, B2 line 8).

Zâyin:
This form displays a diagonal downstroke to the left between the parallel strokes (similar to a Latin H, slanting slightly downwards to the left), whereby the downstrokes run beneath the parallel strokes, similar to the Melqart or Bir-Hadad stela (cf. line 2, the clear z-form from 'zr and line 4) (B1 line 1).

Hêt:
With two stems downwards slanting slightly to the right, this form has three crossbeams that slant somewhat downward to the left (A line 11; B1 line 2).

Kaph:
The shape consists of a long stem from which a v-construction branches off to the left, as in the Kilamuwa inscription, but B1 line 4 closely resembles the Amman Citadel inscription (A line 3, 5 – 9, 12 B1 line 3).

Sâmek:

Here, the grapheme comprises a stem that curves slightly leftward, intersected already above the top by three crossbars, comparable to the Kilamuwa inscription (A line 2; B 2 line 6).

'Ayin:

The letter constitutes a small circle, but the smaller circles of fragment A (lines 1, 12, 13) contrast the smaller ones of B1 (line 3). The Melqart or Bir-Hadad inscription demonstrates the earlier form (!) with a dot in the centre of the circle (line 2) which contrasts the more developed shape as a simple circle (line 4) (A line 1, 12–13 B1 line 3).

Qoph:

Here the grapheme consists of a leftward leaning stem with an oval overlapping in its upper part, a form also present in the Melqart or Bir-Hadad inscription (line 2) though as a leftward leaning steam of an open oval (A line 4–6, 10, B 1 line 5).

Summary:

Formal analysis of the letters written in fragments B (= B1 + B2) and A of the early Aramaic Têl Dan stela would classify it between the Melqart/Bir-Hadad and Kilamuwa inscriptions, more specifically, in the second half of the ninth century, between 845/840 and 825, with a precise date likely at 835/830. The inscription is slightly earlier than the Kilamuwa inscription but later than that of Mesha. This conclusion conforms to the assessment of Joseph Tropper[262]. However, such datings also require an evaluation of political history as reflected in the content of the fragments.

6.3 The Textual Analysis: Persons, Toponyms, and Deities

Agreeing with the scholarly majority in the arrangement of the Têl Dan fragments—namely, B (= B1 + B2) to the left of A—the following infor-

---

262 See Joseph Tropper (1993, 398, 400 ff., 1994, 487 ff.) and Gotthard G.G. Reinhold (2003, 124/125). John T. Willis (1995, 219 ff.) is dating the inscription "between 852 and 843 BCE." (223) and Paul E. Dion (1999, 145 ff.) "between the Kulamuwa and the Zakkur inscriptions." (147).

mation emerges from the reconstructed text with respect to 1. persons, 2. Toponyms, and 3. deities:

6.3.1 Persons

According to my own German translation[263] of the Têl Dan inscription, line 1 and the beginning of line two constitute a preface[264]:

"1....*sagte er: ... [Den (?) Bu[nd schließe mit mir] wie dein Vater]*
2. *mit meinem Vater [-hdd ?/ -el ?] geschlossen hat etc.*".[265]

Preceeding the main text, the author could refer to his "father" in the sense of patron. In this case, he would be seeking an alliance and mentioning an earlier one, that of his predecessor with the father of the would-be ally. A number of scholars read the name of the predecessor with the theophoric element –*hdd*—hence completed by *brhdd*—which thus diverges from my own transcription and historical reconstruction. As yet another possibility, the name of the predecessor might end with the consonant < L >. Based on computer enhancement, W. H. Schniedewind/Bruce Zuckermann[266] propose reconstruction of the upper right broken basalt surface of fragment A as *[b]rq'l. 'by*. Baraq'el, "the lightning of El," would thus designate the name of the predecessor. If the El name could be confirmed, a clan of El would have then acted within the royal house of Damascus to ursurp dynastic succession. Yet the usurper was, in fact, Hazael of Damascus (842/841–805) from Beth Rehob. The postulated home "Hazael of 'Amq" finds confirmation in the Samos-inscription[267]: *zy ntn hdd lmr'n hz'l mn 'mq bšnt 'dh*

---

263 See note 302.
264 The proposal, that Jehu did write the Tel Dan-inscription, was also discussed after the construction from J. W. Wisselius. To this reconstruction see Bob Becking, Did Jehu write the Tel Dan Inscription, *SJOT* 13/2 1999, 187–201, esp. 189 ff.
265 With this reconstruction of the preface also the alliances in Kgs (Ahab, Joram) could have more historical probability. To this matter see section 6.5, although Winfried Thiel (2006, 483) wants to refer 1 Kgs 20:34 (2 Kgs 13:25) to the later time of Joash of Israel.
266 William M. Schniedewind/Bruce Zuckerman, A Possible Reconstruction of the Name of Haza'els Father in the Tel Dan Iscription, *IEJ* 51 2001, 88–91.
267 N. Na'aman, Hazael of 'Amqi and Hadadezer of Beth-rehob, UF, Bd. 27, Kevelaer, Neukirchen-Vluyn: Neukirchener Verlag, 1995, 381–394.

mr'n nhr ("That which [the god] gave our lord Hazael from 'Umqi in the year that our Lord crossed the river"). The "father," or patron, also appears in line 3, which speaks of his illness and death, and again in line 4, where the king of Israel marched militantly in the "father's" country.[268] In line 4/5 the stela reports specifically Hadad had enthroned himself as king. Certainly referring to the deity Hadad, this figure led the battle after seven days of rule. Evidently, he was not the designated successor of Aram-Damascus. According to line 7/8 the kings "Joram, son of Ahabs of Israel" and "Ahaziah, son of Joram, the king of the house of David" were killed in the battle by the king of Aram (the stela's author). In the chronology of Edwin R. Thiele,[269] Joram reigned over Israel from 852 to 841, Ahaziah of Judah until 841. Finally, line 11 indicates Jehu became king over Israel. Jehu, the Ia-ú-a mar ḫu-um-ri of the Black Obelisk, also paid tribute to Assur, reining—according to Thiele—from 841 to 814. Although P. E. Dion[270] reconstructs line 8 as *yhw.br[nmšy]*, the logic of the stela's author prevents Jehu's demise from preceding his succession in line 11/12.

6.3.2 Toponyms

At the end of fragment B1 line 2, reconstruction after *.b'* could read either b or p as two certain consonants. Thus, several readings have arisen: *b'b[l]*, "at/near Abel (-Bet Maacah)"[271], (i.e., Tel Âbel el-Qamah, 7 km away from

---

268 See also J.A. Emerton, Two Issues in the Interpretation of the Tel Dan Inscription, *VT* L 1 2000, 27–41, esp. 27/28, 36.

269 Edwin R. Thiele, A Chronology of the Hebrew Kings (Contemporary Evangelical Perspectives), Grand Rapids: Zondervan Publishing House, 1977, 75.

270 P. E. Dion, *Les Araméens à l'âge du fer: Historie politique et structures sociales* (É Bib NS No. 34, Paris: Gabalda, 1997), 197.

271 With the recent excavations of Tel Âbel el-Qamah the reading b'b[l] the second line of the Tel Dan-Stele gains in importance. See the reconstruction in the contribution Tel Abel Beth Maacah Excavations, htpp://www.abelbeth-maacah.org/index.php/about:
1' [ ]............[ ] and cut [....................]
2' [ ]my father went up[....................f[ighting at/against Ab[el Beth Maacah]
3' And my father lay down, he went to his [fathers]. And the king of I[s-]
4' rael penetrated into my fathers land[. And] Hadad made me -myself-king.

Dan), *b'b [yl]*, "at/near Abil"[272], or *b'pq*, "at/near Aphek"[273]. While all three represent good geographic reconstructions, *b'b[l]* may correspond to the importance of this town as an Aramaean vassal state in the ninth

---

Here I refer especially to Nava Panitz-Cohen in her lecture 'Aram-Maacah? Arameans and Israelites on the Border:
Excavations at Tel Abil al -Qamah (Abel Beth Maacah) in Northern Israel' at the IWH Heidelberg Colloquium, 1. Sept. 2014 and in the Summary of the Colloqium, p. 2: "A recent article Prof. Nadav Naaman has proposed a Scenario for the kingdoms of Geshur and Maacah during the Iron II, where Geshur was an ally of David, but Maacah entered into an unsuccessful anti-David alliance, and as a result, became Israelite vasall or stronghold in the 10th century BCE. Both kingdoms were possibly annexed to Dan when that town became an Aramean vassal of Aram-Damascus in the 9th century BCE, an act commemorated by the Dan Stele, which might also mentioned Abel."

272 In the view of E. Lipinski, The Aramaeans in the West (13th-8th centuries, in: LAOS 3 2013, 123–147, esp. 128/129 the fragmentary first lines of the Tel Dan-Inscription seem to refer to Hadad-ezer (assyr. Adad-'Idri), king of Aram-Damaskus, and to Omri, king of Israel, dealing with the period of time around 875 B.C., which indicate an earlier source in the biblical account 2. Sam. 10, 15–19, but which was changed then in the Deutoronomistic tradition. So E.Lipinski attempted to reconstruct the following Tēl Dan-text:
Transliteraton:
1' ['dy.'rm/'by.lš]mr. '[mry.mlk.yšr'l.]wgzr['.'dn
2' 'm.šn'y.]'by.ysq[.'lwh.b']tlhmh.b'b[yl]
Translation:
"O[mri, king of Israel, did not k]eep [the treaties of Aram/my father], but he concluded [treaties with the enemies] of my father, so that he want up [against him when] the latter was fighting at Ab[īl]."
In this view Omri had concluded an alliance with the enemies of Hadad-ezer, ruling in the land of Tahat, in the Hauran, where he intervened in a battle at Abīl, i.e. Tell al-Qâdi. But here see the reconstruction of Gotthard G.G. Rein-hold (2003, 131) and the further results.

273 For this see Gotthard G. G. Reinhold (2003, 131/ 132), William M. Schniedewind, The Tel Dan Stela: New Light on Aramaic and Jehu's Re-volt, *BASOR* 302 1996, 75– 90, esp. 79 and Stuart A. Irvine, Critical Note. The Last Battle of Hadadezer, *JBL* 124/2 2005, 341–347, esp. 342, 345/46: Abila of Lysanias, city of the tetrarchy of Abilene in Roman times (Jos. Ant. 19.5.1; 20.7.2). See also the proposal from Shuichi Hasegawa, Aram and Israel during the Jehudite Dynasty (= BZAW Bd. 434), Berlin/Boston: Walter de Gruyter 2012, p. 38 "tlhmh.b'[pq.]", translated as "in the fighting at A[pkek ?...]" (p. 40); but he has no comment, explanation and special analysis for the historical background !

century, thereby reflecting the real historical context. However, since the "father" appears at the beginning of the line, with respect to the alliance, *.b'b[y]* seems more likely than a toponym. Aaron Demsky[274] had attempted to reconstruct the fragmentary *'rq.'by* as *'rq. 'by[lh]*, that is, Abila (Têl Âbila, 8 km northwest of Irbid). After the discovery of B1, though, this reconstruction proved no longer tenable. Up until now, I have agreed with Lemaire[275] in reading qdm as local adverb, to paraphrase wy'l, in the sense of the German "hinein-ziehen" (Eng. "to go in[to]") or "vor-rücken" (Eng. "to advance"),[276] and therefore translated "…. *und zog hinein in das Land meines Vaters.*" S. Mittmann[277] seeks to give the passus more of a locative sense, reading *wy'l.mlk y[s](4)r'l qdm.b'rq.'by.* and translating …"*Und es drang der König von I[s]r(4)rael vornweg ein in das Land meines Vaters.*"

With this translation, Mittmann sees an interregnum that occurred after the death of Adad-'Idri, which neighbouring states (especially Israel) used to invade the territory of Damascus.[278] G. Galil[279] reconstructs *qdm b'rq 'by* as "ruled over the land of Ubi/Upe," but this proposal contains a certain inconsistency as he employed the previous toponym for the region of Damascus[280].

A new suggestion has come from Ingo Kottsieper and merits attention. He interprets qdm as "Ostland" (Eng. "Eastern country") referring spe-

274 Aaron Demsky, On Reading Ancient Inscription: The Monumental Aramaic Stela Fragment from Tel Dan, *JANES* 23 1995, 33.

275 A. Lemaire, The Tel Dan Stela as a Piece of Royal Historiography, *JSOT* 81 1998, 5. The other possibility is, to translate "and Hadad went i n f r o n t of me". See Giovanni Garbini, L'iscrizione Aramaica di Tel Dan, AAL.R, Anno CCCXCI, 16–21, esp.465: "Oltre all'avverbio qdm, la nostra epigrafe documenta anche la preposizione qdm (tipica dell'arama), nella frase wyhk hdd qdmy, tradotta Naveh "and Hadad went in front of me."

276 But here is little lexical support for the rendering qdm in the Tel Dan stela as "advanced in." See Stuart A. Irvine, *JBL* 124/2 2005, 344.

277 See Siegfried Mittmann, Zwei "Rätsel" der Mêša'-Inschrift. Mit einem Beitrag zur aramäischen Stelainschrift von Dan (Tell el-Qâdi), *ZDPV* 118 2002, 33–65, esp. 48; S. Hafthórsson, 56: "*And the king of I[s]rael entered.* "

278 Ibid., 50/51.

279 Gershon Galil, *PEQ* 133, 2001, 16–21, esp. 20.

280 See Gotthard G.G. Reinhold, *EHS.T* XXIII/368, 1989, 86 ff.

cifically to the Transjordan region in the area of Ḥaurân, east of Gilead.[281] Despite Mittmann's opposition, this solution does have the undoubted strength of accounting for troop movement from the north to northeast, advancing in the direction of Ramoth-Gilead, a frequent target of military attacks. Furthermore, as Omar Sergi has recently demonstrated[282], the region of Gilead—the northern Transjordan plateau from the Yarmuk River in the north to the higher hill country north of Heshbon (Tell Ḥesbân)[283] and the Madaba plain in the south—was affiliated to Damascus more than Israel, its material culture under Aramaean influence. As a result, Kottsieper[284] translates this passage (line 3–4) as follows:

"*Da drang der König von I[s]rael in QDM ein, das im Lande meines Vaters liegt.*"

Two possible homelands of the father, or patron, emerge in this regard, 'mq = 'Amq (Beth Rehob) or qdm (Ḥaurân). In a new reconstruction of the ivory inscription from Arslan Tash (Ḥadatu), Puech[285] has illuminated the political situation in the northern Transjordan shortly after Hazaels succession.

Already early in Hazael's reign Aram-Damascus may have intended to execute a surprise attack and engage military troops in the area of the Ḥaurân. Hazael would have then marched into Gilead from the southeast, making Ramoth-Gilead the target for attacks, to restore its hegemony over an expanded region in the Transjordan.

281 See Ingo Kottsieper, Die Inschrift von Tell Dan und die politischen Beziehungen zwischen Aram-Damaskus und Israel in der 1. Hälfte des 1. Jahrtausends vor Christus, in: "Und Mose schrieb dieses Lied auf". Studien zum Alten Testament und zum alten Orient, FS für Oswald Loretz. Manfred Dietrich/Ingo Kottsieper, hrsg. (AOAT, Bd. 250, Münster: Ugarit-Verlag, 1998), 475–500, esp. 481, 487.

282 See Omer Sergi, Gilead between Aram and Israel: Some Historical Considerations, lecture at the IWH Colloquium Heidelberg, 3. Sept. 2014.

283 Here I refer to David Merling and Lawrence T. Geraty (1994), Gloria A. London and Douglas Clark (1997) and to Paul J. Ray Jr. (2001, 2003, 71 ff.).

284 Ingo Kottsieper, Aramäische und phönizische Texte. A. Aramäische historische Inschriften, Otto Kaiser (ed.) *TUAT* Ergbd. Gütersloh: Gütersloher Verlagshaus, 2001, 176–179.

285 E. Puech. L' ivorie inscrit d'Arslan Tash et le rois de Damas, *RB* 88/4 1981, 544–562 and Gotthard G.G. Reinhold, EHS.T XXIII/386 1989, 156–157.

However, the Northern Kingdom of Israel was also seeking to gain control of Gilead and Ḥaurân, when the Aramaean dynasty fell into political crisis, caused by the violent (845; later 842/41) or natural death (842/41) of Adad-'Idri (= 'ezer) and his son Bir-Hadad (III), who was murdered by the usurper Hazael (Excursus I). Joram marched in the Ḥaurân (l. 3–4: QDM); but his military movements generated a counter-attack from Hazaels troops, which had already penetrated the southeastern part of the Haurân. Forced to retreat, Joram's forces first tried to protect the most strategic point, the fort of Tell er-Rumeith/Ramith, and then fought for the town of Ramtha (Er-Remta), 15 km east of Irbid.

Indeed, Tell er-Rumeith/Ramith was a "military bridgehead," at the terminal point of the Kings Highway from Damascus to Rabbat-Ammon in the south, the main road from the southeastern El-Mefrağ/Mafrağ (Ḫīrbet el-Fedēn) around Irbid (Beth-Arbeel/Gilead) to the Jordan valley in the northwest. This highway overlooked and controlled the entire Irbid --- El-Hösn (=Lidbir) --- Er-Remtā---plateau.[286] The Aramaean troops might have invaded Gilead from the southeast of Ḥaurân this time, conquered the fort of Tell er-Rumeith/Ramith, and won the town of Ramtha (Er-Remtā). Even if E. Puech's Arslan Tash reconstruction proves correct here, a military celebration honored Hazael: *['rs'. zy. q]rb. 'm'. lmr'n. ḥz'l. bšnt[.'ḥ]zt. ḥwrn]* (*"[Das Bett, welches ge]stiftet hat die Truppe unserem Herrn Hazael im Jahre der [Annex]ion von H[auran]."*[287]

The Tel Dan stela also elucidates these events in the year 841:

Line 7 refers to the killing of "Jo[ram] the son A[habs], the king of Israel," while the following lines 8/9 offer a parallel with that of "[..Ahaz]iah, the son [Jorams, the kin-]/g of the house of David."[288] Scholarly debate has long discussed line 9. Dating the Tēl Dan stela later than 800, as proposed by Athas,[289] would force the phrase *bytdwd* ("house of David") to signify

---

286 Here I refer to Israel Finkelstein, Oded Lipschitz and Omer Sergi, Tell er-Rumeith in northern Jordan: Some Archaeological and Historical Observations, *Semitica* 55 2013, 7–23, esp. 8 Fig.1.

287 Gotthard G.G. Reinhold, *EHS.T* XXIII/386 1989, ebd., 156; S. Hafthorsson, CB OT Series 54 2006, 41.

288 See to the position of Omer Sergi, Judah's Expansion in Historical Context, *Tel Aviv* 40 2013, 226–246, esp. 233.

289 Georg Athas, 2003, 298–309, esp. 226, 308.

not a dynasty, but the settlement of Jerusalem, like 'irdwd ("city of David") as geographical toponym. As I have argued in my 2003 discussion,[290] however, the Aramaean king clearly sought to boast over his annihilation of the kings of Israel and Juda[291], above all the "House of David,"[292] and celebrate his defeat of a powerful enemy.

Employing the term dynasty,[293] the Aramaean successor projected an earlier, successful reign in the near south on to his own. Already well-attested in the Hebrew Bible as well as the Mesha stela (line 31),[294] the term bytdwd does not indicate a locality, sacred shrine, or divine epithet, as some scholars have indicated. For the Tel Dan stela in particular, Israel and Judah appear in parallel, the context being celebratory rhetoric of vanquished kings.

---

290 Gotthard G.G. Reinhold (2003, 140/141).

291 See here the typically used round number 70 of the killed kings or commanders and the defeated 2000 chariots and 2000 horses in his battle/s! See Gotthard G.G. Reinhold, hrsg., Die Zahl Sieben im Alten Orient. The Number Seven in the Ancient Near East. Studies on the Numerical Symbolism in the Bible and Its Ancient Near Eastern Environment, Frankfurt am Main, Berlin, Bern, Bruxelles, New York, Oxford, Wien: Peter Lang, Internationaler Verlag der Wissenschaften, 2008, 65–67 [c] ; A. Lemaire, The Tel Dan Stela as a Piece of Royal Historiography, JSOT 18 1998, 3–14, esp. 11.

292 See Eilat Mazar, The Palace of King David. Excavations at the Summit of the City of David. Preliminary Report Of Seasons 2005–2007, Jerusalem, New York: Shoham Academic Research and Publication, The Old City Press, 2009, and Discovering the Solomonic Wall in Jerusalem. A Remarkable Archaeological Adventure, Jerusalem: Shoham Academic Research and Publication, 2011.

293 See Gary N. Knoppers, The Vanishing Solomon: The Disappereance of the United Monarchy from Recent Histories of Ancient Israel, JBL 116/1 1997, 19–44, esp. 36: The expression "house of David" may refer specifically to the Davidic dynastie or, as is more likely in an Aramaic context, to the state of Juda headed by the Davidic dynastie."

294 See Gotthard G.G. Reinhold (2003, 140). More difficult is the interpretation of the meaning from 'r'l dwdh (l. 12), 'r'l as personal name and dwdh as title or together in meaning of a cultic vessel. See here Andrew Dearman (1989, 112/113), A. Lemaire (1994 [b], esp. 23, 35/36), Hans-Peter Müller (1994, 379), Bruce Routledge (2000, 249), and S. Mittmann (2002, 53 ff.).

Therefore, my conclusion fully aligns with the explanation of Lawrence J. Mykytiuk, who has concluded in his 2001 dissertation,[295] *"The house of David" named in inscriptions and in the Bible was a political entity referred to us as such by use of international terminology appropriate for political entities. Not only the Arameans but also the Moabites applied this terminology to the Davidic dynasties, as did the authors of the book of the Hebrew Bible that pertain to the monarchic period."*

6.3.3 Deities

In line 4 the stela's author records his enthronement by the god Hadad: *[.w]yhmlk.ddd[.] 'lyty]*, (*"[Aber] Hadad machte [mich selbst] zum König"*). Such a declaration finds parallel in the Zakkur inscription (A line 3–4), where the god Ba'alšamin enthrones Zakkur as king over Hazrak: *whmlky.b'lšm[yn.b]/hzrk.* Line 5 continues with *wyhk.hdd.* recounting how Hadad walked to the forefront in battle, which itself resembles Yahweh's military leadership in Deut 1:30 and 31:8. Hadad thus holds pride of place as chief deity in the Aramaean pantheon (cf. the Pannamuwa inscriptions of Sam'al).[296] In the end, Athas[297] wants to restore *[...]'lby* in line 4 to *'lby[t'l...* and thus read "every/ancient [earth on ground of El-Bay[tel..." Even further, he describes El-Baytel as an

---

295 Lawrence J. Mykytiuk (2001: Appendix E, 14–15; 2004, 132; 2009, 117; 2012, 41 ff.).
See also the comments from William H. Schniedewind (1996, 80), Kenneth A. Kitchen (1997, 39): "dynastically oriented term for the kingdom of Judah, stemming from David as the dynastic founder," from Jan -Wim Wesselius, (1999, 183), Carl S. Ehrlich (2001, 63): "Dynasty of David, that is the land of Judah," Guy Couturier (2001, 95): "expression ... 'maison de David'... appellation du Royaume de Juda" and from Victor Sasson (2005, 23 ff.).
In difference to this, see: Niels Peter Lemche, Thomas L. Thompson (1994, 21). But in renewed discussions see also André Lemaire (2012, 305): "Now it is generally agreed that the phrase BYT DWD in line 9' designates the Judean kingdom of Jerusalem as founded by David, which fits very well the Biblical historiographic tradition even though it does not give any detail nor any date." and "It (i.e. The Mesha stela) probably also mentions BT DWD (at the end of line 31) in parallel to Israel in the preceeding lines."
296 KAI, 214, 215.
297 George Athas, 2003, 193, 210–211, 309–315.

Aramaean/Phoenician deity honoured with the erection of a large monument. Yet his consideration of Bethel cult (Tyr, Phoenicia and Israel [Jer. 48: 13]) reflects much more the latere period of the seventh century. In fact, Charles Virolleaud[298] published an Ugaritic cuneiform text already in 1929 that clearly presents the house and deity *bt.'l* ("house of god" or "divine house") followed by a list of multiple *b'l* – that is, members from different houses. In this instance, *bt.'l* indicates less a sacred Bethel stone than a temple with cella, where the *b'ly* could offer sacrifices to the deity on behalf of their houses or families. Similar dynamics occur in Jud. 9: 4 (*b'l-bryt*), 46 (*bt'l-bryt*), 9: 6, 20–25 (*b'ly škm*), 46, 47 (*b'ly mgdl-škm*), although the "God of the Covenant" appears here.[299]

In like manner, Bob Becking considers Athas' proposal "interesting, intriguing and innovative, but not convincing." He then concludes, "I hope to have made clear that the Aramaic inscription from Tel Dan only refers to the Aramaic deity Hadad (A: 5) and (B: 4) but not to other divine beings, neither Dod nor Bethel."[300]

Given the foregoing analysis of line 4 and the reconstruction *r'l. qdm.b'rq.'by[.w]yhmlk .hdd[.'yty.]*, I offer a different reading, one closer to that of Ingo Kottsieper[301]: "…Da zog (bzw. rückte vor) der König von I[s]rael in Qdm (= Ostland, transjordanisches Gebiet im Bereich des Ḥauran) ein, das im Lande meines Vaters liegt. [Aber] Hadad machte [mich selbst] zum König."

298 Charles Virolleaud, Les textes cuneiformes qui ont été decouverte…, *Syr* X 1929, Pl. LXX No. 14; Hans Bauer, Die Entzifferung der Keilschrifttafeln von Ras Schamra, Halle a.d. Saale: Niemeyer, 1930, 47; Cyrus H. Gordon, Ugaritic Manual. Newly Revised Grammar Texts in Translation Cuneiform Selections Paradigms-Glossary-Indice (Anal Or 35, Rom: Pontificium Institutum Biblicum, 1955), 133 Text, 14 (2) f..
See also Sergio Ribchini, Baetyl, in: Dictionry and Demons in the Bible (DDD), Leiden, New York, Köln: E. J. Brill, 1995, 299–304.

299 To the Schechemite deity (or deities?) see M. J. Mulder, Baal-Berith, in: Dictionary of Deities and Demons in the Bible (DDD), Leiden, New York, Köln: E.J. Brill, 1995, Sp. 266–272, esp. 266–268 and Theodore J. Lewis, The Identity and Function of El/Baal Berith, *JBL* 115/3 1996, 401–423, esp. 401–403.

300 Bob Becking, Does the Stela from Tel Dan refer to a Deity Bethel? *BN* 118 (2003), 19–23, esp. 23.

301 I. Kottsieper, AOAT Bd. 250, Münster: Ugarit-Verlag, 1998, 378.

6.4 Transliteration and Translation[302]

Transliteration

1. ....['] mr.'[d'.tgzr.ly] wgzr[.'bk]
2. [...hdd ?/'l ?].'by.ys[q.y'l.lh]tlhmh.b'b[y]
3. wyškb.'by.yhlk.'l[.'bhw]h.wy'l.mlky[s]
4. r'l.qdm.b'rq.'by[.w]yhmlk.hdd[.'yty]
5. 'nh.wyhk.hdd.qdmy[.w]'pq.m[n].šb'[t.ywm]
6. y.mlky.w'qtl.m[lk.šb']n.'sry.'[lpy.r]
7. kb.w'lpy.prš.[w'qtlt.'yt.yw]rm.br'r[h'b.]
8. mlk.ysr'l.wqtl[t.'yt.'hz]yhw.br.[.ywrm.ml]
9. k.bytdwd.w'sm.['rq.hm   ']
10. yt.'rq.hm.lš[mmh   ]
11. 'hrn.wlhp[k.   wyhw.m]
12. lk.'l.ys[r'l.   w'sm.]
13. msr.'l[.   ]
14. ....

Translation

1. ...he said: [The ?] cove[nant cut (i.e. make) with me] like [your father]
2. had cut (i.e. made) a covenant [with] my father [-hadad ?/-el ?]. He went up [(and) went in (?), to] ally himself with [my] father.

---

302   The German translation in Reinhold (2003, 145) is corrected now in line 3–4:
    1. .... sagte er: [Den (?)] Bu[nd schließe mit mir,] wie [dein Vater]
    2. [mit] meinem Vater [-hadad ?/ -el ?] geschlossen hat. So zog er hinauf [(und) ging hinein (?), um sich] mit [meinem] Vater zu verbünden.
    3. Und mein Vater legte sich (krank) nieder und ging hin zu seinen Vätern (d.h.. er starb). Da zog (bzw. rückte vor) der König von I[s]-
    4. rael in QDM ein, das im Lande meines Vaters liegt. [Aber] Hadad machte [mich selbst] zum König,
    5. Ja, mich! Und Hadad zog vor mir her[und] ich brach na[ch siebe]n Tage]
    6. n meines Herrschens auf. Und ich schlug [sieb]zig Kö[nige], die anspannt-en 2[000 Streitwa]-
    7. gen und 2000 Pferdereiter. [Dann tötete ich Jo]ram, den Sohn A[habs]
    8. den König von Israel. Und [ich] töte[te Ahaz[iahu, den Sohn [Jorams, den Kön]-
    9. ig des Hauses Davids. Da setzte ich (in Ruinen) ihr Land......(ihre Stä-
    10. dte, ihres Landes in Ver[wüstung
    11. andere(r/s). Und wan[delte um ... Und Jehu wurde Kö-]
    12. nig über Is[rael... und ich legte]
    13. einen Belagerungs (wall) gegen [ ]
    14. ....:

3. And my father lay down, he went to his [ancestors] (viz. became sick and died). And the king of I[s]-
4. rael penetrated (i.e. moved to) in QDM, which is in the land of my father. [And] Hadad made [me] king,
5. Yes, me. And Hadad went in front me, [and] I departed af[ter] se[ven day-]
6. s of my kingdom. And I slew [seven]ty kin[gs], who harnessed 2[000 of cha-]
7. riots and 2000 horsemen. [Then I killed Jo]ram, the son of A[hab],
8. the king of Israel. And [I] kil[led Ahaz]iahu, the son of [Jehoram, the ki-]
9. ng of the House of David. And I set (in ruins) their land...(their tow-
10. ns, their land into deso[lation
11. Oth(er/s). And tur[ned ...And Jehu ru-]
12. led over Is[rael... and I laid]
13. a siege (wall) upon [   ]
14. ....

6.5 Historical Background and Considerations

The author of the Têl Dan inscription, dated palaeographically to ca. 835/30 B.C., could only be Hazael of Damascus (842–805). Indeed, this suggestion finds confirmation in content and context alike. Jehu (841–814) killed Joram from Israel (852–841) and Ahaziah from Juda (841), *bytdwd* (A line 9), in battle and then seized the throne in Israel (A line 12/13). The inscription itself mentions two important alliances: between the "father" (Nu. 2), the patron of the stela's author, and his ally (Nu. 2), on the one hand, and an earlier one between the "father," the patron, (Nu. 1) and his ally (Nu. 1). If Hazael was the stela's author[303] then his "father" (Nu. 2) or patron—a high person at the courtyard or the king of Aram, Adad-'Idri (ante 853–845/841)—could have lent him his an important position for service at the royal house of Damascus. The ally (Nu. 2) of the "father" (Nu. 2) must have been Joram of Israel (852–841), certainly at the end of his predecessors reign. Adad-'Idri and Ahab of Israel (874–853) were battling at the time of the Assyrian threat under Shalmaneser III. at the battle of Qarqar (853). Furthermore, I suggest Adad-'Idri's father was Ben-/B(i/)ar-Hadad II

---

303 See Victor Sasson, Murderers, Usurpers, or what? Hazael, Jehu, and the Tell Dan Old Aramaic Inscription, UF Bd. 28, Kevelaer, Neukirchen-Vluyn: Neukirchener Verlag, 1996, 547–554, esp. 553; Nadav Na'aman, Prophetic Stories as Sources for Histories of Jehoshaphat and the Omrides, *Biblica* 78/2 1997, 153–173, esp. 170.

(in the early years of Ahab, post 874–ante 853) of Aram-Damascus' royal line of succession, who reigned after Ben-/B(i/)ar-Hadad I (900–870). On his initiative, the Aramaean dynasty allied themselves with Israel in Aphek (854), one year after the siege of Samaria (855) and further established commercial ties between Damascus and Israel (cf. 1 Kgs 20:34)[304]. However, the Assyrian threat increased after 850, as reflected in Assyrian royal chronicles, which report the campaigns of Shalmaneser III in 849 (10 th palû), 848 (11th palû), and 845 (14 th palû). In light of new research on the Melqart or B(i/)ar-Hadad stela (Excursus I) Adad-'Idri (Heb. Hadad-'Ezer) along with his son, Bir-Hadad ("br.hdd. br.'zr", line 2), could have led the campaign against Assur in 845 (14 th palû: Bull Inscription) together. This Bir-Hadad, third in the line of Aramaean rulers named br.hdd, may have been no more than a crown prince, co-regent, or young king (845–842), who was seriously injured in this campaign and thus received special aid— as with a rescue operation, perhaps led by a Tyrian contingent—so he was able to treat his wounds and make sacrifices to his deity. For this reason, he dedicated a stela to the god Melqart (post 845), whose relief appears with the insignia of a war deity. Back in the Damascene royal house, Bir-Hadad remained ill until his own father, Adad-'Idri (842/841)[305] became illness and died a natural death, as reported in the Têl Dan stela (line 3). This precarious political and military situation of Aram-Damascus led to Joram of Israel marching into QDM, the homeland of Hazaels "father" (line 3/4), and battling for the fort of Tell er-Rumeith as well as the town of Ramtha (Er-Remtā) in Gilead.

The Assyrian annals register Adad-'Idri died while Hazael, "son of nobody" (Basalt-statue)[306] seized the throne:

---

304 A structure termed the "hussot," found in area A of Tel Dan in 1997, is similar to the scriptual reference of 1 Kings 20:34, which refers the "hussot" of Damascus. In Tel Dan this building is an "outside structure," outside of the gate complex, which can often mean a street or a bazaar. See also Avraham Biran, The Hussot on Dan, *Eretz Israel* 26 1999, 25–29, esp. 25 (picture).

305 Stuart A. Irvine, *JBL* 124/2 2005, 345 decided against a later date: "Hadadezer's death in 845 or 844 B.C.E."

306 KAH I 30 I 25–27

ID	I
IM–id-ri KUR–šu e-mi id	ḫa– za-'i-DINGIR DU-MU la-ma-ma-na
GIŠ GU-ZA iṣ-bat	

In addition, 2.Kgs. 8:15 reports Hazael killed Bir-Hadad III and usurped the throne Adad-ʻIdri in the royal house of Aram-Damascus.[307] Only seven days after his reign began, he launched a battle (line 5 f.), invading the Ḥaurân and moving to Gilead. He then killed his adversaries from Israel (Joram) and Juda (Ahaziah) (line 7–9) in the battle at Ramoth-Gilead[308], a possible scenario despite the propagandistic nature of the report. Supporting Jehu—a political ally and deserter[309]—the king of Aram-Damascus acted for his own benefit. In 841, when Jehu seised the throne of Israel (line 11/12), Hazael was forced to withdraw his troops from the Transjordan even despite the siege and battle for Ramoth-Gilead.

The royal chronicles suggest the Assyrian threat was omnipresent, for they record campaigns of Shalmaneser III in 849 (10 th palû), 848 (11th palû) and 845 (14th palû). Therefore, recent inquiries into the Melqart or B(i/)ar-Hadad stela (Excursus I) indicate already Adad-ʻIdri (Heb. Hadad-ʻEzer) and his son, Bir-Hadad (br.hdd. br.ʻzr, line 2), were forced to move

---

307 So in her contribution Nili Wazana, "My Father was a Wandering Aramean?": The Implication for Israelite Identity, at the IWH Colloqium Heidelberg, 3. Sept. 2014, pointed out that here the biblical traditions in connection to Aram and Aram-Damascus describe the Arameans not only as fearful and dangerous enemy from the north, but also Israel's unique involvement and vocation to Aram in 1) Political involvement (1 Kgs 19: 15–18 and 2 Kgs. 8: 7–15), 2) Religion points of contact (2 Kgs 1: 2; 5: 1–6, 17; 8: 7–9; 16: 10–16; 18: 34) and 3) Ethnic Identity (Deut 26:5; Gen 28: 1–2,6; Gen 30: 27).

308 Already Robert M. Porter, Dating the Stela from Tel Dan, *JACF* Vol. 7 1994/95, 92–96, esp. 92 decribed the stela as "strong confirmation of the second biblical battle at Ramoth-Gilead (II Ki 8:28–29)."

309 To this assessment see also Ziva Shavitsky, The Mystery of the Ten Lost Tribes: A Critical Survey of Historical and Archaeological Records relating to the People of Israel in Exile in Syria, Mesopotamia and Persia up to ca. 300 B.C.E, Newcastle upon Thyne: Cambridge Scholars Publishing, 2012, 18. "It is possible that Jehu was perceived by Hazael as his agent, just as he was perceived as Yahwe's instrument by the compiler of the biblical narrative."

the greater part of their military forces to the north, just as Hazael would do some years later, in 841.

The town of Dan (Têl Dan) was conquered admidst the break between Jehu and Hazael, who crushed Israel (2 Kgs 10:32 f.). He had personal reasons to justify his move against Israel, as outlined in the Têl Dan stela (about 835/30), which was subsequently destroyed under the reign of either Jehoahaz (814–798) or Jehoash (798–782) of Israel, around 800, a long time before the ultimate destruction of the city by the Assyrians under Tiglath-Pileser III in 733/732.

The historical table outlines this historical recontruction (Tab. 17):

Tab. 17: *The Historical Events between Israel and Aram-Damascus in the Books of Kings, in the Têl Dan Stela, and the Assyrian Campaigns of the Eponym Chronicle*

Israel	The Books of Kings	Aram-Damascus	Têl Dan-Stele	Eponym Chronicles
Jehoash (798–782) Jehoahaz (814–798) Têl Dan stele: Destruction: ca. 800 [B 1 + B 2], A	2 Kgs 13:1–9, 22–5	Bir-Hadad IV., son of Hazael (805– 773/72 title: Mari)		
			Têl Dan stele 835/30 erected by Hazael, the stela's author	
war against Israel; Jehu's break with Hazael	2 Kgs 10: 32 f.	Conquest of Dan		
				838 21th palû

Israel	The Books of Kings	Aram-Damascus	Têl Dan-Stele	Eponym Chronicles
death of Joram and Ahaziah; succession of Jehu	2 Kgs 8: 15, 28; 9, 14–15	Hazael, title: Mari (842/41–805), usurper; murderer of Bir-Hadad III (br..'zr); annexion of Haurân; battle and withdrawal from Ramoth-Gilead; troops against Assur (841)	line 4–8, 11	841 18th palû
Desertation of Jehus to Hazael				
Joram's invasion of QDM and fight for Ramoth-Gilead			line 3–4	
		Adad-'Idris illness and death 842/41; sickness of Bir-Hadad III.; political crisis in Damascus	line 3	
	2 Kgs. 8:7 f.	Bir-Hadad III., son of [Adad] 'Idri (845–841), potential successor without ruling, coregent, young king, injury, rescue in battle; Melqart stela erected post 845		845 14th palû

Israel	The Books of Kings	Aram-Damascus	Têl Dan-Stele	Eponym Chronicles
				848 11th palû.
				849 10th palû
Second alliance post 853.; Joram (852–841); ally from Israel		the author's high patron or the king Adad-'Idri (ante 853--845/41); ally of Aram	line 1	
				battle of Qarqar 853: 6th palû of Shalmaneser III
First alliance 854, Ahab's early time (874–853); father of the ally from Israel	1 Kgs 20:34	Bir-Hadad II. (874– ante 853); the patron's father; ally from Aram	line 1/2	
Baesa, king of Israel (908–886)	1. Kgs 15:16–22[309]	Bir-Hadad I (890–874)		

---

310 According to E. Lipinski, OLA 100, 2000, 372, S. Hafthórsson, CB OT Ser 24 2006, 141–144, 181 and Angelika Berlejung, LAOS 3 2013, 72, here we have a reliable historical information.

References

Abbreviations

AAAS	Annales archéologiques Arabes Syriennes, Damaskus
AALR	Atti della Accademia Nazionale dei Lincei. Rendiconti. Scienze Morali, Roma, Rome
ÄAT	Ägypten und Altes Testament, Wiesbaden
ABG	Arbeiten zur Bibel und ihrer Geschichte, Leipzig
AbLA, ABLAK	M. Noth, Aufsätze zur biblischen Landes- und Altertumskunde, hrsg. H.W. Wolff, I–II, Neukirchen-Vluyn 1971
Abr-n	Abr-Nahrain. An annual under the auspices of the Department of Semitic Studies, University of Melbourne, Leiden
Act Ant Hung	Acta Antiqua Academiae Scientiarum Hungaricae – A Magyar Tudományos Akadémia klasszika-filológiai közleményei, Budapest
ADAJ	Annual of the Department of Antiquities of Jordan, Amman, Jordan
AfO	Archiv für Orientforschung, Graz
AION	Annali dell' Istituto Universitario Orientale di Napoli, Napoli, Neapel
AJSL	American Journal of Semitic Languages and Literatures, Chicago, Ill.
Anal Or, AnOr	Analecta Orientalia, Rome
ANES	Near Eastern Studies, Louvain: Peeters
ANET	Ancient Near Eastern Texts Relating to the Old Testament, ed. By J. B. Pritchard, Princeton, New Jersey 1950, 1955²
Ann A Stor Ant	Annali del Dipartimento di Studi del Mondo Classico e del Mediteraneo Antico. Sezione di Archeologia e Storia Antica, Napoli

An St	Anatolian Studies. Journal of the British Institute of Archaeology at Ankara, London
AOAT	Alter Orient und Altes Testament, Kevelaer
AOF, AoF, AltorF	Altorientalische Forschungen, Berlin
APA	Acta Praehistorica et Archaeologica, Berlin
ARI	A. K. Grayson, Records of the Ancient Near East. Assyrian Royal Inscriptions, I–II, Wiesbaden 1972, 1976
ARM	Archives Royales de Mari, Paris 1950 ff.
ARRIM	Annual Review of the Royal Inscription of Mesopotamia Project, Toronto
ASOR NEA	American School of Oriental Research. Near Eastern Archaeology, Boston, MA.
ASOR SBL	American School of Oriental Research. The Society of Biblical Literatures, Atlanta, Georgia
Atti Acc Toscana Sci Lett	Toscana Atti dell' Academia Toscana di Scienze e lettre "La Columbara", Firenze, Florence, Florenz
Aula Or	Aula Orientalis. Revista de estudios del proximo Oriente, Barcelona
AUSS	Andrews University Seminary Studies, Berrien Springs, Michigan
BAIAS	Bulletin of the Anglo-Israel Archaeological Society, London
BAR, BARev	The Biblical Archaeology Review, Washington
BAR International Series	The Biblical Archaeology Review. International Series, Oxford
BBB	Bonner Biblische Beiträge, Bonn
BBVO	Berliner Beiträge zum Vorderen Orient, Berlin
Bib, Bibl, Bb	Biblica, Rome
BKAT	Biblischer Kommentar zum Alten Testament, Neukirchen-Vluyn
BL Calwer	Calwer Bibellexikon, hrsg. K. Gutbrod, R. Kücklich, Th.Schlatter, Stuttgart: Calwer-Verlag, 1967

BL Haag	Bibel-Lexikon, hrsg. H. Haag, Leipzig: St. Benno-Verlag GmbH, 1969
BMB	Bulletin du Musée de Beyrouth, Paris, Beyrouth, Beirut
BN	Biblische Notizen. Beiträge zur exegetischen Diskussion, Bamberg
BO	Bibliotheca Orientalis, Leiden
BTS	Beiruter Texte und Studien, hrsg. Orient-Institut der Deutschen Morgenländischen Gesellschaft, Beirut, Wiesbaden
CAH	The Cambridge Ancient History, Cambridge
CANE	Civilizations of the Ancient Near East, New York: Charles Scribner's Sons
CB OT Ser.	Coniectanea Biblica. Old Testament Series, Stockholm
CBQ	The Catholic Biblical Quarterly, Washington, D.C.
COS II	W.W. Hallo, K. Lawson Younger, eds., The Context of Scripture: Canonical compositions, monumental inscriptions, and archival documents from the biblical world, II Monumental inscriptions from the biblical world, Leiden, Brill 2000
CRAIBL	Comptes-rendus des séances de l' Académie des inscriptions et belles-lettres, Paris
CUOS	Columbia University Oriental Studies, New York
DDD	Dictionary of Deities and Demons in the Bible, Leiden. New York. Köln
DOTT	D. Winton Thomas, Documents from Old Testament Times, London 1958
EAZ	Ethnographisch-Archäologische Zeitschrift, Berlin
EB. NS	Études bibliques. Nouvelles Série, Paris
EHS.T	Europäische Hochschulschriften, Reihe XXIII Theologie, Frankfurt am Main

Enc Brit, Ebr	The Encyclopedia Britannica. A new survey of universal knowledge, London, Chicago, Geneva, Sydney, Toronto
EI, Eretz Israel	Eretz Israel. Archaeological, Historical and Geographical Studies, publ. Israel Exploration Society, Jerusalem
EThSt	Erfurter Theologische Studien, Leipzig
FO	Folia Orientalia. Revue des études orientales, Kraków
FRLANT	Forschungen zur Religion und Literatur des Alten und Neuen Testaments, Göttingen
FuF	Forschungen und Fortschritte. Nachrichtenblatt der deutschen Wissenschaft und Technik, Berlin
GBL	Das Grosse Bibellexikon, Bd. 1–3, Wuppertal, Giessen, 1987–1989
IEJ	Israel Exploration Journal, Jerusalem
IMJ	The Israel Museum Journal, Jerusalem
Iraq	Iraq. British School of Archaeology in Iraq, London
JACF	Journal of the Ancient Chronology Forum, London
JANES	The Journal of Ancient Near Eastern Society of Columbia University, New York, N.Y.
JBL	Journal of Biblical Literature, Philadelphia, Pa., New York, D.C., New Haven, Conn.
JCS	Journal of Cuneiform Studies, New Haven, Conn.
JESHO	Journal of the Economic and Social History of the Orient, Leiden
JNES, JNESt	Journal of Near Eastern Studies, Chicago, Ill.
JSS, JSSt	Journal of Semitic Studies, Manchester
JKF	Jahrbuch für Kleinasiatische Forschung, Heidelberg
JSOT. SS	Journal for the Study of the Old Testament, Supplement Series, Sheffield
KAI	H. Donner, W. Röllig, Kanaanäische und aramäische Inschriften, Wiesbaden, 1962–1964

Kbo	Keilschrifttexte aus Boghazköi, WDOG 1916 ff., Berlin und Leipzig
KUSATU	Kleine Untersuchungen zur Sprache des Alten Testaments und seiner Umwelt. Im Auftrag der Forschungsstelle für Althebräische Sprache an der Universität Mainz, hrsg. Reinhard G. Lehmann, Waltrop
LAOS	Leipziger Altorientalistische Studien, Wiesbaden
LIBRARY OF HEBREW BIBLE/ OLD TESTAMENT STUDIES	Library of Hebrew Bible/Old Testament Studies. Formerly Journal for the Study of the Old Testament Supplement Series, London. New Delhi. New York. Sydney
Maarav	Maarav. A Journal for the Study of the northwest Semitic languages and literatures, Santa Monica, Calif.
MAD	Materials for the Assyrian Dictionary, Chicago
MBAG	Mitteilungen der Berliner Gesellschaft für Anthropologie, Ethnologie und Urgeschichte, Berlin
MDAI. A	Mitteilungen des Deutschen Archäologischen Instituts, Athenische Abteilung, Berlin
NEAEHL	Stern. E. Ed., 1993–2008, The New Encyclopedia of Archaeological Excavations in the Holy Land, 5 Vols. Jerusalem: The Israel Exploration Society
NESE	Neue Ephemeris für semitische Epigraphik, Wiesbaden
NIDB	The New International Dictionary of the Bible, Pictorial Edition, J.D. Douglas, Merill C. Tenney, eds., Grand Rapids, Michigan: Zondervan Publishing House/Basingstoke, Hants, UK: Marshall-Pickering, 1987
OEANE	Meyers, E.M., Ed., The Oxford Encyclopedia of Archaeology in the Near East, Oxford: The Oxford University Press
OIP	Oriental Institute Publications, Chicago

OLA, OL Anal	Orientalia Lovaniensia Analecta, Leuven, Paris, Sterling, Virginia
OLZ	Orientalische Literaturzeitung. Zeitschrift für die Wissenschaft vom ganzen Orient und seine Beziehungen zu den angrenzenden Kulturkreisen, Berlin, Leipzig
Or	Orientalia, Rom
Orient & Occident	Orient & Occident. Newsletter of the German Protestant Institute of Archaeology in Amman, Amman, Jordan
Or NS	Orientalia, Nova Series, Rom
Or O.S.	Orientalia Old Series
OTS	Oudtestamentische Studiën, Leiden
PEQ	Palestine Exploration Quarterly, London
RA	Revue d'Assyriologie et d'Archéologie Orientale, Paris
RBib, Riv Bibl	Rivista Biblica, Associazione Biblica Italiana, Rom
RIMA	The Royal Inscriptions of Mesopotamia, Assyrian Periods, Toronto, 1987 ff.
RLA	Reallexikon der Assyriologie und vorderasiatischen Archäologie, hrsg. A. Ebeling, B. Meißner, Berlin, New York 1928 ff.
RQ	The Restauration Quarterly, Abilene, Texas
RSF, Riv St Fen	Rivista di Studi Fenici, Roma, Rom
RSO	Rivista degli Studi Orientali, Rome
SAA	State Archives of Assyria, Helsinki
SAAB	State Archives of Assyria Bulletin, Padua
SBANE	Studies in the Bible and the Ancient Near East, Jerusalem
SBL	Society of Biblical Literature. Archaeology and Biblical Studies, Atlanta
SBoT	Studien zu den Bogazköy-Texten, Wiesbaden
SEMITICA	SEMITICA. Cahiers Publiès par l'Institute d'Études Sémitiques du Collège de France, Paris

SJOT	Scandinavian Journal of the Old Testament, Aarhus
St Ans	Studia Anselminana, Philosophica (et) theologia. Institutum Pontificium Sancti Anselmi de Urbe, Rom
Syr, Syria	Syria. Revue d'Art Oriental et d'Archéologie, Paris
Tel Aviv	Tel Aviv. Journal of the Tel Aviv University, Institute of Archaeology, Tel Aviv
TRE	Theologische Realenzyklopädie, Berlin, New York
TSSI	J.C.L. Gibson, Textbook of Syrian Semitic Inscriptions, II 1975, III 1982, Oxford
TUAT	Texte aus der Umwelt des Alten Testaments, I 1982–1985, II 1986 f., Gütersloh
Tyn B	Tyndale Bulletin. Organ of the Tyndale Fellowship for Biblical and Theological Research and of Tyndale House, Cambridge
UF	Ugarit-Forschungen, Neukirchen-Vluyn
VD	Verbum Domini. Commentari de Re Biblica Ponteficum Institutum Biblicum de Urbe, Rom
VT	Vetus Testamentum Quarterly, publ. By the International Organization of Old Testament Scholars, Leiden
VT.S, VTS	Vetus Testamentum, Supplements, Leiden; siehe auch: SVT Supplements to Vetus Testamentum, Leiden: Brill, Paris
WdO, WDO, WO	Die Welt des Orients. Wissenschaftliche Beiträge zur Kunde des Morgenlandes, Göttingen, Wuppertal, Stuttgart
WMANT	Wissenschaftliche Monographien zum Alten und Neuen Testament, Neukirchen
ZAH	Zeitschrift für Althebraistik, Stuttgart, Berlin, Köln
ZAW	Zeitschrift für alttestamentliche Wissenschaft, Berlin, Gießen
ZDPV	Zeitschrift des Deutschen Palästina-Vereins, Leipzig, Wiesbaden

Bibliography

Abramski, Samuel	The Resurrection of the Kingdom of Damascus and its Historiographic Record, in: SBANE, Presented to S.E. Loewenstamm, Jerusalem: Rubinstein, 1978, 183–184
Aharoni, Y.	The Land of 'Amqi, IEJ 3 1953, 153–161
Akkermanns, Peter M.M. Glen M. Schwartz	The Archaeology of Syria, Cambridge: Cambridge University Press, 2003
Albright, William Foxwell	A Votive Stele erected by Ben-Hadad I. of Damascus to the God Melcarth, BASOR 87 1942, 23–29
	Emergence of the Arameans, CAH³ 2/2 1975, 529–536
Amadasi Guzzo, Maria Giulia	TELL AFIS IN THE IRON AGE. The Aramaic Inscriptions, ASOR NEA Vol . 77 No. 1 (March 2014), 54–57
Arnaud, Daniel	Textes sumériens et accadiens, Tome 3 (Recherches au pays d'Aštata. Emar VI/3), Paris: Editions Recherche sur les Civilisations, 1986, 42: 8–9
Arav, Rami	A Chronicle of a Pre-know Destruction. Analysis of the Stages of the Conquest and Destruction of the City of Bethsaida by Tiglathpileser III. (734–732 B.C.E.), in: Eretz-Israel. Archaeological, Historical and Geographical Studies, Vol. 29, Publ. The Israel Exploration Society in cooperation with the Institute of Archaeology, Hebrew University of Jerusalem, Jerusalem 2009, 328*–338*
	Geshur: The Southwesternmost Aramean Kingdom, LAOS 3 2013, 1–29
Athas, George	The Tell Dan Inscription. A Reppraisal New Interpretation (JSOT SS 360. Copenhagen International Seminar 12), London, New York: Sheffield Academic Press, 2003

Avetisyan, Hrayr	On the Role of Aramaen Principalities in the History of Northern Mesopotamia, in: Šulmu IV. Everyday Life in Ancient Near East. Papers Presented at the International Conference Poznan, 19.–22. Sept. 1989, ed. Julia Zablocka and Stefan Zawadski, Universytet im. Adama Mickiewicza w Poznaniu. Seria Historia Nr. 182, Poznan:Adam Mickiewicza Universytet 1993, 21–26
Bardtke, Hans	Art. Benhadad, BHH I 1962, Sp. 215–216
Barnett, R. D.	Arameans, Enc Brit Vol. II 1963, 207–208
Bastert, Katrin, Hans Dieter Bienert, Roland Lamprichs, Dieter Vieweger	Ba'ja Regional Project Report on the First Field Season, 1999, Occident & Orient 5/ 1& 2 Dec. 2000: 39–42
Bauer, Hans	Die Entzifferung der Keilschrifttafeln von Ras Schamra, Halle a.d. Saale: Niemeyer, 1930
Becking, Bob	Review. Wayne T. Pitard, Ancient Damascus…, Winona Lake 1987, BO XLVI No. 1/2 Januari-Maart 1989, 146–150
	The Second Danite Inscription. Some Remarks, BN 81 1996, 21–29
	Did Jehu Write the Tell Dan Inscription, SJOT 13/2 1999, 187–201
	Does the Stele from Tel Dan refer to a Deity Bethel?, BN 118 2003, 19–23
Beek, Martinus Adrianus	Das Problem des aramäischen Stammvaters (Deut. XXVI 5), OTS VIII 1950, 197–212
Begrich, G.	Der wirtschaftliche Einfluß Assyriens auf Südsyrien und Palästina, Diss. Theol., Humboldt Universität, Berlin 1975
Berlejung, Angelika	Nachbarn, Verwandte, Feinde und Gefährten: Die "Aramäer" im Alten Testament, in: Arameans, Chaldeans, and Arabs in Babylonia and Palestine in the First Millennium B.C., ed. By Angelika Berlejung and Michael P. Streck, LAOS 3 2013, 57–86

Berner, U.	Bemerkungen zur Streitwagenfrage, (MBAG 3/2 1969–1971. FS zum Hundertjährigen Bestehen der Berliner Gesellschaft für Anthropologie, Ethnologie und Urgeschichte (1869–1969), Zweiter Teil, Fachwiss,. Reihe), Berlin 1970, 236–239
Beyer, Klaus	Die Sprache der moabitischen Inschriften, KUSATU 11 2010, 5–40
	Der Wandel des Aramäischen veranschaulicht durch Transkriptionen alter aramäischer Texte, in: Alejandro F. Botta, ed., In the Shadow of Bezalel. Aramaic, Biblical, and Ancient Near Eastern Studies in Honor of Bezalel Porten, Leiden. Boston: Koninklijke Brill NV, 2013, 13–28
Beyerle, Stefan	Aram und Israel im 9./8. Jh. v. Chr. aus der Perspektive der aramäischen und assyrischen Inschriften, in: Michael Pietsch, Friedhelm Hartenstein, hrsg. Israel zwischen den Mächten, FS für Stefan Timm zum 65. Geburtstag, AOAT 364, Münster: Ugarit-Verlag, 2009, 47–78
Bienert, Hans Dieter, Roland Lamprichs, Dieter Vieweger, et. al.	Baʻja – The Archaeology of a Landscape. 9000 Years of Human Occupation: A preliminary Report on the 1999 Field Season, ADAJ XLIV 2000, 119–148
	Baʼja: Archäologie einer Landschaft in Jordanien – Bericht über archäologische Feldforschungen, in: Ricardo Eichmann (hrsg.), Ausgrabungen und Surveys im Vorderen Orient I, (Deutsches Archäologisches Institut Orient-Abteilung. Orient Archäologie, Band 5), Rahden/Westf.: Verlag Marie Leidorf–GmbH, 2002, 161–213
Bimson, John J.	Archaeological data and the dating of the Patriarchs, in: Essays on the Patriarchal Narratives. ed. A. R. Millard and D.J. Wisemann, Winona Lake, Indiana: Eisenbrauns, 1980, 59–92
	Shoshenk and Shishak. A Case of Mistaken Identity?, JACF Vol. 6, 1992/93, 19–32
Biran, Avraham	An Aramaic Stele Fragment from Tel Dan, IEJ 43/2–3 1993, 81–93

	Biblical Dan, Jerusalem: Israel Exploration Society. Hebrew Union College – Jewish Institute of Religion, 1994 [a]
	The Aramaic Inscription from Tel Dan, IMJ 12 1994, 50–60 [b]
	The Hussot on Dan, Eretz Israel 26 1999, 25–29
Biran, Avraham, Joseph Naveh	An Aramaic Inscription from the First Temple Period from Tel Dan, Qadmoniot 26 1993, 74–81
	The Tel Dan Inscription: A New Fragment, IEJ 45/1 1995, 1–18
Black, M.	The Milqart Stele, in: DOTT 1958, 239–241
Blenkinsopp, Joseph	Ahab of Israel and Jehosaphat of Judah: The Syro-Palestinian Corridor in the Ninth Century, in: Civilizations of the Ancient Near East, II, New York: Charles Scribner's Sons, 1995, 1309–1319
Bonnet, Corinne	Melqart, Iconography of Deities and Demons in the Biblical World. Electronic Pre Publication Last Revision: 26 Apr. 2007 (IDD website: http://www.religionswissenschaft.unizh.ch/idd/Prepublications/e_idd_melqart.pdf (accessed 20. Dec. 2005)
Bonnet, Corinne, Herbert Niehr	Religionen in der Umwelt des Alten Testaments II, Phönizier, Punier, Aramäer (= Kohlhammer Studienbücher Theologie Band 4, 2), Stuttgart: Verlag W. Kohlhammer GmbH, 2010
Bordreuil, Pierre	A propos de l'inscription de Mesha' deux notes*, in: The World of the Arameans III. Studies in Language and Literature in Honour of Paul-Eugène Dion, 158–167
Bordreuil, P., J. Teixidor	Nouvel Examen de l'inscription de Bar-Hadad, Aula Or 1983, 271–276
Borger, Rykle	Die Inschriften Assarhaddons König von Assyrien, AfO Beiheft 9, Graz: Weidner, 1956
	Einleitung in die assyrischen Königsinschriften I., Das zweite Jahrtausend v. Chr., HO I. Erg. Bd. V/1, Leiden, Köln: E.J. Brill, 1961

	Der Vertrag Assur-Niraris mit Mati'ilu von Arpad, TUAT 1/2 1983, 155–177
Bowman, Raymond A.	Arameans, Aramaic and the Bible, JNES VII/2 1948, 65–90
	Ben-Hadad, in: IDB, New York -Nashville: Abingdon Press, 1962, 381–382
Brinkman, J.A.	A Political History of Post-Kassite Babylonia 1158–722 B.C., Anal Or 43, Rome: Pontifical Institute Press, 1968
Bron, Francois, André Lemaire	Les inscriptions araméennes de Hazael, RA 83/1 1989, 35–44
Brueggeman, W. / W. D. Hankins	"The Affirmation of Prophetic Power and Deconstructions of Royal Authority in the Elisha Narratrives", CBQ 76 2014, 58–76
Bruins, Hendrik J., Johannes van der Pflicht, Amihai Mazar	14C Dates from Tel Rehov: Ron-Age Chronology, Pharaos, and Hebrew Kings, Science 300, No. 5615 (11 April 2003), 315–318, http://www.rehov.org/Rehov/publications/p05.html (Internet 2013)
Bucellati, Giorgio	'Apirû and Munnabtûtu – The Stateless of the First Cosmopolitan Age, JNES 36 1977, 145–147
Bunnens, Guy	Tradition, Innovation and Cultural Borders in Aramean Syria, Heidelberg Colloquium, Aram and Israel: Cultural Interaction Political Borders and Construction of Identity during the Early Iron Age (12th – 8th Centureis BCE), Sept. 2, 2014, lecture
Burnett, Joel S.	The Question of Divine Absense in Israelite and West Semitic Religion, CBQ 67/2 2005, 215–235
Buttery, Alan	Armies and Enemies of Ancient Egypt and Assyria, Goring by Sea: Sussex 1974
Caplice, Richard	Introduction to Akkadian, Studia Pohl: Series Maior 9, Rome: Biblical Institute Press, 1983
Cazelles, H.	Une nouvelle stèle d'Adadnirari d' Assyrie et Joas d'Israël, CRAIBL 113/1 1969, 6–117
Chang-Ho, Ji	Iron Age in Central and Northern Transjordan: An Interim. Summary of Archaeological data, PEQ Nu. 2, Dec. 1995, 122–140

	The East Jordan Valley During Iron Age I, PEQ 129 1997, 19–37
Chapman, Rupert L. III	The Dan Stele and the Chronology of Levantine Iron Age Stratigraphy, BAIAS (1994) 13 1993, 23–29
Chapman, R.	"Putting Sheshonq I in his Place", PEQ 141/1 2009, 4–17
Charbonnet, A.	Le dieu aux lions d'Eretrie, Ann A Stor Ant 8 1986, 117–156, Pls. 33–41.
Chatonnet, Francoise, Briquel	Book Review: Les Araméens a l'âge du fer: Histoire politique et structures sociales, by P.-E. Dion (Études bibliques, nouvelles série, no. 34), Paris: Gabalda, 1997, JNES 61/2 Apr. 2002, 125–127
Childs, B.S.	Deuteronomic Formulae of the Exodus Tradition, in: Hebräische Wortforschung. FS W. Baumgärtner, SVT 16, Leiden: Brill, 1967, 30–39
Cody, Aelred	A New Inscription from Tell Rimah and King Joash of Israel, CBQ 32 1970, 325–340
Choi, Jongwon	Zur Bedeutung der Zahl Sieben. Eine literar- und kompositions-kritische Studie zu den Vorstellungen von Fluch und Strafe im Alten Orient und im Alten Orient und im Alten Testament, Kleine Arbeiten zum Alten und Neuen Testament 11, hrsg. Jan Christian Gertz, Jens Herzer, Wolfgang Kraus und Wolfgang Zwickel, Kamen: Hartmut Spenner 2011
Conklin, Blane W.	Arslan Tash I and other Vestiges of a Particular Syrian Incantory Thread (*), Biblica 84/1 2003, 89–101
Cornwall, P.	Two Letters from Dilmun, JCS 6 1952, 137–142
Couturier, Guy	Quelques Observations le BYTDWD de la Stele araméénne de Tel Dan, in: World of the Arameans II. Studies in History and Archaeology in Honour of Paul-Eugène Dion (JSOT SS), Sheffield: Sheffield Academie Press, 2001, 72–97
Cross, Frank Moore	Epigraphic Notes on the Amman Citadel Inscription, BASOR 193 1969, 13–19

The Stele dedicated to Melcarth by Ben-Hadad of Damascus, BASOR 205 1972, 36–42

Costa, Benjami, Jordi H. Fernandez — Ibiza und Formentera von der Prähistorik bis zur islamischen Epoche. Führer durch das archäologische Museum, Ibiza: Museo Arqueologic d'Eivissa I Fornamentera, 1995

Culican, W. — "Melqart Representations on Phoenician Seals", Abr-n 2 1960–1961, 41–54

Davis, Conn Grayson — The Aramean Influence upon Ancient Israel to 732 B.C., The Southern Baptist Theological Seminary, Ph.D. 1979 (University Microfilms International, Ann Arbor, Michigan, 1984)

Dearman, Andrew, ed. — Studies in the Mesha Inscription and Moab, ASOR. SBL, ed. by Andrew Dearman. Archaeology asnd Biblical Studies, Philip J. King, ed., Nu. 02, Atlanta, Georgia: Scholar Press, 1989

Dearman, J. Andrew J. Maxwell Miller — The Melqart Stele and the Ben-Hadads of Damascus: Two Studies, PEQ 115/2 1983, 95–96, 97–101

De Canales, Gonzáles, F., L.Serrano, J. Llompart — Tarshish and the United Monarchy of Israel, ANES 47 2010, 137–164

Del Fabro, Roswitha — A New Archaeological Look at Sefire, FO Vol. 51 2014, 177–188

Della Vida, G.L., W.F. Albright — Some Notes on the Stele of Benhadad, BASOR 90 1943, 30–34

Deimel, P. Anton — "Miszellen", Or O.S., Roma: ed. a Pontificio Instituto Biblico, II 1920, 53–64

Delsman, Wilhelmius C. — Aramäische historische Inschriften. Die Inschrift des Königs Birhadad von Damaskus, in: TUAT I/6, Gütersloh: Gütersloher Verlagshaus Gerd Mohn, 1982/83/84/85, 625

Demsky, Aaron — On Reading Ancient Inscription: The Monumental Aramaic Stele Fragment from Tel Dan, JANES 23 1995, 29–35

Deutsch, Robert	A Hoard of Fifty Hebrew Clay Bullae from the Time of Hezekiah, in: Shlomo. Studies in Epigraphy, Iconography, History and Archaeology in Honor of Shlomo Moussaieff, Robert Deutsch, editor, Tel Aviv-Jaffa: Archaeological Center Publication 2003, 45–98
De Vaux, Roland	La Chronologie de Hazael et de Benhadad III. Rois de Damas, RB 43/4 1934, 512–518
	Les prophétes de Baal sur l Mont Carmel, BMB 5 1941, 7–20
Dion, Paul-Eugène	Book Review Wayne T. Pitard, Ancient Damascus. A Historical Study of the Syrian City-State from Earliest Times until its Fall to the Assyrans in 732 B.C.E, Winona Lake, Indiana: Eisenbrauns, 1987, BASOR Nu. 270 May 1988, 97–99
	Review Gotthard G.G. Reinhold, Die Beziehungen Altisraels zu den aramäischen Staaten in der israelitisch-judäischen Königszeit, EHS.T, Reihe XXIII Theologie Bd. 368, Frankfurt am Main, Bern, New York, Paris: Peter Lang, 1989, BO No, 1/2 Januari-Maart 1993, 217–219
	Aramean Tribes and Nations of First-Millennium Western Asia, in: Civilizations of the Ancient Near East II, New York: Charles Scribner's Sons, 1995, 1281–1284
	Syro-Palestinian Resistance to Shalmaneser III in the Light of New Documents, ZAW 107. Bd. 1995, 482–489
	Les Araméens à l'âge du Fer: Historie politique et structures sociales. Études Bibliques NS No. 34, Paris: Gabalda, 1997
	The Tel Dan Stele and its Historical Significance, in: Y. Avi-shur et al., Historical Epigraphical and Biblical Studies in Honor of Prof. Michael Heltzer, Tel Aviv – Jaffa: 1999, 145–156
Dhorme, R.P.P.	Les Pays Bibliques et l'Assyrie, RB 19/7 1910, 54–75

Donbaz, V.	Two Neo-Assyrian Stelae in the Antakya and Kahramanmaras Museum, ARRIM 8 1990, 4–24
Dubovský, Peter	Tiglath-pileser III's Campaigns in 734–732 B.C.: Historical Background of Isa 7; 2 Kgs 15–16 and 2. Chr. 27–28, Biblica 87/2 2006, 153–169
	Assyrian downfall through Isaiah's eyes (2 Kings 15–23): the histiography of representation, Biblica 89/1 2008, 1–16
Dupont-Sommer André	Les Araméens, L'Orient ancient illustre 2, Paris: Adrien-Maisonneuve, 1949
	Sur le débuts de l'histoire aramméenne, Congres Volume Copenhagen 1953, VT.S 1. Leiden: E.J. Brill, 1953, 40–49
Dunand, Maurice	Stele aramménne dédiée à Melqart d'Alep, BMB 3 1939, 65–76, Pl. 13
	A propos de la stêle de Melqart du Musée d'Alep, BMB 6 1942/43, 41–45
Edel, Elmar	Die Ortsnamenlisten aus dem Totentempel Amenophis III, BBB 25 Bonn: Peter Hanstein Verlag GmbH, 1966
Edel, Elmar, Manfred Görg	Die Ortsnamenlisten im nördlichen Säulenhof des Totentempels Amenophis III. (ÄAT 50), Wiesbaden: Harrassowitz, 2005
Ehrlich, Carl S.	Coalition Politics in Eight Century B.B.C. Palestine: The Philistines and the Syro-Ephraimite War*, ZDPV 107, 1/ 2 1991, 48–58
	The bytdwd-Inscription and Israelite Historiography: Taking Stock after Half a Decade of Research, in: The World of the Arameans II. Studies in History and Archaeology in Honor of Paul-Eugène Dion (JSOT SS 325), Sheffield: Sheffield Academic Press, 2001, 57–76
Elat, Moshe	The Campaigns of Salmaneser III. against Aram and Israel, IEJ 25 1975, 25–35
Emerton, J.A.	The Issues in the Interpretation of the Tel Dan Inscription, VT L/1 2000, 26–41

	Lines 25–6 of the Moabite Stone and a recently-discovered Inscription, VT LV/3 2005, 293–303
Eph'al, Israel, Joseph Naveh	Hazael's Booty Inscriptions, IEJ 39 1989, 192–200
Eshel, Esther	A Late Iron Age Ostracon Featuring in Term לערכך, IEJ 53/2 2003, 151–163
Eshel, Hanan	Short Notes. Isaiah: VIII 23: An Historical-Geographical Analogy, VT 40/1 Jan. 1990, 104–109
Ewing, W.	Aphek, International Standard Bible Encyclopedia, http://topicalbible.org/a/apek.htm, sowie http://bibleatlas.org/regional/aphek_3.htm (Internet 2013)
Fales, Frederick Mario	Istituzioni a confronto tra mondo semitico occidentale e Assiria nel I Millenio a.C.: Il trattato di Sefire, in: L. Canfera, M. Liverani, C. Zaccagnini, eds, I tratti nel mondo antico. Forma, ideologia, funzione, Saggi di Storia Antica 2, Roma: L'Erma di Bretschneider, 1990, 149–173
Feldman, Steven	Return to Aphek, http://fontes.Istc.edu/~rklein/Documents/Aphek.htm (Internet 2013)
Finkelstein, Israel	Hazor and the North in the Iron Age: a Low Chronology Perspective, BASOR 14 1999, 55–70
	The Great Wall of Tell en-Nasbeh (Mizpah), The First Fortification in Judah, and 1 Kings 15:16–22*, VT 62 (2012), 14–28
Finkelstein, Israel, Oded Lipschitz, Omer Sergi	Tell er-Rumeith in Northern Jordan: Some Archaeological and Historical Observations, Semitica 55 2013, 2–23
Finkelstein, J.J.	Subartu and Subarians in Old Babylonian Sources, JCS 9 1955, 1–7
Fitzmyer, Joseph A.	The Aramaic Inscription of Sefire, Biblica et Orientalia 19, Rome: Pontifical Biblical Institute, 1967
	Assyrian Rulers of the Early First Millennium BC I (1114–859), (The Royal Inscriptions of Mesopotamia. Assyrian Periods/Volume 2) Toronto, Buffalo, London: University of Toronto Press, 1991

Fitzmyer, Joseph A. Stephen A. Kaufmann	An Aramaic Bibliography Part 1. Old Official and Biblical Aramaic, Baltimore and London: The John Hopkins University Press, 1992
Fohrer, G.,	Art. Uz, in: BL Calwer, Stuttgart: Calwer Verlag, 1967, 2. Aufl., Sp. 1378
Forrer, E.	Art. Aramu, RLA I 1932, 131–139
Frame, Gane	The Political History and Historical Geography of the Aramean, Chaldean, and Arab Tribes in Babylonia in the Neo-Assyrian Period*, LAOS 3 2013, 87–121
Free, J.P.	The Excavations of Dothan, BA 19 1956, 43–48
	The Seventh Season at Dothan., BASOR 160 1960, 6–15
Freedman, R. David	Woman, A Power Equal to Man. Translation of Woman as a "Fit Helpmate" for Man is Questioned, BAR Jan./Febr. Vol. IX/1 1983, 56–58
Gadd, C. J.	Prism of Sargon II. From Nimrud, Iraq 16 1954, 173–201
Gadot, Yuval	Aphek in the Sharon and the Philistine Northern Frontier, BASOR No. 341 (February, 2006), 21–36
Gadot, Yuval, Esther Yadin	Bronze and Iron Age Remains (Area X) of the Upper City of Aphek, http://www.tau.ac.il/humanites/archaeology/projects/proj_past_aphek.html (Internet 2013)
Galil, Gershon,	Conflicts between Assyrian vassals, SAAB VI/I 1992, 55–63
	A New Look at the Inscriptions of Tiglath-pileser III, Biblica 81/4 2000, 511–520
	The Boundaries of Aram-Damascus in the 9th-8th BC, VT.S 81, Leiden, New York, Cologne: E. J. Brill 2000, 35–41
	A Re-arrangement on the Fragments of the Tel Dan Inscription and the Relations Between Israel and Aram, PEQ 133 2001, 16–21
	Shalmaneser III in the West, RB T.109/1 2002, 40–56

Garbini, Giovanni	Israele e gli Aramei di Damasco, Rbib I + VI /3 1958, 199–209
	L'iscrizione Aramaica di Tel Dan, AAL.R, Anno CCCXCI 1994, 461–471
Garelli, Paul	The Achievment of Tiglath-Pileser III: Novelty or Continuity?, Scripta Hierosolymitana 33, FS Hayim Tadmor, Jerusalem: The Magnes Press, 1991, 46–51
Gates, John F.	Ben-Hadad, in: NIDB, Pictorialv Edition, J.D. Douglas/Merill C. Tenney, ed., Grand Rapids: Zondervan Publishing House, U.S.A./Basingstoke, Hants, UK.: Marshall-Pickering, 1987, 134–135
Gelb, Ignace J.	Inscriptions from Alishar and Vicinity, OI P Vol. XXVII (Researches in Anatolia Vol. V), Chicago: University of Chicago Press, 1935
	Sargonidic Texts from the Diyala Region, MAD No. 1, Chicago, Illinois: The University of Chicago Press, 1952
Gelb, Ignace J., P. Purves, A. MacRae	Nuzi Personal Names, OIP 57, Chicago: University of Chicago Press, 1943
Gibson, John C. L.	Textbook of Syrian Semitic Inscriptions Vol. II Aramaic Inscriptions including inscriptions in the dialect of Zenjirli, Oxford: Claredon Press, 1975
	Textbook of Syrian Semitic Inscriptions Vol. III Phoenician Inscriptions including inscreiptions in the mixed dialect of Arslan Tash, Oxford: Claredon Press, 1982
Geller, Mark J. and Tuviah Kwasman	Two More Triangular Aramaic Tablets, in: Robert Deutsch, ed., Shlomo. Studies in Epigrapy, Iconography, Hitory and Archaeology in Honor of Sholomo Moussaieff, Tel Aviv – Jaffa: Archaeological Center Publication, 2003, 99–104
Goetze, A.	The Texts Ni 615 and Ni 641 of the Istanbul Museum, JCS 6 1952, 142–145 (Appendix)
Gonella, Julia, Wahid Khayyata, Kay Kohlmeyer	Die Zitadelle von Aleppo und der Tempel des Wettergottes.Neue Forschungen und Entdeckungen, Münster: Rhema 2005

Gordon, Cyrus H.	Ugaritic Handbook, Anal Or 25, Roma: Pontificium Institutum Biblicum 1947
	Ugaritic Manual. Newly Revised Grammar Texts in Translation Cuneiform Selections Paradigms – Glossary – Indices, Anal Or 35, Roma: Pontificium Institutum Biblicum, 1955
Görg, Manfred	Aram und Israel, VT 26 1976, 499–500
	Namenstudien III: Zum Problem einer Frühbezeugung von Aram, BN 9 1979, 7–10
Grayson, Albert Kirk	Assyrian Royal Inscriptions Part 2 (= Records of the Ancient Near East, ed by Hans Goedecke, Vol. II), Wiesbaden: Otto Harrassowitz, 1976
	Assyrian Rulers of the Early First Millennium BC I (114–859 BC), (The Royal Inscriptions of Mesopotamia. Assyrian Periods Vol. 2), Toronto, Buffalo, London: University of Toronto Press, 1991
Greßmann, Hugo	Die älteste Geschichtsschreibung und Prophetie Israels: von Samuel bis Amos und Hosea, Göttingen: Vandenhoeck & Ruprecht, 1921
Gubel, Eric	An Essay on the Axe-bearing Astarte and their Role in a Phoenician Triad Author, RSF 8 1980, 1–17
Gadot, Yuval	Aphek in the Sharon and the Philistine Northern Frontier, BASOR February 2006, 21–36
Grosby, Steven	Biblical Ideals of Nationality Ancient and Modern, Winona Lake, Ind.: Eisenbrauns, 2002
Hafthórsson, S.	A Passing Power. An Examination of the Sources for the History of Aram-Damascus in the Second Half of the Ninth Century B.C., Coniectanea Biblica. Old Testament Series 54 Stockholm: Almqvist & Wiksell, 2006
Hallo, W.W.	From Qarqar to Carchemish, BA 23/2 1960, 34–61
Halpern, Baruch	The Stela from Dan: Epigraphic and Historical Consideration, BASOR 296 1994, 63–80
Hasegawa, Shuichi	Aram and Israel during the Jehuite Dynasty, BZAW Bd. 434, Berlin, Boston: Walter de Gruyter GmbH & Co. 2012 [a]

	Looking for Aphek in 1 Kgs 20*, VT 62 2012, 501–514 [b]
Hawkins, J.D.	The Neo-Hittite States in Syria and Anatolia, in: CAH III/1 1982, 372–441
	The Hittite Name of Til Barsip: Evidence from a New Hieroglyphic Fragment from Tell Ahmar, An St 33 1983, 131–136
Heltzer, Michael	An Old-Aramaic Seal-Impression and some problems of the History of the Kingdom of Damascus, in: M. Sokoloff, ed., Arameans, Aramaic and the Aramaic Literary Tradition, Ramat Gan: Bar-Ilan, 1983, 9–13
Hentschel, Georg	Die Eliaherzählungen. Zum Verhältnis von historischem Geschehen und geschichtlicher Erfahrung, Erfurter Theologische Studien, hrsg. Wilhelm Ernst und Konrad Feiereis, Bd. 33, Leipzig: St. Benno-Verlag GmbH, 1977
Herdner, A.	'Dédicace araméenne au dieu Melqart', Syr 25 1946–1948, 329–330
Herles, Michael	Zur geographischen Einordnung der aḫlamû – eine Bestandsaufnahme, AltorF 34/2 2007, 319–341.
Herr, Larry G.	Jordan in the Iron I and II A Periods, in: The Ancient Near East in the 12 th – 10 th Centuries, ed by Gershon Galil, Ayelet Gilboa, Aren M. Maeir, Dan'el Kahn: Culture and History. Proceedings of the International Conference held at the University of Haifa 2.–5. May 2010, AOAT Bd. 392, Münster: Ugarit-Verlag 2012, 207–220
Herrmann, Siegfried	Geschichte Israels in alttestamentlicher Zeit, München 1973, 1. Aufl. Berlin: Evangelische Verlaganstalt, 1981
Herzog, Chaim, Mardechai Gichon	Battles of the Bible. A Modern Military Evaluation of the Old Testament, London: Grennhill Books/ Lionel Leventhal Limited of Park House, 1978
	"Mit Gottes Hilfe" Die biblischen Kriege, München: Langen Müller, F.A. Herbig Verlagsbuchhandlung, 1998

Hindawi, Abdel-Nasser	The archaeology of the Northern Jordanian plateau during the Iron Age ca. late 13th – 6th centuries BC. Tell Ya'amoun as a key site, Freiburger Dokumentenserver (FreiDok), http://www.Freidok.uni-freiburg.de/volltexte/4574/ (Internet 2013)
Hitti, P.K.	History of Syria, London: Macmillan and Co. Ltd., 1951, 1957[2]
Höhne, Ernst, Red., Hermann Wahle, Kartogr.	Palästina. Historisch-archäologische Karte, Göttingen: Vandenhoeck & Ruprecht, 1981
Horn, Siegfried H.	The Amman Citadel Inscription, BASOR 193 1969, 2–13
	Art. Ben-Hadad, in: ABD Comm. Ref. Vol. 8, Washington, D.C. 1979, 135–136
	Relics of the past: The world's most important Biblical artifacts, Washington D.C.: Ministerial Association of the General Conference of SDA, n.d.) 1–16 (Lit. in: The Archaeology of Jordan and Other Studies, ed. Lawrence T. Geraty and Larry Herr, Berrien Springs, Michigan: Andrews University Press, 1986, 645)
Howard-Carter, T.	The Tangible Evidence for the Earliest Dilmun, JCS 33 1981, 210–223
Hrouda, Barthel	Der assyrische Streitwagen, Iraq 25/2 1963, 155–158
Hulster, Izaak J., de	A God of the Mountains? An Iconographic Perspective on the Aramean Argument in 1 Kings 20:23, in: Izaak J. de Hulster and Joel M. LeMon, IMAGE, TEXT, EXEGESIS. Iconographic Interpretation and the Hebrew Bible, LIBRARY OF HEBREW BIBLE/ OLD TESTAMENT STUDIES 588, London, New Delhi, New York, Sydney: Bloomsbury T & T Clark, 2014, 226–250
Ikeda, Yutaka	Once again KTK in the Sefire Inscriptions, EI 24 1993, 104*–108*

Irvin, Stuart A.	Critical Note. The last Battle of Hadadezer, JBL 124/2 2005, 341–347
Isserlin, B.S.J.	Das Volk der Bibel. Von den Anfängen bis zum Babylonischen Exil. Kulturgeschichte der antiken Welt Bd. 84, Mainz: Verlag Philipp von Zabern, 1998
Jackson, Kent P.	The Language of the Mesha' Inscription, in: Studies in the Mesha Inscription and Moab, ed. By Andrew Dearman, ASOR.SBL Archaeology and Biblical Studies, Philip J. King, editor, Nu 02, Atlanta, Georgia: Scholars Press, 1998, 96–130
James, Peter, Peter van der Veen	When *did* Shoshenq I Campaign in Palestine?*, in: Peter James, Peter van der Veen, ed., Solomon and Shishak. Current Perspectives from Archaeology, Epigraphy, History and Chronology. Proceedings of the Third BICANE Colloqium held at Sidney Sussex College, Cambridge 26–27 March, 2011, BAR International Series 2732, Oxford: Archaeopress. Publishers of British Archaeological Reports, 2015, 127–136
Jepsen, Alfred	Israel und Damaskus, AfO 14 1944, 153–172
	Zur Melqart Stele Barhadads, AfO 16 1952, 315–317
Jeremias, Jörg	Der Prophet Amos, ATD Teilbd. 24/2, Göttingen: Vandenhoeck & Ruprecht, 1995
Jirku, Anton	Der assyrische Name des Königs Benhadad III. von Damaskus, OLZ 21 1918, 279
	Art. Benhadad, RLA I 1928, 482–483
	Die ägyptischen Listen palästinensischer und syrischer Ortsnamen, KLIO Beih. 38 1932 (N.F. 25), 5–22
	Geschichte Palästina-Syriens im orientalischen Altertum, Aalen: Scientia Verlag, 1963
Kahn, Dan'el	The Kingdom of Arpad (Bît Agûsi) and 'all Aram': International Relations in Northern Syria in the Ninth and Eighth Centuries BCE, ANES 44, Louvain: Peeters, 2007, 66–85

Kapelrud, A.S. Israel – From Earliest Time to the Birth of Christ, translated by J.M. Moe, Oxford: Blackwell, 1966

Kaswalder, Pietro, Massimo Pazzini La Stele Aramaica di Tel Dan, Rbib 42 1994, 193–201

Keel, Othmar, Amihai Mazar Iron Age Seals and Seal Impressions from Tel Rehov, in: Eretz Israel. Archaeological, Historical and Geographical Studies, Vol. Twenty-Nine. Publ. The Israel Exploration Society in cooperation with the Institute of Archaeology, Hebrew University of Jerusalem, Jerusalem 2009, 57*–69* http://www.academie.edu/2579762/Iron_Age_Seals_and_Seal_Impressions_from_Tel_Rehov

Keiser, Clarence E. Cuneiform Bullae of the Third Millennium B.C. by Clarence E. Keiser New York MCMXIV. Babylonian Records in the Library of J. Piermont Morgan, ed by Albert T. Clay, New Haven: Yale University Press/ London-Humphrey Milford – Oxford University Press, MDCCCCXX

Kelle, Brad What's in a Name? Neo-Assyrian Designations for the Northern Kingdom and their Implications for Israelite History and Biblical Interpretation, JBL 121/4 2002, 639–666

Khayata, Wahid, ed. Guide to the Museum of Aleppo. Ancient Oriental Departmemt. Guide to the Old Oriental Department, Aleppo: Arab National Printing House, 1977

Kitchen, Kenneth A. Aram, Arameans, in: The New Bible Dictionary, ed. T.D. Douglas, London: Eerdmans 1967, 55–59

Art. Aram/Aramäer, in: Das Grosse Bibellexikon Bd. I, Wuppertal, Giessen 1987, 93–97

Art. Ben-Hadad, in: Das Grosse Bibellexikon Bd. I, Wuppertal, Giessen, 1987, 181–182 [b]

The Patriarchal Age. Myth or History?, BARev 21/2 1995, 48–57, 88, 90–92, 94–95

A Possible Mention of David in the Late Tenth Century B.C.E. And Deity * Dod as dead as the Dodo?, JSOT 76 1997, 29–44

	On the Reliability of the Old Testament, Grand Rapids, Mich., Cambridge, U.K.: William B. Eerdmans Publ. Comp., 2003
Klengel, Horst	Handel und Händler im alten Orient, Wien, Köln, Graz: Böhlau 2. Aufl. 1979.
	City and Land of Damascus in the Cuneiform Tradition, AAAS XXXV 1985, 49–57
	Syria 3000 to 300 B.C., Berlin: Akademie Verlag, 1992
Klengel-Brandt, Evelyn	Syrien. Kleinasien (VAM Kleine Schriften 6), Vorderasiatisches Museum zu Berlin, 1986
Knoppers, Gary N.	The Vanishing Solomon: The Disappearance of the United Mo narchy from Recent Histories of Ancient Israel, JBL 116/1 1997, 19–44
Kochavi, Moshe, Timothy Renner, Ira Spar, Esther Yadin	Rediscovered ! The Land of Geshur, BARev July/August 1992, 30–44
Kochavi, Moshe, A. Tsukimoto	'En Gev, in: The New Encyclopedia of Archaeological Excavations in the Holy Land. 5. Suppl. Vol. 2008, 1724–1726
Kottsieper, Ingo	Die Inschrift von Tell Dan und die politischen Beziehungen zwischen Aram-Damaskus und Israel in der 1. Hälfte des 1. Jahrtausends vor Christus, in: "Und Mose schrieb dieses Lied auf". Studien zum Alten Testament und zum Alten Orient FS für Oswald Loretz. Manfred Dietrich/Ingo Kottsieper, hrsg., AOAT Bd. 250, Münster: Ugarit-Verlag, 1998, 475–500
	Aramäische und phönizische Texte. A. Aramäische historische Schriften, TUAT, ed. Otto Kaiser, Ergbd., Gütersloh: Gütersloher Verlagshaus, 2001, 176–179
Kraeling, Emil G. H.	Aram and Israel or the Arameans in Syria and Mesopotamia, CUOS XIII, New York: Columbia University Press, 1918

Kupper, Jean-Robert   Les nomades en Mésopotamie au temps des rois de Mari, Paris: Society d'Edition Les Belles Lettres, 1956

Kyrieleis, Helmut   Ein altorientalischer Pferdeschmuck aus dem Heraion von Samos, MDAI. A Bd. 103, Berlin: Gebr. Mann Verlag, 1988, 37–61, Taf 9–15

Lamprichs, Roland   Die Westexpansion des neuassyrischen Reiches. Eine Strukturanalyse. Inaugural-Dissertation, Freie Universität Berlin, Berlin 1993

Der Expansionsprozeß des neuassyrischen Reiches: Versuch einer Neubewertung, in: Zwischen Euphrat und Indus. Aktuelle Forschungsprobleme in der Vorderasiatischen Archäologie, hrsg. Karin Bartl, Reinhard Bernbeck und Marlies Heinz, Deutsches Archäologisches Institut. Abt. Baghdad, Hildesheim, Zürich, New York: Georg Olms Verlag, 1995, 209–365

Lamprichs, Roland, Ziad al-Saad   International Workshop on 'The Northern Jordan Plateau during the late Bronze- and Iron Age based on studies of ceramics" 30. Oct. – 01. Nov. 2008 coorganized by Dr. Roland Lamprichs and Prof. Dr. Ziad al-Saad within the Alexander von Humboldt Stiftung/ Foundation. Partnership Program. Abstracts and Participants, Institut für Altorientalische Philologie und Vorderasiatische Altertumskunde. University of Münster, Münster

Lappin, David F.   Neue Untersuchungen zur Chronologie der Ersten Dynastie von Babylon auf der Grundlage der Venus-Tafeln des Ammizaduga und überlieferter 30-Tage-Mondmonats-Reihen* (Anhang C), in: Peter van der Veen/Uwe Zerbst, VOLK OHNE AHNEN? Auf den Spuren der Erzväter und des frühen Israel, STUDIUM INTEGRALE, Holzgerlingen: SCM Hänssler, 2013, 279–325

Layton, Scott C., Dennis Pardee, ed.   Literary Sources for the history of Palestine and Syria. Old Aramaic Inscriptions, BA Sept. 1988, 172–189

Lehmann, Gunnar	2008. North Syria and Cilicia, ca. 1200–330 B.C.E. Pp. 205–246 in Beyond the homeland: Markers in Phoenician Chronology, ed. Sagona. Ancient Near Eastern Studies, Supplement 28. Louvain: Peeters Press http://www.academia.edu/1194858/ Lehmann_Gunnar_2008_ North_Syria and Cilicia_ca_1200_-_330_ ....
Leineweber, Wolfgang	Die Patriarchen im Licht der archäologischen Entdeckungen. EHS.T Reihe XXII Bd. 127, Frankfurt am Main: Peter Lang, 1980
Lemaire, André	La stèle de Barhadad, Or 3 1984, 337–349
	Hazaël de Damas, roi d'Aram, in: D. Carpin, E. Joannès, ed., Marchands, Diplomates et Empereurs. Etudes sur la civilisation mèsopotamienne offertes à Paul Garelli, Paris: Edition Recherche sur le Civilisations, 1991, 91–108
	Epigraphic Palestinienne: Nouveaux Documents. Fragment de Stele Arameenne de Tel Dan, Henoch XVI, 1994, 87–93 [a]
	"House of David" Restored in Moabite Inscription, BARev 1994, 30–37 [b]
	The Tel Dan Stele as a Piece of Royal Historiography, JSOT 81 1998, 3–14
	Les premiers rois Araméens dans la tradition biblique, in: The World of the Arameans I. Biblical Studies in Honour of Paul-Eugènie Dion (JSOT SS 324), Sheffield: Sheffield Academic Press, 2001, 113–143
	Les formulaires juridiques des tablettes araméennes, in: Sophie Démare-Lafont & André Lermaire, Trois millénaires de formulaires juridiques (École Pratique des Hautes Études. Sciences Historiques et Philologiques – II. Hautes Études Orientales – Moyen et Proche-Orient 4 48), Genève: Librairie Droz S.A., 2010, 187–219, Fig. 1–5

West Semitic Epigraphy and the History of the Levant during the 12 th – 10 th Centuries BCE., in: The Ancient Near East in the 12 th – 10 th Centuries: Culture and History. Proceedings of the International Conference held at the University of Haifa, 2.–5. May 2010, ed. By Gershon Galil, Ayelet Gilboa, Aren M. Maeir, Dan'el Kahn, (AOAT Bd. 392), Münster: Ugarit-Verlag 2012, 291–308

Lemaire, André, Jean-Marie Durand — Les inscriptions araméennes de Sfiré et l'Assyrie de Shamshi-ilu, École pratique des hautes études. Ive Section, Sciences historiques et philologiques II. Hautes Etudes Orientales 20, Genève-Paris: Librairie Droz, 1984

Joas de Samarie, Barhadad de Damas, Zakkur de Hamat. La Syrie-Palestine vers 800 av. J.-C., Eretz Israel 24 1994, 148*– 157*

Lemche, Niels Peter, Thomas L. Thompson — Did Biran kill David? The Bible in the Light of Archaeology, JSOT 64 1994, 3–22

Lewis, Theodore J. — The Identity and Function of El/Baal Berith, JBL 115/3 1996, 401–423

Lidzbarski, Mark — Handbuch der nordsemitischen Epigraphic, II. Teil, Tafeln, Weimar: Emil Felber, 1898

Lipinski, E. — Le Benhadad II de la Bible et l'historie, in: Proceedings of the Fifth World Congress of Jewish Studies T. 1, Jerusalem: R. H. Hacohen, 1969, 157–173

'Attar-hapêš, the Forefather of Bar-Hadad II., AION N.S. XXI 31 1971, 101–104 [a]

The Assyrian Campaign to Mansuate in 796 B.C. and the Zakir Stela, AION 31 1971, 393–399

Notes on the Bar-Hadad and the Zakir Inscription, in: Studies in Aramaic Inscriptions and Onomastics I, OL Anal 1, Leuven: Leuven University 1975, 15–23

'Attar-sumki and related Names, ibid, 58–78

Art. Aramäer und Israel, TRE III, Berlin, New York, 1978, 590–599

Aram et Israel du X e au VIII e siecle av. N.e., Act Ant Hung 27 1979, 49–102

The Arameans. Their Ancient History, Culture, Religion (OLA 100), Leuven, Paris, Sterling Virginia: Peeters, 2000

The Aramaeans in the West (13th – 8th centuries), LAOS 3 2013, 123–147

London, Gloria A., Douglas R. Clark, ed. Ancient Ammonites & Modern Arabs. 5000 Years in the Madaba Plains of Jordan, The Madaba Plains Project, Andrews University, Berrien Springs, Mich., 1997

Luckenbill, Daniel David Benhadad and Hadadezer, AJSL 27 1910/1911, 267–284

The "Wandering Arameans", AJSL 36 1920, 244–245

The Annals of Sanherib, OIP (The University of Chicago Oriental Institut Publications) Vol. II, Chicago, Illinois: The University of Chicago Press) 1924

Malamat, A. Art. 'rm dmsq, in: Encyclopaedia Biblica I, 1954, 577–580 [a]

Cushan Rishataim and the decline of the Near East around 1200 B.C., JNES XIII/4 1954, 231–242 [b]

The Arameans, in: Peoples of the Old Testament Times, ed. By D.T. Wiseman, Oxford: Claredon Press, 1973, 134–155

Ein neuer Vorschlag zur Identifizierung von Ktk in den Sefîre-Inschriften (hebr.), in: M. Razin, mifkâdîm u-m' gillot-jahas u-mašmš' ûtâm ha-historît l-îmê ša'ûl we-dåwîd, Oranim, Haifa-University, 1976, VII–IX

Mallowan, M.E.L. Nimrud and its Remains, Vol. II London: A Colonnade Book. British Museum Publications Ltd., 1966/ and London: Collins, 1966

Mazar, Amihai Archaeology in the Land of the Bible. 10 000–586 B.C., New York: Doubleday – Anchor, 1990

	Looking for Aram in the Beth-Shean Valley in Light of the Excavation at Tel Beth Shean and Tel Rehov, lecture at the IWH Symposium Heidelberg, Sept. 1, 2014
Mazar, B.	The Arameans Empire and its Relations with Israel, BA 25 1962, 98–120
Mazar, Eilat	The Palace of King David. Excavations at the Summit of the City of David. Preliminary Report of Seasons 2005–2007, Jerusalem, New York: Shoham Academic Research and Publication, Jerusalem: The Old City Press, 2009
	Discovering the Solomonic Wall in Jerusalem. A Remarkable Archaeological Adventure, Jerusalem: Shoham Academic Research and Publication, 2011
Mazzoni, Stefania	Tell Afis and the Lu'ash in the Aramean Period, in: The World of the Arameans II, Studies in History and Archaeology in Honour of Paul-Eugènie Dion (JSOT.SS 325), Sheffield: Sheffield Academie Press 2001, 99–114
	Syria and the Chronology of the Iron Age, www.researchgate. net/publication/41491660_SYRIA_AND_THE_CHRONOLOGY_OF_THE_AGE, pág. 121–138 (Internet 2015)
McCarter, Peter Kyle, Jr.	Ancient Inscriptions. Voices from the Biblical World, Washington D.C.: Biblical Archaeology Society, 1996
McCarthy, Dennis J.	Treaty and Covenant. A Study in Form in the Ancient Oriental Documents and in the Old Testament, Analecta Biblica 21 A, Rome: Biblical Institute Press, 1981
McKane, William	Studies in the Patriarchal Narratives, Ediburgh: The Handsel Press 1979
McLellan, Thomas L.	Twelfth Century B.C. Syria: Comments on H. Sader's Paper, in: The Crisis Years: The 12 Th Century B.C.. From Beyond the Danube to the Tigris, Dubuque, Iowa: Kendall/ Hunt Pub., 1992, 164–173

McNamara, M.	De populi Aramaeorum primordis, VD 35 1957, 129–142
Meir, Aren M.	The Historical Background and Dating of Amos VI 2: An Archaeological Perspective from Tell es-Safi/Gath, VT LIV/3 2004, 319–334
	Review of Jonathan Miles Robker, The Jehu Revolution: A Royal Tradition of the Northern Kingdom and Its Remifications, Review of Biblical Literature [www.book-reviews.org] (Internet 2015)
Meir, Aren, Carl S. Ehrlich	Excavating Philistine Gath. Have we found Goliath's Hometown?, BARev 27/6 2001, 22–31
Merendino, Rosario Pius	Das Deuteronomische Gesetz – Eine literarkritische, gattungs- und überlieferungsgeschichtliche Untersuchung zu Dtr. 12–26, BBB 31, Bonn: Hanstein, 1969
Merling, David, Lawrence T. Geraty	Hesban. After 25 Years, Institute of Archaeology, Siegfried H.Horn Archaeological Museum, Andrews University, Berrien Springs, Mich. 1994
Millard, Alan R.	Alphabetic inscriptions on ivories from Nimrud, Iraq 24/1 1962, 41–51
	Fragments of Historical Texts from Niniveh: Middle Assyrian and Later Kings, Iraq 32 1970, 167–176
	Adad-nirari III, Aram and Arpad, PEQ 105/2 1973, 161–164
	A Wandering Aramean, JNES 39 1980, 153–155
	Israelite and Aramean History in the Light of Inscriptions, Tyn B 41.2 1990, 261–275
	The Homeland of Zakkur, Semitica 39 1990, 47–52
	Arameans, in: The Anchor Bible Dictionary, Vol. I A – C, New York, London, Toronto, Sydney, Auckland: Doubleday, 1992, 345–350
Millard, Alan R., Hayim Tadmor	Adad-nirari III in Syria. Another Stela Fragment and the Dates of His Campaigns, Iraq 35 1973, 57–64
Miller, J. Maxwell	The Elisha Cycle and the Account of the Omride Wars, JBL 85/4 1966, 441–454

	Geshur and Aram, JNES 28 1969, 60–61
	Site Identification: A Problem Area in Contemporary Biblical Scholarship, ZDPV 99 1983, 119–129
Miller, Patrick D.	Ugaritic ĠZR and Hebrew 'ZR II, UF 2 1970, 159–175
Mitchell, T.C.	Rehob, in: GBL, Wuppertal, Giessen, Bd. 3 1989, Sp. 1279
Mittmann, Siegfried	Die aramäische Inschridft von Tel Dan, ZAH VIII/2 1995, 121–139
	Zwei "Rätsel" der Mêša'-Inschrift. Mit einem Beitrag zur aramäischen Steleninschrift von Tell Dan (Tell el-Qâdî), ZDPV 118/1 2002, 33–65
Morrow, William	The Sefire Stipulations and the Mesopotamian Treaty Tradition, in: The World oft he Arameans III. Studies in Language and Literature in Honour of Paul-Eugenie Dion (JSOT SS 326, Sheffield: Sheffield Academia Press, 2001), 83–99
Moscati, S.	Sulle origini degli Aramei, RSO 26 1951, 16–22
	The Aramean "Achlamu", JSS 4/4 1959, 303–307
Müller, Hans-Peter	König Mêša' von Moab und der Gott der Geschichte, Ugarit-Forschungen, Bd. 26, Kevelaer, Neukirchen-Vluyn: Neukirchner Verlag, 1994, 373–395
	Die aramäische Inschrift von Tel Dan, ZAH VIII/2 1995, 121–139
Mulder, M.J.	Baal-Berith, in: Dictionary of Deities and Demons in the Bible (DDD), Leiden, New York, Köln: E.J. Brill, 1995, Sp. 266–272
Münger, Stefan	Early Iron Age Kinneret – Early Aramean or Just Late Cananite? Remarks on the Material Culture of a Border Site in Northern Palestine at the Turn of an Era, LAOS 3 2013, 149–182
Muffaddi Abu Taleb, Mahmud	Investigations in the History of North Syria 1115–717 B.C., Diss. University of Pennsylvania, Philadelphia 1973 (University Microfilms International, Ann Arbor, Michigan, 1983)

Mykytiuk, Lawrence J.	Identifying Biblical Persons in Hebrew Inscriptions and Two Stelae from before the Persian Era, Dissertation Ph.D., University of Wisconsin-Madison, 1998, Rev. Ed. 2001, 1–340, Appendix
	Identifying Biblical Persons in Northwest Semitic Inscriptions of 1200–539 B.C.E., SBL Academia Biblica 12, Atlanta: Society of Biblical Literature, 2004
	Corrections and Updates to "Identifying Biblical Persons in Northwest Semitic Inscriptions of 1200–539 B.C.E.", Maarav 16.1 2009, 49–132
	Sixteen Strong Identifications of Biblical Persons (Plus Nine Other IDs) in Authentic Northwest Semitic Inscriptions from before 539 B.C.E., in: SBL Archaeology and Biblical Studies, Atlanta 2012, 35–58
	50 People in the Bible Confirmed Archaeologically, thedailyhatch.org/2015/05/20/50-people-in-the-bible-confirmed-archaeologically/ (Internet 2015)
Na'aman, Nadav	Sannacherib's "Letter to God on his Campaign to Juda, BASOR 214 1974, 25–39
	Rezin von Damascus and the Land Gilead, ZDPV 111/2 1995, 105–117
	Hazael of 'Amqi and Hadadezer of Beth-rehob, Ugarit-Forschungen, Bd. 27, Münster: Ugarit-Verlag, 1995, 381–394
	Prophetic Stories as Sources for Histories of Jehoshaphat and the Omrides, Biblica 78/2 1997, 153–173
	Royal Inscriptions and Histories of Joash and Ahaz, Kings of Juda, VT XLVIII/3 1998, 333–349
	Was Ahab Killed by an Assyrian Arrow in the Battle of Qarqar?, Ugarit-Forschungen, Bd. 37, Münster: Ugarit-Verlag 2005, 461–474

	The Northern Kingdom in the Late Tenth-Ninth Centuries BCE., in: H.G.M. Williamson, Unterstanding the History of Ancient Israel. Proceedings of the Bristish Academy, Vol. 143, The Bristish Academy Oxford/New York: Oxford University Press Inc. 2007, 399–418
Nicholson, E.W.	Exodus and Sinai in History and Tradition, Oxford: Basil Blackwell, 1973
Niehr, Herbert	The Religion of the Arameans in the West: The Case of Sam'al, LAOS 3 2013, 183–221
Noth, Martin	Könige 1. Teilbd. BK IX/1, Neukirchen: Neukirchener Verlag, 1968
	Geschichte Israels, Sechste unveränderte Aufl., Berlin: Evangelische Verlagsanstalt GmbH, 1968 [b]
	Die Ursprünge des Alten Israel im Lichte neuer Quellen, AbLA 2 1971, 245–272
Nougayrol, J.	Les Palais Royale d'Ugarit III Textes, Accadiens et Hourrites des Archives East, Quest et Centrales, MRS 6, Paris: Imprimerie Nationale/ Klincksiek 1955
O'Callaghan, Roger T.	Aram Naharaim – A Contribution to the History of Upper Mesopotamia in the second Millennium B.C, Anal Or 26, Rome: Pontificum Institutum Biblicum, 1948
Oded, B.	Observations on Methods of Assyrian Rule in Transjordan after the Palestinian Campaign of Tiglath-pileser III., JNES 29/3 1970, 177–186
	The Historical Background of the Syro-Ephraimite War Reconsidered, CBQ 34 1972, 153–165
Oeming, Manfred	"And the King of Aram was at War with Israel" – The Construction of the Aramean as an Enemy in the Elisa Cycle 2 Kings 2–3, in: Heidelberg Colloquium. Aram and Israel: Cultural Interaction, Political Borders and Contruction of Identity during the Early Iron Age (12th- 8th Centuries BCE, Sept. 1–4, 2014, 16–17

Owen, David I.	Some new Evidence on Yamadiu = Ahlâmû, in: The Tablet and the Scroll. Near Eastern Studies in Honor of William W. Hallo, ed. by Mark E. Cohen, Daniel C. Snell, David B. Weinsberg, Bethesda, Maryland: CDL Press, 1993, 181–184
Page, Stephanie	A Stela of Adad-nirari III and Nergal-Ereš from Tell al Rimah, Iraq 30 1968, 139–153
	Joash and Samaria in a new Stela excavated at Tell al Rimah, Iraq, VT 19/4 1969, 483–484 [a]
	Adad-nirari III and Semiramis: the Stele of Saba'a and Rimah, Or NS 38 1969, 457–458 [b]
Parpola, Simo Kazuko Watanabe	Neo-Assyrian Treaties and Loyalty Oaths (SAA II), Helsinki: Helsinki University Press, 1988
Parrot, André	Bibel und Archäologie III.: Samaria, die Hauptstadt des Reiches Israel, Babylon und das Alte Testament, Zollikon – Zürich: Evangelischer Verlag, 1957
Pettinato, Giovanni	L'atlante geografico del Vicino Oriente attestato a Ebla e ad Abū-Ṣalābīkh (I), Or 47 1978, 50–73
Puech, E.	L'ivorie inscrit d'Arslan Tash et le rois de Damas, RB 88/4 1981, 544–562
	La Stele de Bar-Hadad à Melqart et les Rois d'Arpad, RB T. 99/2 1992, 311–334 [a]
	VII Les Traités Araméens d Sfiré, 19 Traités de BarGayah, roi de KTK, avec Mati'el, roi d'Asrpad, Traités et serments le Proche-Orient Ancien 88 n 107 (Supplement au Cahier Evangile 81), Paris: Editions du Cerf., 1992, 88–107 [b]
Pitard, Wayne T.	Who is the Bir-Hadad of the Melqart Stele? unpubl. paper, 1985, (presentation of W. H. Shea to Gotthard G.G. Reinhold)
	Ancient Damascus: A historical Study of the Syrian-State from Earliest Times until Its Fall to the Assyrians in 732 B.C.E., Winona Lake, Ind.: Eisenbrauns, 1987
	The Identity of Bir-Hadad of the Melqart Stela, BASOR 272 1988, 3–21

Arameans, in: People of the Old Testament World, ed by Alfred J. Hoerth, Gerald Mattingly & Edwin M. Yamauchi, Cambridge: The Lutherword Press, Baker Books, 1996, 207–230

The Melqart Stela (2.33), COS II, 2000, 152–153

Pohl, A. Kurze Bemerkungen zu den Ortsnamen der Tafel Wengler 22, JKF 11 1965, 363–364

Pope, Marvin H. 'Attar, in: WdM I, Stuttgart: Ernst Klett-Verlag, 1965, 249–250

Porter, Robert M. Dating the Stela from Tel Dan, JACF Vol. 7 1994/95, 92–96

Priese, Karl-Heinz 'rm und '; m, das Land Irame. Ein Beitrag zur Topographie des Sudan im Altertum, AOF 1 1974, 7–41

Studien der Topographie des ‚äthiopischen' Niltales im Altertum und zur meroitischen Sprache, EAZ 17 1976, 315–329

Puech, È. L'ivorie inscrit d'Arslan Tash et les rois de Damas, RB 88/4 1981, 544–562

La Stele de Bar-Hadad à Melqart et les Rois d'Arpad, RB T. 99/2 1992, 311–334

VII Les Traités Araméens de Sfiré, 19 Traités de BarGayah, roi de KTK, avec Mati'el, roi d'Arpad, Traites et serments dans le Proche-Orient Ancien 88n 107 (Supplement au Cahier Evangile 81), Paris: Editions du Cerf., 1992, 88–107 [a]

Radner, Karen The Stele of Adad-nērārī III and Nergal-ēreš from Dūr-Katlimmu (Tell Šaiḫ Ḥamad), AOF 39/2 2012, 265–277

Ray, Paul J., Jr. Tell Hesban and Vicinity in the Iron Age (= Hesban 6), Institute of Archaeology. Andrews University, Berrien Springs, Mich.: Andrews University Press, 2001

Hesbân and Vicinity in the Late Bronze Age, in: Gotthard G.G. Reinhold, hrsg. Bei Sonnenaufgang auf dem Tell. At Sunrise on the Tell. Essays about decades researches in the field of Near Eastern Archaeology, Remshalden: Verlag Bernhard Albert Greiner. 1. Aufl. 2003, 72–87

Reinhold, Gotthard G.G.

Some Remarks on the Second Line of the Bir-Hadad Stele Inscription, Andrews University, Berrien Springs, Michigan, 1985, unpubl. paper

The Bir-Hadad Stele and the Biblical Kings of Aram, Andrews University, Berrien Springs, Michigan, 1985, unpubl. paper

The Bir-Hadad Stele and the Biblical Kings of Aram, AUSS 24/2 1986, 115–126

Die Beziehungen Altisraels zu den aramäischen Staaten in der israelitisch-judäischen Königszeit, EHS.T Bd. 386, Frankfurt am Main, Bern, New York, Paris 1989

Zu den Stelenbruchstücken der altaramäischen Inschrift von Tell Dan. Gewidmet dem Deutschen Evangelischen Instutut für Altertumswissenschaft des Heiligen Landes, Amman, Zweigstelle Amman, Jordanien, 1999, manuscript.

Die altaramäischen Steleninschriften von Sefîre/Syrien im Blickpunkt neuer Forschungen, Sulzbach an der Murr 2000, manuscript.

Zur Liste der ammonitischen und nicht-ammonitischen Herrscher und Verwalter von Ammon bis zur Zeit der achämenidischen Vorherrschaft, in: Gotthard G.G. Reinhold, Bei Sonnenaufgang auf dem Tell. At Sunrise on the Tell. Essays about decades researches in the field of Near Eastern Archaeology, Remshalden: Verlag Bernhard Albert Greiner, 1. Aufl. 2003, 101–118

Zu den Stelenbruchstücken der altaramäischen Inschrift von Têl Dân, in: ibid., Gotthard G.G. Reinhold, 2003, 121–155

Zur Forschungsgeschichte und Neuinterpretation der altaramäischen Sefîre-Vertragsinschriften, Sulzbach an der Murr 2004, manuscript, handed over to Prof. Dr. Wolfgang Zwickel, Johannes Gutenberg-Universität Mainz (2008) and Dr. Izaak de Hulster, Georg August-Universität Göttingen (2011)

Die Melqart und Tel Dan Stelen. Investigations into Persons and Deities of the Aleppo-Stele/Syria and the Têl Dan Stele fragments, Israel, Fachtagung für Biblische Archäologie vom 4.-6. November 2005, Schönblick/Schwäbisch Gmünd, Vortrag, manuscript

The Earliest References to Aram and its Rises to Power (2–1 Millennia B.C.), ABA Seminar Woltersdorf/Berlin, 15–17 Dezember 2006, Vortrag, manuscript

Israel und die Aramäer. Archäologieseminar -Reise in die Vergangenheit III – Die Welt von David und Salomo, ETL, Löwenstein, 18. – 20. Jan. 2008, Vortrag, manuscript [a]

Abraham, ein wandernder "Aramäer", Fenster zur Vergangen heit der Bibel – Abraham und seine Welt, Seminar für Biblische Archäologie, Schönblick/Schwäbisch Gmünd, 10.–12. Okt. 2008, Vortrag, manuscript [b]

Die Zahl Sieben im Alten Orient. The Number Seven in the Ancient Near East. Studies on the Numerical Symbolism in the Bible and Its Ancient Near Eastern Environment, Frankfurt am Main, Berlin, Bern, Bruxelles, New York, Oxford, Wien: Peter Lang, 2008 [c]

Die Aramäer und Altisrael. Zur Frühbezeugung Arams in Schriftquellen des 3./2. Jahrtausends v. Chr. aus dem syrischen und mesopotamischen Raum, in: Peter van der Veen/Uwe Zerbst, Volk ohne Ahnen? Auf den Spuren der Erzväter und des frühen Israel, Studium Integrale, Holzgerlingen: SCM Hänssler, 2013, 204–205

Ribchini, Sergio	Baetyl, in: Dictionary of Deities and Demons in the Bible (DDD), Leiden, New York, Köln: E.J. Brill, 1995, 299–304
	Melqart mlk sr "King of Tyr", in: Dictionary of Deities and Demons in the Bible (DDD), Leiden, New York, Köln: E.J. Brill, 1995, 1053–1058
Richter, W.	Beobachtungen zur theologischen Systembildung in der alt-testamentlichen Literatur anhand des "kleinen geschichtlichen Credo", in: Wahrheit und Verkündigung, FS für M. Schmaus zum 70. Geburtstag, München, Paderborn, Wien: Verlag Ferdinand Schöningh, 1967, 175–212
Röllig, Wolfgang	Melqart, in: Wörterbuch der Mythologie, Bd. I, Götter und Mythen im Vorderen Orient, hrsg. H.W. Haussig, Stuttgart: Ernst Klett-Verlag, 1965, 297–298
	Alte und neue Elfenbeininschriften, in: NESE II, Rainer Degen, Walter W. Müller und Wolfang Röllig, Wiesbaden: Otto Harrassowitz 1974, 37–64
	Die aramäische Inschrift für Haza'el und ihr Duplikat, MDAI. A Bd. 103 1988, 62–75
Rössler, Otto	Die Verträge des Königs Bar-Ga'yah von Ktk mit König Mati'-Il von Arpad, TUAT 1/2 1983, 178–189
Rost, Leonhard	Das kleine Credo und andere Studien zum Alten Testament, Heidelberg: Quelle und Meyer, 1965
Routledge, Bruce	The Politics of Mesha: Segmented Identities and State Formation in Iron Age Moab, JESHO 43/3 2000, 221–256
Sacchi, P.	Osservazioni sul problema degli Armei, Atti Acc Toscana Sci Lett 25 1960/61, 85–142
Sader, Hélène S.	Les ètats araméens de Syrie depuis leur fondation jusqu' à leur transformation en provinces assyriennes, BTS Bd. 36, hrsg.. Orient-Institut der Deutschen Morgenländischen Gesellschaft, Beirut, Wiesbaden: Franz Steiner Verlag, 1987

Saggs, Henry W.F.	Babylonians, 1. publ. London: British Museum Press, 2000, 128–139
Sass, Benjamin	The Alphabet at the Turn of the Millennium. The West Semitic Alpabet CA. 1150–850 BCE. Tel Aviv. Journal of the Institute of Archaeology of Tel Aviv University. Occasional Publications No. 4, Tel Aviv: Emery and Claire Yass Publications, 2006
Sasson, Victor	The Old Aramaic Inscription from Tell Dan: Philological, Literary, and Historical Aspects, JSS XL/1 Spring 1995, 11–30
	Murderers, Usurpers, or what? Hazael, Jehu and the Tell Dan Old-Aramaic Inscription, Ugarit-Forschungen, Bd. 28, Kevelaer, Neukirchen-Vluyn: Neukirchner Verlag 1996, 547–554
	Some observations on the use and original purpose of the *WAW* consecutive in Old Aramaic and biblical Hebrew, VT XLVII/1 1997, 111–127
	The Tell Dan Aramaic inscription: The Problem of a new minimized reading. A review article, JSS L/1 Spring 2005, 23–34
Sauer, J.A., Larry G. Herr	Transjordan: Transjordan in the Bronze and Iron Age, in: The Oxford Encyclopedia of Archaeology in the Near East, ed. E.M. Meyers, Vol. 5, New York: Oxford University Press1997, 231–235
Sauerwein, R.	Elischa. Eine redaktions- und religionsgeschichtliche Studie, BZAW 465, Berlin: de Gruyter 2014
Schaalje, Jacqueline	Tel Afek, http://www.jewishmag.com/38mag/afek/afek.htm (Internet 2013)
Šanda, Albert	Die Aramäer, AO 4/3 1902, 1–32
Scheil, V.	"Notules", RA 14 1917, 139–163
Schiffer, Sina	Die Aramäer. Historisch-geographische Untersuchungen, Leipzig: J. C. Hinrichs'sche Buchhandlung, 1911
Schmitt, H. Chr.	Elisa.Traditionsgeschichtliche Untersuchungen zur vorklassischen nordisraelitischen Prophetie, Gütersloh: Gerd Mohn, 1972

Schneider, Nikolaus	Aram und Aramäer in der UR III-Zeit, Biblica 30 1949, 109–111
	Die Keilschrifturkunden der Ur III-Archive und die Bibel, St Ans 27.28 1951, 453–475
Schneider, Tammi J.	Rethinking Jehu, Biblica 77/1 1996, 100–107
Schniedewind, William M.	Tel Dan Stela: New Light on Aramaic and Jehu's Revolt, BASOR 302 1996, 75–90
	The Rise of the Aramean States, JSOT.SS 341, London: Sheffield Academic Press 2002, 276–287
	Ibid, in: Mesopotamia and the Bible: Comparative Explorations, M.W. Cavalas, K. Lawson Younger, eds, Grand Rapids: Baker, 2002, 276–287
	Review, Athas George. The Tel Dan Inscription: A Reppraisal and a New Interpretation, RBL 10 2003, Society of Biblical Literature 2003
Schniedewind, William M., Bruce Zuckermann	A Possible Reconstruction of the Name of Hazael's Father in the Tel Dan Inscription 2001, IEJ 51 2001, 88–91
Schott, Erika	Die Namen der Pharaonen, Göttingen: Weender Druckerei GmbH, 1989
Schwartz, Glenn M.	The Origins of the Arameans in Syria and northern Mesopotamia: Research problems and potential strategies, in: To the Euphrates and Beyond, ed. by O.M.C. Haex, H.H. Curves & P.M.M. Akkermans, Rotterdam, Brookfield: VT A.A. Balkema, 1989, 275–291
	Pastoral nomadism in Western Asia, in: Civilizations of the Ancient Near East I., New York: Scribner, 1995, 249–258
Seebaß, H.	Der Erzvater Israel und die Einführung der Jahweverehrung in Kanaan, BZAW 98, Berlin: Alfred Töpelmann, 1966
	Geschichtliche Zeit und theonome Tradition der Joseph-Erzählung, Gütersloh: Gerd Mohn, 1978
Sergi, Omer	Judah's Expansion in Historical Context, Tel Aviv 40 2013, 226–246

The Alleged Judahite King List: Its Historical Setting and Possible Date, Semitica 56, 233–247

Shavitsky, Ziva   The Mystery of the Ten Lost Tribes: A Critical Survey of Historical and Archaeological Records relating to the People of Israel in Exile in Syria, Mesopotamia and Persia up to ca. 300 B.C.E., Newcastle upon Thyne: Cambridge Scholars Publishing 2012

Shea, William H.   Adad-nirari III. and Jehoash of Israel, JCS 30 1978, 101–113

The Kings of the Melqart Stela, Maarav 1 /2 1979, 159–176

Israelite Chronology and the Samaria Ostraca, ZDPV 101/1 1985, 9–20

Singer, I.   A New Stele of Hamiyatas, King of Masuwari, Tel Aviv 15/16 1988/89, 184–192

Smith, Marx S.   Melqart, Baal of Tyre and Dr. Bonnet, Ugarit-Forschungen Bd. 28, Kevelaer, Neukirchen-Vluyn: Neukirchner Verlag, 1996, 775–777

Soggin, J.A.   Amos VI: 13–14 und I: 3 auf dem Hintergrund der Beziehungen zwischen Israel und Damaskus im 9. und 8. Jahrhundert, in: Near Eastern in Honor of W. F. Albright, ed. by Hans Goedicke, Baltimore: John Hopkins Press, 1971, 433–441

Spruytte, J.   Etudes technologique la roe du char royal assyrien, RA 88/1 1994, 37–48

Steck, O.H.   Überlieferung und Zeitgeschichte in den Elia-Erzählungen, WMANT 26, Neukirchen: Neukirchener Verlag, 1968

Stiebing, William H.   When Was the age of the Patriarchs? --of Amorites, Canaanites, and Archaeology, BARev 1 June 1975, 17–24

Stieglitz, R.R.   Ebla and Dilmun, in: Eblaitica. Essays on the Ebla Archives and Eblaite Language, ed by Cyrus H. Gordon, Gary A. Rendsburg, Nathan H. Winter, 1, Winona Lake, Indiana.: Eisenbrauns, 1987, 43–46

Strawn, Brent A.	Who's Listening to Whom? A Syntactical Note on the Melqart Inscription, Ugarit-Forschungen, Bd. 37, Kevelaer, Neukirchen-Vluyn: Neukirchner Verlag, 2005, 621–641
Tadmor, Hayim	Historical Implications of the Correct Rendering of Akkadian dâku, JNES 17/1 Jan. 1958, 129–141
	A Note on the Saba'a Stele of Adad-nirari III *, IEJ 19/1, 46–48
	The Historical Inscriptions of Adad-Nirari III., Iraq 35/2 1973, 141–150
Tetley, M. Christine	The Date of Samaria's Fall as a Reason for Rejecting the Hypothesis of Two Conquests, CBQ 64/1 2002, 59–77
Thiel, Winfried	Erwägungen zur aramäisch-israelitischen Geschichte im 9. Jh. v. Chr., in: H. Michael Niemann, Matthias Augustin, Werner H. Schmidt, hrsg., Nachdenken über Israel. Bibel und Theologie. FS für Klaus-Dietrich Schunk zu seinem 65. Geburtstag (Beiträge zur Erforschung des alten Testaments und des antiken Judentums, Bd. 37), Frankfurt am Main, Berlin, Bern, New York, Paris, Wien: Peter Lang, 1994, 117–131
	Erwägungen zur aramäisch-israelitischen Geschichte im 9. Jh. v. Chr., in: Gelebte Geschichte. Studien zur Sozialgeschichte und zur frühen prophetischen Geschichtsdeutung Israels, hrsg. Peter Mommer und Simone Pottmann, Neukirchen-Vluyn: Neukirchener Verlag, 2000, 189–203
	Der Vertrag zwischen Israel und Aram-Damaskus und die prophetische Redaktion (1. Kön. 20, 31–34, 35–43), in: Die unwiderstehliche Wahrheit. Studien zur alttestamentlichen Prophetie. Festschrift für Arndt Meinhold. Arbeiten zur Bibel und ihrer Geschichte Bd. 23, hrsg. RüdigerLux und E.-J. Waschke, Leipzig: Evangelische Verlagsanstalt GmbH 2006, 477–489

Thiele, Edwin R.	A Chronology of the Hebrew Kings (Contemporary Evangelical Perspectives), Grand Rapids: Zondervan Publishing House, 1977
Thompson, Thomas L.	The Historicity of Patriarchal Narratives. The Quest for the Historical Abraham, Berlin, New York: Walter de Gruyter, 1974
Thureau-Dangin, F.	Une Inscription de Narâm-Sin, RA VIII 1911, 199–200
	Une tablette bilingue de Ras Shamra, RA 37 1940, 97–118
Timm, Stefan	König Hesion II. von Damaskus, WdO 24, Göttingen: Vandenhoeck & Ruprecht, 1993, 55–84
Tocci, Franco Michelini	Damasco e Ša imêrišu, RSO XXXV 1960, 129–133
Tropper, Joseph	Eine altaramäische Steleninschrift aus Dan, Ugarit-Forschungen Bd. 25, Kevelaer, Neukirchen-Vluyn: Neukirchner Verlag, 1993, 395–406
	Paläographische und linguistische Anmerkungen zur Steleninschrift aus Dan, Ugarit-Forschungen Bd. 26, Kevelaer, Neukirchen-Vluyn: Neukirchener Verlag, 1994, 487–492
Unger, Eckhard	Die Aramäer auf der Höhe ihrer Macht, FuF 4. Jg. 22/23 1928, 226–228
Unger, Merill F.	Israel and the Arameans of Damascus, London: James Clare, 1957
Van den Born, A.	Art. Benhadad BL Haag, 1969, Sp. 191
Vandersleyen, C.	L'Euphrate, Aram Naharaim et la Bible, in: Le Museon. Revue d'études, 107, Louvain-La-Neuve: Peeters, 1994, 5–14
Van der Veen, Peter Uwe Zerbst, Hg.	Biblische Archäologie am Scheideweg? Für und Wider einer Neudatierung archäologischer Epochen im alttestamentlichen Palästina, STUDIUM INTEGRALE, Holzgerlingen: Hänssler-Verlag 2002
Van der Veen, Pieter Gert	The name Shishak, an update, JACF Vol. 10 2005, 8, 42. [a]

The: Final Phase of the Iron Age II C and the Babylonian Conquest: A Reassessment with Special Emphasis on Names and Bureaucraticd Titles on Provenanced Seals and Bullae from Israel and Jordan, Ph.D. Diss, University of Bristol 2005 [b]

Schischak: Pharao Schoschenk I oder Ramses III?, http//www.scilogs.de/archaeologische-spatenstiche/ schischak-pharao-schoschenk-i-oder-ramse… 18. März 2009

Zeit der geteilten Reiche – Juda, in: W. Zwickel et al. (hrsg.), Herders Neuer Bibelatlas, Freiburg i. Br.: Herder, 2013, 164–189

The Final Phase of Iron Age II in Judah, Ammon and Edom: A Study of Provenanced Official Seals and Bullae as Chronological Markers, AOAT 415, Münster: Ugarit-Verlag 2013

Schoschenk I, Wikipedia. Die freie Enzyklopädie, https://de.wikipedia.org/wiki/scheschonq_I (Internet 2015)

Van Seters, John   Abraham in History and Tradition, New Haven, London: Yale University Press, 1975

Veenhof, Klaas R.   Grundrisse zum Alten Testament, ATD Ergänzungsreihe Bd. 11, Göttingen: Vandenhoeck & Ruprecht, 2001

Virolleaud, Charles   Les textes cuneiformes qui ont été decouverte…., Syr X 1929, Pl. LXX Tablettes de Ras Shamra, No. 14

von Bredow, Iris   Die Geschichte Syriens vom Neolithikum bis zum Ende der Bronzezeit, Abteilung Alte Geschichte, Historisches Institut der Universität Stuttgart, Suttgart, WS 2004/2005, printed manuscript.

von Rad, Gerhard   Das fünfte Buch Mose. Deuteronomium., ATD Neues Göttinger Bibelwerk Teilbd. 8, Berlin: Evangelische Verlagsanstalt, 1965

Theologie des Alten Testament I. Die Theologie der geschichtlichen Überlieferungen, 5.durchges. verb. Aufl., Berlin: Evangelische Verlagsanstalt, 1969 (Nachdruck)

Voos, Joachim	Studien zur Rolle von Statuen und Reliefs im syro-hethitischen Totenkult während der frühen Eisenzeit (etwa 10.–7. Jh. v.u.Z.), EAZ 29 1988, 347–362
Wäfler, Marcus	Zum assyrisch-urartäischen Westkonflikt, APA 11/12 1 1980, 79–97
Wartke, Ralf-B	SAM'AL. Ein aramäischer Stadtstaat des 10. bis 8. Jhs. v. Chr. und die Geschichte seiner Erforschung, Mainz: Verlag Philipp von Zabern, 2005
Wazzana, Nili	Border Description and Cultural Barriers, in: SBoT, Wiesbaden: Harrassowitz, 2001, 696–701
Weidner, E.	Book Review: Arno Poebel, The Second Dynastie of Isin according to a New King-List Tablet. VIII (Assyriological Studies No. 15), Chicago: The University of Chicago Press, 1955, AfO 17 1954–1955, 383–385
	Die Inschriften Tukulti-Ninurtas I. und seiner Nachfolger, AfO Beih. 12, Graz: Weidner, 1959
Weippert, M.	Die Landnahme der israelitischen Stämme in der neueren wissenschaftlichen Diskussion, FRLANT 92, Göttingen: Vandenhoeck & Ruprecht, 1967
	Zu Syienpolitik Tiglatpilesers III., BBVO 1982, 398–498
	Die Feldzüge Adadnararis III. nach Syrien. Voraussetzungen, Verlauf, Folgen*, ZDPV 108/1 1992, 42–67
Wesselius, Jan-Wim	The First Royal Inscription from Ancient Israel: The Tel Dan Inscription Reconsidered, SJOT 13 1999, 163–166
Westermann, Claus	Genesis 1.Teilbd. Genesis 1–11, BKAT, Bd. 1/1, Neukirchen-Vluyn: Neukirchener Verlag, 1974
	Genesis 2.Teilbd. Genesis 12–36, BKAT Bd. 1/2, Neukirchen-Vluyn: Neukirchener Verlag, 1981
Whiting, Robert M.	Amorite Tribes and Nations of Second-Millennium Western Asia, in: Civilizations of the Near East, Jack M. Sasson, ed., Vol. II, New York: Charles Scribner's Sons, 1995, 1231–1242

Wiesner, Joseph	Zum Stand der Streitwagenforschung, APA 1 1970, 191–194
Willis, John T.	The newly discovered fragmentary Aramaic inscription from Tel Dan, RQ 37/5 1995, 219–226
Willoughby, Bruce E.	Amos, in: The Anchor Bible Dictionary, Vol. I A – C, New York, London, Toronto, Sydney, Auckland: 1992, 203–212
Winter, Irene J.	Is there a South Syrian style of ivory carving in the early first millennium B.C., Iraq 43 1981, 101–130
Wiseman, D.J.	The Alalakh Tablets, London: British Institute of Archaeology at Ankara, 1953
without author	Heidelberg Colloqium. Aram and Israel: Cultural Interaction. Political Borders and Construction of Identity during the Early Iron Age (12th – 8th Centuries BCE), IWH Heidelberg, Sept. 1–4, 2014, 1–22, and the program: http://www.iwh.uni-hd.de/oeming2014.html http://www.theologie.uni-heidelberg.de/md/theo/aktuelles/news/aram_and_israel_-_program_-_a... http://blogs.helsinki.fi/sacredtexts/2014/08/28/heidelberg-colloqium-aram-and-israel/ a.o.
Wolf, Hans Walter	Dodekapropheton 2, Joel und Amos, BKAT, Bd. XIV/2, Neukirchen: Neukirchener Verlag, 1969
Worschech, Udo	Abraham. Eine sozialgeschichtliche Studie (EHS.T Reihe 23 Theologie Bd. 225), Frankfurt/M., Bern, New York: Peter Lang, 1983
Yamada, S.	Aram-Israel Relations as Reflected in the Aramaic Inscriptions from Tel Dan, Ugarit-Forschungen, Bd. 27, Neukirchen-Vluyn: Verlag Butzon & Bercker, Kevelaer, 1995, 611–625
Yassine, K., J. Teixidor	Ammonite and Aramaic Inscriptions from Tell El-Mazâr in Jordan, BASOR 264 Nov. 1986, 45–50
Yildez, Efrem	Los Arameos de Lu'aš y Hamat, Arabismo.com ano 2001, 1–10

Younger, K. Lawson   Neo-Assyrian and Israelite History in the Ninth Century: The Role of Shalmaneser III, in: H.G.M. Williamson, ed., Understanding the History of Ancient Israel. Proceedings of the British Academy, Vol. 143, The British Academy, Oxford/ New York: Oxford University Press Inc. 2007, 243–277

Some of What's New in Old Aramaic Epigraphy. ASOR NEA 70/3 2007, 139–146

Zadok, Ran   On the Historical Background of the Sefire Treaty, AION 44 1984, 529–538

Elements of Aramean Pre-History, in: M. Cogan and I. Eph'al (eds.) Ah, Assyria... Studies in Assyrian History and Ancient Near Eastern Historiography Presented to Hayim Tadmor (Scripta Hiersolymitana 33), Jerusalem: The Magnes Press, 1991, 104–117

The Aramean Infiltration and Diffusion in the Upper Jazira, Ca. 1150–930 B.C., in: Gershon Galil, Ayelet Gilboa, Aren M. Maeir and Dan'el Kahn eds., The Ancient Near East in the 12th – 10th Centuries B.C.E.: Culture and History. Proceedings of the International Conference held at the University of Haifa, 2. – 5. May 2010, AOAT Bd. 392, Münster: Ugarit-Verlag 2012, 569–579

Zaccagnini, Carlo   Notes on the Pazarcik Stela, SAAB 7 1993, 53–72

Zimmern, Heinrich   Benhadad, in: Assyriologische und archäologische Studien, Hilprecht Anniversary, Volume, Chicago & Leipzig 1909, 299–303

Zwickel, Wolfgang   Eisenzeitliche Ortslagen im Ostjordanland. Beihefte zum Tübinger Atlas des Vorderen Orients, Reihe B, Nr. 81, Wiesbaden: 1990

Ein Afek im Golan?, in: Peter Mommer, hrsg., Geschichte Israels und deuteronomistisches Geschichtsdenken: Festschrift zum 70. Geburtstag von Winfried Thiel, AOAT Bd. 380, Münster: Ugarit-Verlag 2010, 317–318

Photographic Acknowledgements and Certifications

Author

Gotthard G.G. Reinhold, born December 19 1945, in Erkner/Berlin, studied Theology (1967–1972) and pursued additional studies in Pre- and Early History (1974–1979) at the Humboldt-University of Berlin, receiving a degree in theology in 1972 (Dipl.theol.) and completing an archaeological thesis in 1979.

In 1989, he received a Ph.D. in Religious Sciences from the Johann Wolfgang Goethe-University, in Frankfurt am Main. Besides study trips to Syria, Jordan, Israel, and Egypt (Sinai), he served as square supervisor at Tell el-'Umeiri in Jordan (1987). Since then, he participated in the Madaba Plains Project up through 1998, which was supported by the American Schools of Oriental Research (USA) and the American Center of Oriental Research (Jordan).

During this period Reinhold worked in Khirbet Rufeis (Amman), and at Tell Ḥesbân.

In 1999, he was a member of the excavation team with the Ba'ja Regional Project near Petra, led by the German Protestant Institute for the Archaeology of the Holy Land (Amman).

175

Then in 2005, he excavated at Ramat Rahel. From 2009 to 2011 Reinhold was a member of the ABA (The German Study Group for Biblical Archaeology, in Schorndorf, Germany) in Jerusalem and the environs of Israel. He is also an affiliated member with the Archaeological Institute and S.H. Horn-Museum of the Andrews University (Berrien Springs, USA), and through his digitalization of regional archives in Baden-Wuerttemberg, member of the "Historischer Verein für Württembergisch Franken" (1990– to the present).

Milton Keynes UK
Ingram Content Group UK Ltd.
UKHW022125060923
428148UK00015B/681

9 783631 675991